Mr. Marshall

The Rural Economy of the West of England including Devonshire

Vol. II

Mr. Marshall

The Rural Economy of the West of England including Devonshire
Vol. II

ISBN/EAN: 9783741142536

Manufactured in Europe, USA, Canada, Australia, Japa

Cover: Foto ©knipser5 / pixelio.de

Manufactured and distributed by brebook publishing software
(www.brebook.com)

Mr. Marshall

The Rural Economy of the West of England including Devonshire

THE
RURAL ECONOMY
OF THE
WEST OF ENGLAND:
INCLUDING
DEVONSHIRE;
AND PARTS OF
SOMERSETSHIRE,
DORSETSHIRE,
AND
CORNWALL.
TOGETHER WITH
MINUTES IN PRACTICE.

By Mr. MARSHALL.

VOL. II.

LONDON:
Printed for G. NICOL, Bookseller to His Majesty, Pall-Mall;
G. G. and J. ROBINSON, Paternoster Row;
and J. DEBRETT, Piccadilly.

M,DCC,XCVI.

CONTENTS

OF THE

SECOND VOLUME.

DISTRICT THE THIRD.

THE

MOUNTAINS

OF

CORNWALL AND DEVONSHIRE.

PREFATORY REMARKS, 1.

EXCURSION IN CORNWALL.

BUCKLAND TO BODMIN, 3.

Elevation.

Climature, 4.

Surface.

Soil.

Subsoil,

Subsoil, 5.
Rivers.
Navigations.
Roads.
Mines.
Manufactures, 6.
Townships.
Produce.
Fuel.
Inclosure.
Fields.
Fences, 7.
Buildings.
Crops.
Cattle.
Sheep.
Beasts of Labor.
Implements.
Manure, 8.
Tillage.
Orchards.
Woodlands.
Ornament, 9.
Harvesting.
Furze.
State of Husbandry.
Towns, 10.
Callington.
Leskard.
Bodmin.

BODMIN TO BUCKLAND, 10.

Elevation.
Climature, 11.
Surface.

Soil,

Soil 12.
Mines.
A Stream Work described.
Rivers, 13.
Roads.
Inclosures.
Produce.
Manufactures.
Buildings.
Fields, 14.
Fences.
Crops.
Cattle.
Sheep.
Goats.
Beasts of Labor.
Manure.
Harvesting, 15.
State of Husbandry.
Orchards.
Woodlands.
Ornament.
Towns.
Temple—a deserted Village!
Launceston.
GENERAL OBSERVATIONS ON CORNWALL, 16.

CONTENTS.

DARTMORE,

AND ITS

UNCULTIVATED ENVIRONS.

Prefatory Remarks, 19.

Situation, 20.
Extent.
Elevation, 21.
Surface, 22.
Note on Brent Tor, 22.
Waters, 23.
Soils.
Subsoils, 24.
Productions.
Application of Pasturage, 25.
Rights of Depasture.
Duchy of Cornwall.
Manors appendant.
Venville Tenants.
Cattle, 26.
Sheep.
Objects of Moorside Farming, 27.
Present Value of these wild Lands.
In a political Light, 28.
In a private Point of View.

IMPROVE-

IMPROVEMENTS proposed, 29.

The Mountain Lands, 30.
Objects of Improvement.
Planting.
Herbage, 31.
Hedgemounds.
Climature.
Burning off Heath, 32.
Sodburning.
Grasses and Rape Herbage.
Rape Seed, 33.
Draining.
Watering.
Manuring, 34.
Stock.
Rabbit Warren, 35.
Lower Grounds.
Climature.
Remarks.
Woodland, 36.
Coppice Fences.
Lime, 37.

INLAND NAVIGATION proposed.

Objects to be obtained.
Articles of Carriage.
Direction of the Canal, 39.

DISTRICT THE FOURTH.

NORTH DEVONSHIRE.

Prefatory Remarks, 41.
Note on forming this Journal, 42.
Okehampton and its Environs, 43.
Okehampton to Torrington, 45.
Hatherly, 48.
General Remarks, on this Stage, 52.
Torrington and Environs, 54.
Torrington to Biddeford, 55.
Remark, 56.
Biddeford and Environs, 57.
Walk on the Southwestern Hills, 59.
Biddeford Market, 61.
Walk on the North of the Town, 61.
General Remarks, 64.
Biddeford to Barnstaple, 65.
General Remarks, 68.
Barnstaple and its Environs, 69.
Barnstaple to Moulton, 70.
Valley of Swimbridge, 72.
South Moulton and Environs, 75.
North Devon Cows examined.
General Observations on North Devonshire, 77.
South Moulton to Dulverton, 78.
Exmore, a Remark on, 79.

Dulverton

Dulverton and Environs, 81.
Walk above the Town, 83.
Dulverton to Tiverton, 85.
Bampton, 87.
Limeworks of Bampton.
Horse Barrows described, 88.
Remarks on this Stage, 91.
Further Remarks on North Devonshire, 93.

DISTRICT THE FIFTH.

THE

VALE OF EXETER.

Prefatory Remarks, 95.
The DISTRICT described, 97.
I. Situation.
II. Extent, 98.
III. Elevation.
IV. Surface.
Remarks on examining the natural Face of a Country.
V. Climature, 100.
VI. Waters, 101.

VII. Soils.

VII. Soils.
Honiton to Exeter, 102.
Environs of Exeter.
Exeter to Nutwell, 103.
Environs of Nutwell.
Exeter towards Taunton.
Environs of Tiverton.
VIII. Subsoils, 104.
Remark on the Mixture of Lands in this Vale, 105.
Remark on the Vale Elm.
IX. Political Divisions, 106.
X. Public Works.
Inland Navigation.
A Canal proposed.
Remarks on the Advantages of such a Canal, 107.
Roads.
State of Inclosure, 108.
Conjectures on its Origin.
XI. Present Productions.
Political Remark.
XII. State of Society, 109.
Towns.
Country Habitations.
Employments, 110.
XIII. Face of the Country, 110.

The RURAL ECONOMY of this Diſtrict.

MANAGEMENT of ESTATES.

I. Diſtribution of Farm Lands, 111.
II. Farm Buildings, 112.
Remarks on "Cobwalls," 113.
III. Hedgerows, 113.
Note on Gateways and Gateposts, 114.

WOODLANDS, 114.

Management of Hedgerows.
Lopping Oak Timber Trees! 115.
Remark on Pruning Trees.
The Elm improved by it.

AGRICULTURE, 116.

I. Farms.
II. Beaſts of Labor.
III. Implements, 117.
IV. Plan of Management.
V. Manure.
VI. Wheat, 118.
VII. Beans.
VIII. Turneps.

IX. Graſs-

IX. Grassland.
X. Orchards, 119.
XI. Cattle, 119.
XII. Dairy, 120.
Remark on Clouting Cream.
XIII. Swine, 121.
XIV. Sheep.

DISTRICT THE SIXTH.

THE DAIRY DISTRICT

OF

WEST DORSETSHIRE.

Introductory Remarks, 123.
The DISTRICT Described, 125.
I. Situation.
Note on the Country between Crewkern and Chard.
II. Extent, 126.
III. Elevation.
IV. Surface, 127.
Note on the Valley of Yarcombe, 127.
V. Climature, 128.
VI. Waters.

VI. Waters.
VII. Soils, 129.
VIII. Subsoils, 130.
IX. Fossils.
Limestone.
Chalk, 131.
X. Roads, 131.
XI. State of Inclosure.
Tradition respecting the First Peopling of Devonshire, 132.
Note on the Authenticity of TRADITION, 133.
Remarks on the Cultivation of Commonable Lands, 134.
Common Rights of East Devonshire, 135.
XII. Present Productions, 137.
XIII. Towns.
XIV. Villages.
XV. Habitations, 138.
Note on Laying out Townships.
XVI. Appearance of the Country.
Views from Beaminster Down, 139.

The AGRICULTURE of this District.

I. Farms, 141.
II. Farmers, 142.
III. Beasts of Labor.
IV. Implements, 143.
Insertion of the Yoke Irons.
V. Plan of Management.
Objects.
Arable Crops, 144.
Succession.
Hemp and Flax for Manufactures, 145.

VI. SEM.

VI. Manures, 145.
Red "Marl." as in the Midland District." 146.
VII. Grasslands, 146.
VIII. Orchards, 147.
IX. The Dairy, 148.
Objects.
Formerly Cheese.
Now Butter.
Size of Dairies, 149.
Breed of Cows.
Procuring Cows.
Dairy Management, 150.
Letting Dairies.
X. Sheep, 151.

IMPROVEMENT of this District, 152.
I. Hill or Commonable Lands, 153.
II. Hedgerows, 154.
General Remarks on the Management of OAKLAND HEDGEROWS, 156.
III. Plan of Management, 158.
IV. Management of Soils, 159.
A Principle of Management, 160.
V. Manures, 160.
Burnt Clay, 161.
Black Moory Earth, 162.

DISTRICT THE SEVENTH.

THE
VALE OF TAUNTON,
&c. &c.

Prefatory Remarks, 163.
Situation, 165.
Extent.
Elevation, 166.
Surface.
Climature, 167.
Soils.
Subsoils, 168.
Rivers.
Productions.
State of Inclosures, 169.
Fences.
Termination of the Danmonian Fence, 169.
Management of Farms, 170.
Termination of the Danmonian Husbandry.
Orchards, 171.
Termination of the Devonshire Orchard.

QUANTOC HILLS, 172.

BLACK-

BLACKDOWN HILLS, 174.
Remarks on the Limestone of West Somersetshire, 176.

SOUTH SEDGEMORE, 178.
Natural Boundaries.
Extent, 179.
Elevation.
Surface.
Reflections on the Formation of these Lands.
Note on the Boar or Eagre, 180.
Soil, 181.
Herbage.
Stock, 182.
Cattle.
Sheep.
Geese.
Remarks on the Improvement of the Somersetshire Marshes, 183.

CURSORY REMARKS IN A JOURNEY THROUGH SOMERSETSHIRE.

Tiverton to Taunton, 185.
Taunton, 189.
Market of Taunton, 190.
Taunton to Somerton, 191.
Remark on the Modes of Travelling, 193.
Langport, 196.

Somerton

Somerton and its Environs, 198.
Somerton to Shipton Mallet.
Vale of Glastonbury, 200.
Note on Sheet Cows, 203.
Shipton and its Environs, 205.
Shipton to Frome, 206.
Frome, 209.
Frome to Devizes, 210.
Trowbridge, 212.
Devizes, 214.

GENERAL VIEW of South Somersetshire, 215.

Analysis of the Line of Country.
Elevation, 216.
Surface.
Climature.
Geology, 217.
Inland Navigation.
State of Inclosure.
Productions, 218.
Buildings.
Manufacture.
Farms, 219.
Beasts of Labor.
Note on a TAX ON HORSES, 220.
Cattle, 220.
Sheep, 221.
Swine, 222.
Bees.

RETROSPECTIVE VIEW

OF THE

WEST OF ENGLAND,

A Natural Department, 223.
An Agricultural Department.
Conjectures on its Colonization, 224.
Peculiarities of Practice.
Cultivation of Commonable Lands, 226.
Lifeleasehold Tenure.
Prevalency of Small Farms.
Management of Coppice Wood.
Construction of Fences.
Prevalency and Excellency of Earthen Walls.
Method of Hiring Servants, 227.
Taking Apprentices in Husbandry.
Carriage of all Articles on Horseback.
Singularity of Implements and Tools.
Method of Burning the Surface of Land.
Management of Lime.
Harvest Operations, 228.
Winnowing Corn, &c.
Thrashing Wheat.
Method of Sowing Wheat.
Culture of Turneps.
Prevalency of Ley Grounds.
Watering Slopes of Hills, 229.

Training

Training Orchard Trees.
Breed of Cattle.
Fatting Calves at Grass.
Raising Cream by Heat, 230.
Bleeding Cattle for the Slaughter.
Management of Swine.
Breed of Sheep.
Shepherding of Sheep.
Shearing Sheep without Washing them.

MINUTES IN WEST DEVONSHIRE.

Introductory Remarks, 233.
MIN. I. On the Country between Plymouth and Buckland, 235.
Approach to Buckland Place, 236.
II. On the Farm or Barton of Buckland Place, 237.
III. On the Upper Part of the Valley of the Tamer, 239.
Salmon Weir of the Tamer, 240.
Mountain Horses of Cornwall, 241.
IV. On the Skirts of the Dartmore Hills, 242.
Remarks on the Names of Hundreds, 244.
Remarks on Plymouth Brook.

MIN. V. On the Central Parts of the Valley of the Tamer, 245.
Remark on Surveying a District, 246.
Observations on Tamerton Fair.
On Breeding Cattle, 247.
On the Short-horned Breed, 248.
VI. On the Requisite Preliminaries of Improvement, 249.
Tables of Fields, Stock, &c.
Cautions to be used by an Improver, 251.
VII. On the State of Tillage, in West Devonshire, 252.
A Simple Improvement of its Plow, 253.
Note on the Devonshire Plow.
On the Improvement of Plows, 254.
A Principle of Conduct, on introducing Improvements, 255.
VIII. On the Salmon Fishery of the Tavey, 256.
Salmon Weir described.
Fish of the Tavey, 259.
Net Fishing, 260.
Fish Poachers detected, 261.
IX. On the Rains of West Devonshire, 262.
X. On Inverting the Sward of Orchards, 264.
XI. On Plowing with Whip Reins, 265.
A Regulation on introducing the Use of Whip Reins, 266.
XII. On the Treatment of Coppice Hedges, 266.
Pruning their Sides.
Guarding the Mounds with Brushwood, 268.
XIII. On the Leat or Made Brook of Plymouth, 269.
On the Mill Streams of Devonshire, 271.

Remarks

Remarks on Made Brooks.
Water Mills are Bars to Improvements, 273.
XIV. On the Country between Buckland and Plympton, 273.
On Plympton Fair, 274.
On the Situation of Plympton.
XV. Further on Training Hedges, 275.
XVI. On Reclaiming Land from Stones, 276.
XVII. On Reclaiming Land from Weeds, 277.
Practical Remarks on Fallowing, 278.
On Manuring Fallows, 279.
Remarks on Eighteen-Months Fallows, 280.
XVIII. On Introducing the Hoing of Turneps, with Practical Directions, 281.
XIX. On the Shoeing of Oxen, 283.
The Devonshire Practice.
Thoughts on Facilitating this Operation, 285.
XX. On my General Work, and the Improvements of Buckland, 286.
On Objects of Husbandry, 287.
On Forming River Breaks, 288.
On the Improvement of the Breed of Cattle, 291.
On the Improvement of the Salmon Fishery, 292.
XXI. On the Country round Milton Abbots, 294.
A Geological Remark on this Country.
XXII. On the Coating of Buildings, 295.
The Theory of Roughcast and Stucco Work, 296.
XXIII. On Feeding Cattle with Charlock, 297.
XXIV. On Cutting Cabbages, 300.

MIN. XXV. On Societies of Agriculture, 301.
Their proper Object.
On Associations of Landed Gentlemen, 303.
The Subjects of Discussion, 305.

XXVI. On the Monastery Barn of Buckland Place, 307.
Its Improvement.
On the Nature of Cement, 308.

XXVII. On the Uses of Natural Rills, and the Method of conducting artificial ones, 308.
A new Level constructed, 310.
On the proper Fall of Rills, 311.
On the Uses of Reservoirs to artificial Rills, 314.

XXVIII. On Destroying Earth Worms, and
On Forming Drinking Pools, with Walnut-Tree Leaves, instead of Lime, 315.

XXIX. On Laying out Farm Yards, &c. 317.
On the Farmery of Buckland, and its Improvement, 317.
On Octagonal Ranges of Sheds, 318.

XXX. On Hanging Doors on Stone, 319.
On the Effect of the Rust of Iron, 320.

XXXI. Further on Hanging Doors, 321.
On the Use of Rabbets.
On their proper Dimensions, 322.

XXXII. On Liming Land, 322.
A new Practice struck out.

XXXIII. Further on conducting Rills, 323.
Practical Directions on this Subject, 324.
On conducting a Rill among Trees.
On the Use of Gauges, 325.
On the Dimensions of Rills, 327.

MIN.

MIN. XXXIV. On Laying out Roads, 327.
The Use of the Frame Level and Cross, 328.
Practical Directions.
On Forming Roads, 331.
XXXV. On the Sale of Coppice Wood, 332.
Age of Felling.
Calculations on the Rental Value.
On Reclaiming Coppice Ground, 334.
XXXVI. Further on the Sale of Coppice Wood, 336.
Conditions of Sale.
Calculations on the comparative Advantages of different Offers, 337.
XXXVII. On securing infirm Buildings, 339.
A difficult Case.
Effectually remedied, 340.
On building Buttresses, 341.
XXXVIII. On the general Economy of a Farm, with Respect to Grasslands, 342.
A leading Object, on a Sheep Farm.
On Mowing Temporary Leys the first Year.
On the Value of Watered Lands, 344.
On the Nature of Waters.
On Studying Sites of Improvement, 344.
On Watering Slopes of Hills, 345.
Practical Directions in Irrigation, 346.
Practical Directions on Laying out Lands to be watered, 347.
XXXIX. On Plowing with two Oxen and Reins, 349.
An Instance of full Practice.
XL. Further on the Farmery of Buckland, 351.
On the Eligibility of a semi-octagon Cattle Yard.
On Building against a Bank of Earth.

On

On the Width of Cattle Sheds, 351.
On Erecting Wooden Pillars of Sheds.
On the proper Dimensions of Cattle Stalls, 353.
On Forming a Dung Pit, and Paving Cattle Sheds, 354.
An Instance of Practice in Watering Farm Yards, 356.
On the General Economy of Farm Yards, 357.
On the Expenditure of Dung Water, or Yard Liquor.

DISTRICT

DISTRICT THE THIRD.

THE MOUNTAINS OF CORNWALL AND DEVONSHIRE.

PREFATORY REMARKS.

THE MATERIALS which I collected, respecting these Mountain Tracts, were obtained in different ways.

What relates to CORNWALL, I gathered in an EXCURSION; undertaken for the purpose of gaining some general ideas respecting this remote part of the Island.

But, with respect to DARTMORE, and its uncultivated Environs, the information I am possessed of arose INCIDENTALLY; without any premeditated plan of survey.

 Indeed,

Indeed, theſe wild uncultivated lands reſemble, ſo much, the mountainous parts of Scotland, and the North of England, on which the broad lines of nature remain unobliterated, that a minute examination was the leſs required, by one who has been accuſtomed to read her works; and whoſe only deſire, in this inſtance, was to extract a few leading facts.

My ſources of information being thus diſtinct, I will preſerve the materials ſeparate, and, firſt offer a Tranſcript of my CORNISH JOURNAL, as it was haſtily formed, at the time of making the Excurſion (in AUGUST 1791); whether it relate to the MOUNTAINS or the LOWLANDS of Cornwall.

AN

EXCURSION

IN

CORNWALL.

THIS Excursion was made,---by CALLINGTON and LESKARD, to BODMIN; and back by LAUNCESTON and TAVISTOCK.

BUCKLAND TO BODMIN.

The ELEVATION of the Country, in this ride, is high: the road leads, moſt of the way, between the Mountains, and the broken cultivated Country toward the Sea; and, in paſſing between Leſkard and Bodmin, it croſſes over the chain of Mountains which run through this Peninſula; but not in an elevated part. Some very high hills are ſeen to the North of the road:--- "Hinkſtone," a depreſſed Cone, with a

 Proſpect

Proſpect Houſe on the top, is ſeen at great diſtances; but a hill weſtward of it, overlooking Callington, is ſaid to be the higheſt land, in the County. Many ragged *Tors*, of the true mountain caſt, are ſeen in this ride.

CLIMATURE. On the hangs of the Mountains, corn is ſtill green; but in the lower lands, harveſt is now (the twentythird of Auguſt) at its height:---more than half cut, and ſome carried.

The SURFACE is exceedingly broken, into ſharp ridges, and deep, ſteepſided vallies; eſpecially on the lower declivities of the general range of hills; as between Callington and Leſkard. On the upper parts, as between Leſkard and Bodmin, the ſwells are more rounded, and the vallies wider and leſs ſteep.

The SOIL is very various, as to quality; but even the tops of the lower mountains are far from barren; ſupporting numerous herds of cattle, as well as many ſheep:---much more productive of graſs, than the heaths of Yorkſhire; though every part produces more or leſs heath. Between

St. Ive

St. Ive and Leſkard, and below this toward the Sea, is a tract of charming land: five or ſix quarters of barley, an acre, are now harveſting. The *ſpecies of ſoil* appears to be very much like that of Weſt Devonſhire.

The SUBSOIL is alſo ſimilar:---namely, a ſlatey rock, and a kind of ruſty rotten ſlate, or rubble.

RIVERS. Several large Brooks paſs from the Mountains, ſouthward, to the Sea.

NAVIGATION. None of the Eſtuaries ſtretch up ſo high as this road. That of Looe reaches within a few miles of Leſkard.

The ROADS are of ſtone, and in ſome parts extremely well kept. The gates few, and the tolls moderate. Toll Roads are now formed between moſt or all of the market towns. The Roads of Cornwall were, formerly, very rough and dangerous; eſpecially acroſs the open heaths, among the Mines! yet, at the firſt introduction of them, in this Country, obſtinate riots took place.

MINES. Some, but not many, in this ride:---They are, now, I underſtand, chiefly confined to the Weſtern parts of the County.

 The

The MANUFACTURE of the Diſtrict, I believe, is principally Woollen Yarn, for the Devonſhire Sergemakers and Clothiers.

The TOWNSHIPS appear to be large,---with numerous Hamlets.

The PRODUCE, of the Incloſures, moſtly *Corn*. The *Heaths* ſupport the cattle in ſummer, and great part of the winter months. The principal requiſite is in courſe, Straw, to feed them with, in the depth of winter. Some *Meadows* appear in the bottoms; but little *upland graſs* is ſeen: and but very little *Woodland*; except in the Dingles, at the heads of the vallies, next the heaths.

FUEL. Towards the Mountains, Turf (provincially "vags") and Peat (provincially "Turf.") But little of the Peat, of theſe hills, is firm enough, it ſeems, to be charred (as on Dartmore), for the uſe of Black-ſmiths.

INCLOSURES. The Mountains and their ſkirts are open:---the lower lands all incloſed.

The FIELDS are well ſized, and well formed.

FENCES.

Fences. The banks thinner and lower, than in West Devonshire; but of the same form.

The Buildings are mostly of Stone and Slate: some "Cob"—or Mudwall.

Crops. Wheat and Barley, with some Oats and Turneps (unhoed), with a little Clover and upland Ley. But not a Bean nor a Pea (unless harvested), in this Ride!

The cattle are of the West of England breed: bred and kept on the heaths, in great numbers, from yearlings to aged Oxen: working these occasionally from the heath!

The Sheep of the heaths are tall, and ill formed: some polled, some horned: yet, apparently, all of the same old stock: the Ewes are now at rut: the Rams have mostly large horns.

Beasts of labor. Some Oxen and Horses in carriages. But Packhorses seem still to be much in use.

Implements. A singular kind of two-wheel carriage, for Horses or Oxen, is here in common use; especially, I believe, to carry harvest produce upon. It is called a "WAIN;" and it is a hay cart, or wain, without ſides: having only two arches bending over the wheels, to keep the load from bearing upon them! with a wince behind. How ſimple; and, being low, how eaſily loaded! I met two on the road, laden with wool; each, with two oxen at the pole, and two horſes before them.

MANURE. Lime and Beat aſhes are univerſal. A conſiderable portion of the country is now ſet with roof heaps of Lime, and with velled Beat, now burning. A great quantity of earth, I ſee, is burnt. All, no doubt, for Wheat. Theoriſts I find are, here, againſt burning the *ſoil*; but Farmers, to a man, I underſtand, are for it.

The TILLAGE is apparently better, here, than in Devonſhire. About Leſkard, the land appears to be in a good ſtate of cultivation.

ORCHARDS evidently diminiſh, with the diſtance Weſtward.

WOODLANDS.—Very few: ſome diſtant Oak coppice.—Peeling on the ſtub extends into Cornwall.

ORNA-

ORNAMENT. The views are frequently picturable, and ſometimes grand: but they cloy, through a frequency of repetition, and a degree of ſameneſs.

HARVESTING. Buſy "handreaping:" ſaw ſeveral *women* at work. Make ſhocks of ten ſheaves: nine in a ſquare, and one as a hood, as in Devonſhire. But, unleſs the ſtraw be long, and the hood ſheaf be made large and ſtraight, the covering is incompleat. Mow chiefly with bows; but cradles, I ſee, are to be ſold. About Bodmin, the Wheat in general ſeems to be made into "*arriſh mows*," or field ſtacklets, of about a load each.

FURZE. There are two diſtinct ſpecies, or varieties, now in full blow. The lower ſkirts of the uncultivated hills are gilded with them. One of them is the creeping ſort, which is common to the Southern Counties; the other is called the "French Furze;" and Taviſtock, I underſtand, has long been a market for Furze ſeed.

The GENERAL STATE OF HUSBANDRY, in ſome parts of this ride, is above mediocrity; except in the culture of Turneps. Between

Between St. Ive and Leſkard, is a paſſage of as well cultivated land, as moſt in the kingdom.

TOWNS. *Callington*, is a ſmall market town; and a *borough*. *Leſkard* is a large, populous, decent-looking place, and would appear reſpectable in any part of the Kingdom. It is likewiſe a *borough*. *Bodmin*, though one of the County towns, is much inferior, in ſize and reſpectability. This, too, is a *borough*.

BODMIN TO BUCKLAND.

THE ELEVATION of the Country is very great, between Bodmin and Five Lanes, over Bodmin Down, and Temple Moor. Some very high points of view are reached. Saw the cliff and the eſtuary of Padſtow. In a clear day, both ſeas are obſervable (near Fowey and Padſtow). Some remarkable rugged mountains are ſeen towards the North coaſt. Paſſed "Doſmary Pool," a ſmall lakelet, about a mile in circumference, upon the higher part of theſe heaths;

heaths; and crossed a quaking bog; which has formerly, no doubt, been a lake. From the elevations surmounted in this ride, and from the top of the castle of Launceston, perhaps half of Cornwall, and a very large portion of Devonshire, are seen over: the whole a strongly featured country.

CLIMATURE. Some Wheat *upon* the hills is still quite green. The harvest, in this elevated situation, is in general very late. Sometimes, being prolonged, till after Michaelmas *.

SURFACE. About ten miles of the upper part of the heaths, over which this road passes, is tamely billowy; the swells resembling those of the Downs of the Southern Counties; with lofty mountains on each hand; a charming ride, *in fine weather*. The remaining ten miles, to Launceston, and from thence to Buckland, is the same abruptly broken country, which prevails throughout the more cultivated parts of the two Counties.

The

* An intelligent fellow traveller; formerly of Bodmin: now of Launceston.

The SOIL towards Bodmin is of a mean quality; neverthelefs, the Downs and Moors are thickly ftocked with Cattle and Sheep; efpecially with the former: faw, on one of the higher knolls, fome hundreds in a herd!

About Launcefton, are fome wellfoiled, but very fteep hills. At Milton *Abbots!* is a plot of the fineft grafsland in the Kingdom! Grazing ground of a very fuperior quality. The Midland Counties cannot fhew better. Alfo about Lamerton and Taviftock, is fome good grazing land.

MINES. There is no "mine" within fight of this ride. But two or three confiderable "ftream works" are feen: one of which I ftopt to look into. In a ftream work, there is no "lode" or body of ore; the tin being lodged in fmall particles or fragments, among the earth (at two or three to twenty or thirty feet deep) which is wafhed by a rill or ftream, conveyed, by art, to the required fpot *; the metal and ftones remaining; while the foil is carried away

* Query, Have STREAM WORKS given rife to "LEATS," or made Streams, in this Country?

away with the ſtream: thus annihilating the *land*, in the moſt compleat manner ingenuity could deviſe.

RIVERS. The Tamer and Tavey: alſo the heads of ſome of the Southern rivers.

The ROAD in general is good. For a conſiderable way, the ſtones are covered with a kind of rough ſand, or ſmall gravel, apparently, the looſe materials of which granite is compoſed; making an admirable road.

INCLOSURE.—The moors are open: except ſome ſmall incloſures, about Temple &c. Cultivated lands are everywhere incloſed.

PRODUCE—as before.

MANUFACTURE.—Yarn.

BUILDINGS.—Stône and Slate. At Launceſton the houſes are moſtly faced with Slates: ſome of them three or four feet ſquare. The Church is of Moorſtone, deeply and richly ſculptured! Subſtantial, and beautiful, as a Gothic building: the workmanſhip muſt have been immenſely great; ſeeing the hardneſs of the materials—a ſhining granite.

FIELDS

FIELDS—as before.

FENCES—increaſe toward Devonſhire, ſwelling to their fulleſt magnitude, at Buckland Place.

CROPS—as before; excepting the grazing grounds of Milton and Taviſtock.

CATTLE. The Moor ſtock are of the Weſt of England breed: ſaw ſome oxen which would fat to ſixty or ſeventy ſtone on theſe heathy mountains! All in very good ſtore condition.

SHEEP. The ſame tall, aukward ſort, as about Bodmin.

GOATS. Saw ſeveral browzing on furze. I was told that numbers are kept in Cornwall, for milking; ſome herds conſiſting of a hundred head; and that Goats' and Kids' fleſh are not uncommon in the Corniſh markets.

BEAST OF LABOR—as above.

MANURE. Beat aſhes, and "ſea ſand;" a fine *ſhell marl*; which is brought in great quantities from the North coaſt, by the Padſtow river, to within three miles of Bodmin; and carried, by land, many miles.

TILLAGE—as before.

HAR-

HARVESTING—the ſame.

STATE OF HUSBANDRY,—much the ſame:—ſomewhat inferior.

ORCHARDS—increaſe toward Devonſhire.

WOODLANDS. There are few in Cornwall; except on the banks of the Tamer.

ORNAMENT. The mountain views are extenſive and grand: thoſe from the lower points are frequently pictureſque.

TOWNS. *Temple*, a DESERTED VILLAGE! The only one I have ever ſeen. Some years ago, not a ſingle perſon lived in the townſhip! (a Curacy appendant to Bliſland) and only one little farmhouſe is now inhabited:——the ruins of half a dozen more; the body of the Church down; the Chancel remains. GOLDSMITH, ſurely, muſt have travelled this road!

Launceſton—provincially and univerſally, throughout the country, "*Laanſon*," is a genteel looking place; but aukwardly ſituated; on the brink and ſide of a very ſteep hill. The ſtreet leading to Newport is as ſteep, almoſt, as the roof of a houſe. The caſtle, which has been a very ſtrong fortreſs, com-

commands ſome charming views. *New-port* a paltry *borough*:—a mean looking hamlet; belonging to the pariſh of St. Stephen's, a village which ſtands oppoſite to Launceſton. *Milton Abbots* a charming ſituation. The Abbots were admirable judges of ſoils and ſituations. *Taviſtock* is alſo well ſituated; and was heretofore famous for its *abbotry*.

GENERAL OBSERVATIONS. I am agreeably diſappointed with reſpect to Cornwall. From what I had ſeen on the banks of the Tamer*, I expected to have found, as I went farther Weſtward, a wretched country, wretched roads, wretched towns, wretched accommodations, and wretched inhabitants. On the contrary, the country, whether in point of ſoil or cultivation,—except the higher mountains, and they are good in their kind,—is above mediocrity. The roads, their unlevelneſs apart, are among the beſt in the kingdom. The towns, ſubſtantial and neat. The accommodations, equal to anything met with, out of the great roads. The inhabitants, intelligent, civil, are ſaid to be extremely hoſpitable, are

* See No. 3 of the following MINUTES.

are affable, clean in their appearance, and handſome in their perſons. What moſt diſguſts a ſtranger, in travelling through Cornwall, is the inordinate number of its boroughs; and this impropriety lies not with the people of Cornwall. There are none, indeed, ſo ſenſible of it, as the inhabitants themſelves.

DARTMORE,

AND ITS

UNCULTIVATED ENVIRONS.

THE Incidents, which led me to a knowledge of this Diſtrict, are various. I had repeated occaſions to traverſe the WESTERN SKIRTS of Dartmore. I purpoſely aſcended the SOUTHERN HEIGHTS, to view the ſtriking features which that ſide of it exhibits, and to catch a bird's eye view of the Diſtrict of the South Hams. I croſſed the SUMMIT, in travelling between Morton and Buckland. And I ſkirted the NORTH-WESTERN MARGIN, in paſſing between Taviſtock and Okehampton. I have, therefore, had opportunities of ſeeing almoſt every ſquare mile of its ſurface, and of obſerving its natural characters, in different and diſtant parts.

The SITUATION, of this uncultivated tract of country, is towards the Weſtern ſide of Devonſhire; being, in part, ſeparated from the Corniſh mountains, by the cultivated banks of the Tamer: but, to the North of Taviſtock, the ſkirts of Dartmore, and thoſe of the uncultivated wilds of Cornwall, may be ſaid to unite: for although they are ſtrewed with plots of cultivated lands, there is no regular line of ſeparation; and the ſame mixed country ſpreads wide, on the North-Weſt quarter, towards Launceſton, and to the immediate environs of Okehampton. On the South, lies the fertile Diſtrict of the South Hams; and a continuation of the Chudleigh or Hall Down Hills, broken in a moſt ſtriking manner, ſeparates it on the Eaſt, from the vale of Exeter.

The EXTENT of theſe wild lands is not eaſy to eſtimate; there being no determinate line, on the North-Weſt ſide. A circle of twenty miles diameter, would, perhaps, comprize the whole extent of the open

open lands, in this part of Devonſhire; exclusively of the incloſed lands, which lie intermixed among them. Admitting this ſuppoſition to be ſufficiently near the truth, to give a general idea of the extent of thoſe open lands, we may ſay that they cover more than three hundred ſquare miles of ſurface, —amount to more than two hundred thouſand acres.

In ELEVATION above the ſea, theſe lands are greatly varied. The extended ſummit of the main body of the mountain, is raiſed, in a ſingular manner, above the ſurrounding country; eſpecially on the South ſide. Looking down, even from the midway ſtages, upon the South Hams, an upland Diſtrict, the comparative elevation is ſo great, as to render the idea of difficulty, in travelling acroſs the latter, truly ridiculous. Nevertheleſs, the ſea waſhing, in a manner, the foot of the mountain, its poſitive height is inconſiderable, compared with that of many leſs mountain-like maſſes, which occur in the more central parts of the Iſland. On the North ſide, the ſtages are lengthened, and the general deſcent much leſs abrupt. The outſkirts, round Brent Tor, and towards Launceſton, form an extended flat, mean in elevation, compared with the towering heights, which overlook it, on either ſide *.

The SURFACE, of Dartmore proper, is truly mountainous. The compoſition is grand; the lines in general lengthened, and the features large: not abrupt and broken, like the minor hills of Devonſhire. Nevertheleſs, the ſummits of ſeveral of the higher ſwells of Dartmore are truly ſavage, and rendered finely picturesque, by reaſon of immenſe piles of ſtones, or huge fragments of rock, thrown confuſedly together, in

* The conical hillock of BRENT-TOR, pointed with rugged rocks, and ſurmounted by a Church! riſes in the center of this wide flat. From the grounds of Buckland, this hillock aſſumes the character of a mountain height of conſiderable magnitude; and, in navigating the Sound of Plymouth, it is uſed as a landmark, at more than twenty miles diſtance;—yet, in reality, it is but an inconſiderable hillock. A proof of the extreme levelneſs of this paſſage of country.

LAUNCESTON CASTLE, crowning a higher, but more rotund eminence, is another ſtriking feature of the ſame fine, broad, ſavage face.

in the moſt groteſque manner: ſometimes crowning the knolls, but oftener hanging on their brows.

In ſome parts, the ſurface is thickly ſtrewed with ſtones; which, in many inſtances, appear to have been collected into piles, on the tops of prominent hillocks; as if in imitation of the natural Tors.—The "*ſtone burrows*," of Dartmore, reſemble the *Cairns*, of the Chiviot and Grampian hills.

The WATERS of this tract of mountain are merely the torrents, which pour down its furrowed ſides, in every direction. The DART is the moſt conſiderable ſtream that owes its ſupport to theſe hills.

The SOILS of theſe unreclaimed lands are greatly above the par of mountain ſoils, in the Iſland at large. They are ſuperior to thoſe of the Highlands of Scotland, and very ſuperior to thoſe of the North of England. Some of the higher ſwells, it is true, are covered with black moory earth; and in the dips between them, peat bogs are frequent, and dangerous, not only to ſtrangers who travel the croſs roads, but to pasturing stock. And, in many parts, the soil is much encumbered with stones; which, in some, occupies, perhaps, half the surface. Nevertheless, there are extensive tracts, even of the upper grounds, that enjoy a loamy soil, nearly free from stones, and of a sufficient depth for cultivation: wanting nothing but a genial climature, and a proper supply of manure, to render them valuable, as arable lands. And soils of still better quality are observable, on some of the marginal Commons; though, on others, those of inferior value may be found.

The SUBSOILS are equally various. I have observed a stoney rubble, or foul YELLOW GRAVEL, resembling that of the Yorkshire mountains; also a friable, BROWN ROCK; and, even on the higher hills, LOAM, of a sufficient depth for every purpose of land.

The PRESENT PRODUCTION of Dartmore and its uncultivated environs may with some little licence be said to be HERBAGE!—greensward! even of the highest bleakest hills; frequently intermixed, however, with HEATH; which, indeed, chiefly occupies

occupies the worst-soiled parts of the mountain; while, on the lower grounds, the FURZE, particularly the trailing sort, is prevalent. There is little if any WOOD, I believe, on the unappropriated parts of this tract of country: the FUEL, used by the bordering inhabitants, being the produce of the peat-bogs, and the black moory soils; as in other mountainous Districts *.

The APPLICATION of the pasturable produce, which this uncultivated wild at present throws out, is to CATTLE, SHEEP, and HORSES, and some few RABBITS.

The RIGHT of DEPASTURE belongs to different interests. A considerable part of the mountain is FOREST LAND, subject to the superiority of the DUCHY OF CORNWALL. The outskirts, and parts of the hills, are appendant to the MANORS of the subjoining country; and the right of pasturage vested in the appropriated lands of those manors. And beside this intrinsic right,

* Some of the PEAT is of a superior quality; admitting of being CHARRED; and in this state, it is used by BLACKSMITHS, instead of pit coal.

right, over their respective commons; many of those lands have a prescriptive right, on the forest, by paying an inconsiderable sum —a few pence—annually, under the name of *Venville money*, to the Duchy. The Duchy, nevertheless, preserves the right of stocking the forest lands, by *agistment*: and stock are sent, in numbers, from distant townships; paying a very low price for their pasturage: not more than a shilling or eighteen pence, a head; being paid for the summer's run of cattle!

Beside the CATTLE thus brought together by agistment, great numbers are reared, by the Venville tenants, on the verge of the forest; under a routine of practice that has been already mentioned *.

The SHEEP, being drawn together, from various quarters, differ as to breed. On the Southern hangs, and on the upper parts of the mountain, the polled breed of the South Hams are mostly seen. But, on the Northern and Western sides of it, the partially horned breed, which has been no-

* See Vol. I. P. 244.

noticed *, are prevalent; correſponding, in general appearance, with the eſtabliſhed breed of the Corniſh mountains; but of a better frame. In winter, thoſe ſheep are drawn down to the incloſed country, where the ewes drop their lambs, and return with them, in the ſpring, to their mountain paſture.

Hence, the leading OBJECT of the MOORSIDE FARMER is to raiſe fodder enough for his cattle, and to preſerve graſs enough for his ſheep, to ſupply them, during the winter months; depending, almoſt wholly, on the commonable lands, for their ſummer maintenance; his milking cows and rearing calves excepted: working oxen are, everywhere, ſeen on the commonable land, both of Devonſhire and Cornwall: their work, under this treatment, being in courſe moderate.

The PRESENT VALUE of theſe lands appears, from this general view of their application, to be far from inconſiderable. I had not an opportunity of eſtimating the aggregate

* See Vol. I. P. 259.

aggregate of the ſtock they ſupport. But an eye, accuſtomed to obſervations of this nature, may readily diſcover, that, in a POLITICAL LIGHT, theſe uncultivated lands are, at preſent, of ſome eſtimation. For admitting that a Moorſide Farmer, by the aſſiſtance of theſe lands, in ſupporting his ſtock nine or ten months of the year, is enabled to rear, and forward to market, twice the number of cattle and ſheep (or even one fourth of ſuch additional number), that he could without their aſſiſtance,—the aggregate increaſe of produce to the community, would be found, on calculation, to be worthy of public regard. And, in a PRIVATE point of view, if one may judge from the good eſtimation in which Venville farms are held,—from the extraordinary prices which the Moorſide men give for rearing calves,—namely, fifteen to twentyfive ſhillings, at three days old! a price which they nowhere elſe bear,—and from the comfortable livelihoods which the ſmalleſt of theſe farmers are enabled to make,—theſe lands are not, at preſent, wholly thrown away.

Never-

Neverthelefs, though they are doubtlefs of confiderable value, at prefent, it does not follow that they are, at prefent, in their moft valuable ftate.

To fpeak, in pofitive terms, of the means requifite to the

IMPROVEMENT

of this uncultivated tract of country, might be prefumptuous, in one who has confeffedly given it only a curfory incidental examination. But it has alfo been premifed, that the paffage of country, under confideration, is of a fpecies fimilar to the Moors of Yorkfhire, and the Mountains of Perthfhire,—both of which I have examined with attention, and have, at different periods of time, feparately digefted my ideas, with refpect to their improvement: circumftances which enable me to fpeak, with greater confidence, on the improvement of the moory mountains of Devonfhire; whofe diftinguifhing characteriftics lie, chiefly, in the fuperiority of foil and climature, compared with thofe of the unreclaimed lands of Yorkfhire and Perthfhire.

In

In ſuggeſting hints for the improvement of Dartmore and its uncultivated environs, it will be proper to conſider the mountain or foreſt lands, ſeparately from the commons, and lower grounds of the extenſive flat which has been mentioned; as they appear to me to require ſomewhat different principles of improvement.

In the improvement of the HIGHER LANDS, the leading objects appear, to me, to be WOOD and HERBAGE. Their *climature*, I apprehend, unfits them for the profitable production of CORN: and a want of *manure* is another bar to this ſpecies of produce. Nevertheleſs, there may be dips and unreclaimed vallies, which, *as limited home grounds*, might admit of a courſe of arable management.

But ſpeaking generally of theſe lands, the firſt means of improvement appears to me, to be that of PLANTING, or otherwiſe covering with wood, the STONEY SURFACES: not more to encreaſe the value of theſe particular parts, than to improve the climature of the whole. The *Birch*, the *Mountain Sorb*, and the *Larch*, if judiciouſly pro-

propagated, would flouriſh, I apprehend, on the bleakeſt expoſures.

To improve the HERBAGE of the freer ſurface of theſe expoſed lands, various means might be ſuggeſted.

Running high FENCE MOUNDS acroſs the current of the Southweſt winds, and planting them with Birch, Mountain Sorb, Elder, Holly, Furze, Broom, &c. in the Devonſhire manner; but making the top of the mound hollow, or concave, to collect and retain moiſture, and to ſkreen the young plants, or ſeedlings, in their tender ſtate. It were impoſſible, perhaps, to conceive a better fence, for bleak mountain lands, than the ordinary hedge of Devonſhire. The mound is an immediate fence and ſhelter; and the coppice wood, as it grew up, could not fail, from its relative height above the ſubjoining lands, to IMPROVE their CLIMATURE; and encourage, in a particular manner, the *growth of herbage*; beſide being, at the ſame time, ſingularly friendly to paſturing ſtock. The only doubt, as to the propriety of raiſing ſuch fences, acroſs the bleak lands of Dartmore,

more, lies in the expence of doing it: for, great as the poſitive advantages would doubtleſs be found,—if the expence of raiſing them overbalanced theſe advantages, ſuch means of improvement would be altogether ineligible to be proſecuted, by *Individuals*, however profitable the effect might be to the *Public*. The freer, better-ſoiled parts of Dartmore, I am of opinion, would pay Individuals, amply, for this CARDINAL IMPROVEMENT.

To change the preſent produce to more profitable paſturage, either in the open or an incloſed ſtate, different means might be purſued.

BURNING OFF THE HEATH of the black moory parts, and paſturing them hard with ſheep, would tend to extirpate the heath, and bring up herbage in its place. The Cheviot hills of Northumberland, and ſimilar hills in the South of Scotland, were probably brought to their preſent ſtate of green turf, by this means.

SODBURNING the more loamy ſoils, ſowing RAPE AND GRASS SEEDS, and FOLDING OFF THE PRODUCE, with ſheep, would

would be a ready means of meliorating the herbage.

If, by the intervention of Hedge mounds, the climature of theſe Hills could be rendered ſufficiently genial for the maturation of RAPE SEED, and ſhould their ſoils be found ſufficiently productive of this valuable crop, the propriety of erecting ſuch fences would no longer remain doubtful; as a full crop of this grain would amply repay any reaſonable expence that could be incurred by incloſing; and the incloſure would amply recompenſe the loſs, which the ſoil could ſuſtain, from the exhauſtion of *one grain crop:* graſs ſeeds being, in courſe, ſown with the rape ſeed, or over the plants in the ſpring; or a due portion, at either ſeaſon.

By DRAINING the ſpringy ſlopes of hills, and perhaps ſome of the Peatbogs, the produce of thoſe parts might be very materially improved.

By WATERING, ſuch parts of the lower ſlopes as can command water, the herbage, perhaps, might be eſſentially bettered:

But very much would depend on the quality of the water; and this experience would readily prove.

By MANURING, ſomething might doubtleſs be done, towards the melioration of the herbage. The vegetable mold of the Peatbogs, either in a crude recent ſtate, or in the ſtate of charcoal, or in that of aſhes, would, with moral certainty, be found ſerviceable to the loamy ſoils. And earthy ſubſtances, which, if ſought for, might doubtleſs be found, could not fail of producing beneficial effects, on the black moory lands. It is needleſs to add, that if Lime could be brought to theſe lands, at a moderate expence, there would be little riſque in the free uſe of it. With its powerful aid, even CORN might be produced, on many of the lands under notice; but whether with *eventual* advantage, either to the Proprietor or the Public (unleſs on a ſmall ſcale), is a matter of great uncertainty.

The moſt profitable STOCK for theſe lands, in the ſtate of improvement above ſuggeſted, would probably be found to be *young Cattle*, *Sheep*, and *Rabbits*.

There

There appears to be many ſituations in which the laſt would be moſt eligible. Seeing the local ſituation of theſe weak-ſoiled lands, --- between the markets of Exeter and Plymouth,---and the favorable turn of ſurface, which Nature has given to many of them, for the propagation of this ſpecies of farm ſtock, it is rather extraordinary that RABBIT WARRENS ſhould not be more common, in this Diſtrict, than they appear to be at preſent. But, perhaps, the true reaſon has been already aſſigned. See Vol. I. Page 271.

In the improvement of the LOWER GROUNDS of this extenſive tract of unreclaimed lands;

CLIMATURE is the firſt object of attention. It is well known, to thoſe who have embraced opportunities of obſerving natural effects, that the Climature of an extended and naked plain is frequently more ſevere and chilling, both to the animal and the vegetable creation, than that of a billowy ſurface, of much greater elevation. The wind, in paſſing over the latter, is broken into eddies, and its effects are thereby

 ſoftened:

ſoftened: beſide, let the blaſt blow from whence it may, ſome part of ſuch a ſurface will always afford a degree of ſhelter, to animals that have free range over it; and even vegetables, that are fixed, enjoy by turns, as the wind ſhifts, the advantages of its ſhelter---while, over an extent of naked level ſurface, the current ruſhes forward with unabating force; and let it ſet from whatever quarter, vegetables and animals are equally expoſed to its unrelenting ſeverity. Some Oaks, ſcattered over the flat of wild lands now under conſideration, might be adduced, with numberleſs other facts, in evidence of the truth of this theory. They are cut down flat, as with an edge-tool. Had they ſtood on the heights of Maker, expoſed to the immediate ſea blaſt, they would not probably have ſuffered more.

Hence, in this ſituation, as on the hills, the firſt ſtep towards improvement would be to convert to Woodland, ſuch parts as are unfit for cultivation; and to raiſe Coppice Hedges acroſs the line of the moſt miſchievous winds, as ſkreens to the culturable lands.

In

In a Climature thus improved, and with a ſufficient ſupply of LIME, at a moderate price, I am of opinion that ſome conſiderable proportion of theſe flat lands might be ſubjected, with profit, to a courſe of arable Management. But without a plentiful ſupply of Lime, or other calcareous MANURE, it appears to me more than probable, from what I have ſeen of theſe lands, that very few of them would pay for cultivation, as arable lands.

I am therefore of opinion, that, without the aſſiſtance of INLAND NAVIGATION, this extenſive tract of Country muſt neceſſarily remain in its preſent ſtate, or be improved as paſture grounds, in the manner which has been already ſuggeſted, for the higher lands of Dartmore.

Viewing this wide extent of Country, which, with moral certainty, might be highly improved, by means of a plentiful ſupply of LIME: Viewing, next, the numerous tracts of uncultivated lands between Okehampton and Biddeford, which are evidently ſtill more improveable, as will preſently be ſhewn, and by the ſame

MANURE:---And, laſtly, viewing the extenſive tracts of Woodland, ſeen in paſſing between the places laſt mentioned, and the value of SHIP TIMBER at Plymouth,---there can be little riſque in ſaying, that there is no other Diſtrict in this Iſland in which the LANDED INTEREST calls equally loud for Inland Navigation, as the line of Country between PLYMOUTH and BIDDEFORD.

And ſeeing, at the ſame time, the length, and ſtill more the uncertainty, of the paſſage, between Wales and the port of Plymouth, by ſea; and the quantity of CULM which is now uſed for burning Lime, on the banks of the various Eſtuaries that branch out of it, as well as COALS for the uſe of Plymouth and its neighbourhood,---it appears that the INTERESTS of TRAFFIC are alſo concerned.

Finally, admitting, what I believe. is known to be a fact, that it is the bulky articles, here particularized --- namely, LIME, COALS, and TIMBER, not the Boxes and Bales of Trade, that render Inland Navigation profitable,--- it may be fairly concluded,

concluded, that no Line of Canal is more likely to *pay*, than that now under consideration.

The proper direction, of the Southern part of the Line, is evident. The TIDE flows within the Estuary or Mouth of the TAVEY: and, where the Tide ends, the CANAL should commence; winding up the valley of the Tavey, to TAVISTOCK; a branch being thrown off, up the valley of the Walkham, to HARROW BRIDGE, for the use of the extensive Commons in that neighbourhood, and to catch the use of the public road which there crosses the valley. Above Tavistock, the main line would still wind with the valley of the Tavey, to the FOOT OF THE DARTMORE HILLS (a most desirable point to be gained),---and thence bend across the uncultivated flat, towards OKEHAMPTON.

In travelling between Tavistock and Okehampton, I observed (between Lydford and the latter place) that the road was repaired with LIMESTONE!---black marble; a circumstance which renders it more than probable, that the raw materials of improvement lie within the field to be improved ; and that FUEL only would be wanted, to render the profecution eafy and profitable.

Without intending to cenfure the fupineness, which has lately prevailed in this Country, with refpect to the permanent improvement of its furface, I will not hefitate to fay, that had advantages, like thofe which are here adduced, occurred within the interior of the Ifland, they would long ago have been feen and embraced : and that whenever the fpirit of enterprize, in this extreme part of it, fhall fhift its ground, from MINING to AGRICULTURE, the Improvement which is here pointed out, will be carried into effect.

DISTRICT THE FOURTH.

NORTH DEVONSHIRE.

PREFATORY REMARKS.

AN accurate Definition of what is familiarly called "NORTH DEVON," or "the North Country," I ſhall not attempt to give. It is generally applied, I believe, to the Country lying towards the North Coaſt; round Biddeford, Barnſtaple, and South Moulton. But the Diſtrict to which this name aptly applies, is ſituated between the Mountain of Dartmore and the Sea;--- comprizing a wide extent of Country: diverſified, it is true, in ſoil and ſurface; but it has no diſtinct ſeparation of parts, large enough to warrant its being divided into ſeparate Diſtricts.

As the only opportunity I had of collecting information, reſpecting this Diſtrict, was

was obtained by an EXCURSION, undertaken for the purpose of viewing its prominent features, and of remarking the overt practices, which meet the eye of every Traveller, who looks attentively round him, --- I will not attempt a digested Register, either of the District, or its Rural Management; but offer a Transcript of my Travelling Journal *.

The route which I thought it proper to take, was from OKEHAMPTON to HATHERLEY, TORRINGTON, BIDDEFORD, BARNSTAPLE, SOUTH MOULTON, and across the Country to DULVERTON (to catch

* It is, however, with diffidence and some reluctance, I adopt this mode of publication. And I have only to say, in its behalf, that the series of remarks, which are here published, arose from facts and reflections, that occurred, in passing through the District under review; and were in general *dictated*, while the several subjects of Remark—remained under the eye.

The defective style, in which they appear, is the convenient one of a Journal,—or *verbal sketch book*. It is concise; and the pronoun, or the verb, which may frequently be wanting, is readily to be *understood*. If the first person were used, egotism would disgust: if the second (as it is in the ordinary style of Journals) sense would be sacrificed.

catch a view of Exmoor and the fine ſcenery of its Environs); and thence, to BAMPTON and TIVERTON.

OKEHAMPTON

AND ITS

ENVIRONS.

SUNDAY 14 SEPTEMPER, 1794.

THE TOWN, well ſized and reſpectable, conſidering the recluſeneſs of its ſituation, is ſeated in a deep baſon, broken into three parts, by the narrow wooded vallies of the Oke and its two principal branches: the former winding towards the North, the latter ſpreading wide to the Eaſt and Weſt; and embracing, as with arms, the Northern point of the Dartmore Mountain; which here forms a flattened ſtage, of conſiderable extent and elevation; overlooking the town, and forming one ſide of the baſon in which it is ſituated. The face of the ſteep is finely hung with wood; —moſtly large full-headed Oaks; being part

part of the ancient demeſne lands, belonging to the Caſtle of Okehampton; whoſe ruins ſtill occupy a peninſular hillock that faces this bold woody ſteep; being divided from it by the Weſtern branch of the Oke. The ſcenery truly alpine.

Sheep, of a diminutive ſize, are grazing among the ruins of the Caſtle. Various in head, as thoſe of Weſt Devonſhire and Cornwall. Some of them reſembling very much, in head and carcaſe, the ſize apart, the improved breed of Dorſetſhire.

The ſite of the Caſtle, and the ſteep rugged height, on the face of which it ſtood, appears to be compoſed of ſlatey rock, ſimilar to that of Weſt and South Devonſhire.

Upon this eminence, and on the Weſtern brink of the Baſon, ſtands the principal Church of Okehampton: proudly ſituated; and forming a good object from the oppoſite height; making one feature of a fine landſcape.

The entire Environs, and the views from them are rich and beautiful; but the ſcale is ſmall. A truly monaſtic ſituation; ---rich

—rich and recluſe---yet, I believe, without the veſtige of a monaſtery!

The fertile ſwells are now loaded with graſs; and ſome of them ſtocked with good Cows, of the North Devonſhire breed. But little corn; and moſt of this is ſtill in the field. The North ſide of a Mountain Diſtrict is naturally liable to a backwardneſs of climature.

OKEHAMPTON

TO

TORRINGTON.

(17 Miles)

MONDAY 15 SEPTEMBER, 1794.

ASCEND, by a ſteep ill conducted road, the Weſtern banks of the Oke, and leave the cultivated Environs, at one mile from the Town.

Delightful morning!

The Okehampton hounds are gone out, towards the hills of Dartmore, another pack now

now paſs the carriage, towards the oppoſite hills. A finely wild ſporting country.

Enter an extenſive furze-grown Common; apparently well ſoiled, and the ſubſoil rotten ſlate. Land fit for almoſt any purpoſe of Huſbandry.

Several plots of this Common are now ſodburnt and liming for Wheat! The entire Common lies in narrow ridges, as if it had undergone the ſame operation, and been ſuffered to lay down again to reſt, after one crop of corn had been thus taken.

The Stock, now on this ill applied tract, are ſmall Sheep; ſimilar to thoſe near Okehampton.

A rich Valley opens to the right: to the left, a mixed Country; marked by the Church of Ingerley: a pleaſing though gayly coloured object. But the morning is fine; and Nature herſelf appearing gay, a white waſhed ſteeple aſſimilates with the ſcene.

Enter an incloſed, but rough, upland Country.

Farm houſes and Cottages mean; moſtly of mud and thatch.

Hedgemounds

Hedgemounds in the manner of West Devonshire; but not, in general, so high.

See red soil, in the valley to the right.

More furze-covered Commons;—highly improveable: a waste of property to suffer them to remain in their present unproductive state. A patch of Wheat stubble on one of these Commons, discovers, in its own strength, that of the land.

Some rubbishly ill bred Cattle, on these Commons. The natural produce of commonable lands.

Cross a cold clayey Dip; and enter more extensive Commons. Thousands of acres of dwarf furze, which ought to be supplanted by Wheat, Beans, and Clover.

Some Timber Trees seen scattered over the Inclosures.

Grass Inclosures velled for Wheat; as in the South of Devonshire.

The spring and the autumn furzes are here intermixed, as in Cornwall and West Devonshire.

A billowy, wooded, Kentish view opens to the left.

A newly

A newly planted Hedgemound. The plants as thick as the arm, and cut down to two or three feet high, as in West Devonshire. The Hedgewoods Birch, Hazel, Ash.

Enter a cold-soiled Woodland District. Instance of Scotch Firs planted on this cold retentive soil!

Still more extensive tracts of dwarf furze. Not only the Commons, but some Inclosures, are cropped with this unprofitable plant; the whole of these furze grounds lying in narrow Wheat ridges.

The common Sheep, here, are small and mostly polled.

A large parcel of hewn Timber, fit for Ship Building, collected by the side of the road.

The subsoil of these Commons is a red clayey gravel.

Enter an inclosed, red soiled plot of Country,—the immediate Environs of

HATHERLY: a mean market Town: mostly or wholly built with red earth and thatch. Some of the houses white-washed, others

others rough-caſt. Obſerved Reed in ſheaves; as in the Weſtern parts of the County.

A beautifully wooded Dip breaks, to the left: the valley of the Torridge.

Leave the red ſoil, about a mile from Hatherly. The ſubſoil a deep grouty rubble: red as oker.

Enter a cold, vale Country. The ſubſoil a pale coloured clay.

A narrow flat of river-formed land.

Buildings entirely of clay.

Four Oxen, two Horſes, two Men, and a Boy, at plow!

A ſhameful fall of young Timber.

A charming broad wooded Baſon, now opens to the Weſt;---between Hatherly and Sheepwaſh.

And, now, a wide flat of Marſhes to the right; apparently in a wild, neglected, unproductive ſtate.

Hewiſh, Sir James Norcliff's, appears on the oppoſite banks of theſe marſh lands.

A bad Turnpike road traces a high ridge of cold white clay,---commanding a ſtrongly featured country.

Ridges of Lime and Earth, for Wheat, are common in the adjoining Inclosures.

Coppice Hedges universal.

Descend, by a steep road, into a well soiled Dip of Land. The subsoil slatey rubble, or rotten slate rock.

Very few Orchard Grounds in this Country.

Ascend "Padstow" Hill: an insulated eminence; commanding a fine circle of views. To the South, the Mountain of Dartmoore rising bold to the view, and forming a remarkably strong feature from this point. To the East, the rising banks of the Oke and the Taw; apparently, well soiled, and well cultivated; the foreground of this view, the Valley of "Marland"--- or Marshland, in a state of neglect,---much of it occupied by furze; to appearance, highly improveable. To the North, a ridge of well soiled arable upland. To the West, a well wooded District.

A delightful morning: with the Lark in full song:---and with hounds in full cry!

A distant view of the North Country, now begins to open.

The

The Country, here, wholly incloſed: moſtly in large ſquare *Devonſhire* Fields.

Paſſed the firſt Cart: drawn in the Cleveland manner! three horſes; one in the ſhafts, the other two abreaſt, and guided by reins: loaded with bark, for the port of Biddeford; to be there ſhipped for Ireland.

Croſs a well timbered Hollow. Much valuable Ship Timber, in this Diſtrict.

Cloſe woody lanes,---how tantalizing to a Traveller!

Enter a well ſoiled paſſage; moſtly arable. Some patches of Turneps and Clover.

Very few Field Potatoes in this Diſtrict.

A Box: Winſcot: the firſt *Houſe* I have paſſed, in this ſtage.

Still a well ſoiled arable Country. Farms ſeemingly of good ſize; and not ill cultivated.

Obſerve ſeveral good Horſes. Q. Bred in this Diſtrict?

Another paſſage of good upland Country. Skirted by a cold ruſhy bottom.

Meet a ſtring of Lime Horſes, from Biddeford; eight or ten miles.

Lime, here, a prevailing manure.

Hedgemounds increaſe in height: this, altogether, a South-Devonſhire-like Diſtrict.

An extenſive view opens to the left.

Inſtance of a cropt Hedge. What a loſs to the Traveller, that the practice is not prevalent.

Large white Pigs, in a good form.

A fine view of the Valley of Torrington burſts upon the eye.

Orchard Grounds encreaſe.

A charming back view of the Valley above Torrington: well formed ground, happily enriched with wood and water.

An extenſive and rich view, to the right, including the Eaſtern banks of the Taw.

An inſtance of limed Graſsland.

Dip down to the Bridge of Torrington.

GENERAL REMARKS.

THE Townſhips, in this ſtage, appear to be of the middle ſize. The Churches, in general, tall and conſpicuous.

Of

Of the State of Inclosure, it may be said, that about half the lands, which fall immediately under the eye, are inclosed; the rest, in coarse furzey Commons, capable of great improvement.

The Fields are generally well shaped, and well sized; as in West and South Devonshire.

The Fences, throughout, are similar to those in the Southern parts of the County. But the Mounds are somewhat narrower and lower.

Woodlands extensive. Oak the prevailing wood. Much fine Timber: much also in a state of Coppice.

The Orchard Grounds are few and small.

The Arable Crops appear, by the stubbles, to be chiefly Wheat and Oats: but altogether small, in proportion to the Grasslands and Furze Grounds, which occupy this Line of Country; especially towards Okehampton.

The Climature somewhat forwarder than about Okehampton. The crops mostly harvested.

The preparations, now going on for the next year's crop of Wheat, are the very ſame, here, as in the South of Devonſhire; namely, ley ground burnt and limed.

Very few Cattle, or Sheep, are ſeen in the Incloſures; which are now full of graſs.

The ſtate of Huſbandry, on the whole, is conſiderably below par.

TORRINGTON AND ITS ENVIRONS.

THE TOWN is proudly ſituated on the brink, and partly hanging on the brow, of the Eaſtern bank of the Oke. It is a large inland Market Town; but has no thorofare to ſupport it. There is no poſting inn, in the place! and only one chaiſe kept for hire. Nevertheleſs, the Town is neat, and the people alive. Circumſtances to be accounted for, only, in the many family reſidences, which appear in its neighbourhood, and which ſeldom fail to meliorate the manners

manners of every claſs of thoſe, who fall within the ſphere of their influence.

The view from the ſite of the Caſtle---now a Bowling Green---is uncommonly fine. A wooded amphitheatre, richly diverſified: with a lengthened bend of water in the middle ground:---and with fox-hounds in the woods!

TORRINGTON

TO

BIDDEFORD.

(Seven Miles)

MONDAY, 15 SEPTEMBER, 1794.

A well ſoiled Common near the Town; ſtocked with ſmall neat ſheep.

Paſs between well ſoiled Incloſures: a rich and beautiful Country.

Croſs a lovely wooded valley: thriving Oak Timber; well thinned, and ſet out.

A ſmall Yorkſhire plow. The firſt I have obſerved in the County.

The ſurface broken, abruptly, into hill and dale: a truly Danmonian paſſage.

Surmount a clean upland Country. The ſubſtratum brown ruſty rock.

Reach the ſummit of the ridge: a furze-grown waſte. A broad view of the Briſtol Channel meets the eye; with extenſive land views, on either ſide. On the one hand, Hartland Point is a prominent and ſtriking feature; on the other, Exmore? riſes boldly to the view.

Deſcend towards Biddeford.

Meet ſtrings of Lime Horſes, with pack-ſaddles and bags of Lime. Alſo two-horſe Carts, with Lime and Sea ſand.

General Remark.

This Paſſage of Country, in Soil, Surface, and apparent General Management, perfectly reſembles the South-Weſtern parts of Devonſhire.

BIDDEFORD

AND ITS

ENVIRONS.

TUESDAY, 16 SEPTEMBER, 1794.

THE Town is remarkably forbidding. Meanly built houses (timber, brick, or mud, covered with bad slate or thatch), stuck against a steep hill. The streets, of course, are aukward; and most of them are narrow. In the vacant spaces between the streets, immense piles of furze faggots rise, in the shape of houses, and make the houses themselves appear more like hovels than they really are.

These dangerous piles of fuel are for the use of the pottery, for which only, I believe, this Town is celebrated: chiefly, or wholly, the coarser kinds of earthen ware.

The Bridge of Biddeford is an extraordinary erection: a high thick wall, run across

acroſs the river or narrowed eſtuary; with Gothic gateways, here and there, to let the water paſs.

The tide out: many men employed in loading packhorſes, with ſand, left in the bed of the river: and, in every vacant corner about the Town, compoſts of earth, mud, aſhes, &c. are ſeen. Shell ſand is ſaid to be plentiful on the coaſt; but little, if any of it, is brought up this river.

On the ſhore of the eſtuary, oppoſite to the Town, are ſeveral limekilns, now in full work. Numbers of packhorſes, and a few carts, loading, or waiting for loads. The ſtone, chiefly, and the culm with which it is burnt, wholly, brought acroſs the channel, from the coaſt of Wales. The kilns ſimilar to thoſe of West Devonſhire. This lime is carried fourteen or fifteen miles; chiefly on horſeback.

STROLL UPON THE HIGH LANDS, TO THE SOUTH AND WEST OF THE TOWN.

The ſubſoil of the ſkirts of the hill, is a Slate rubble. A baſe kind of Slate is uſed as a covering.

Some charming views, from the midway ſtages of this eminence. To the North, the conflux of the eſtuaries of the Taw and the Oke,—backed by the cultivated hills of the coaſt. To the South, a beautiful bend of the narrowing eſtuary of the Oke, loſing itſelf in the winding wooded valley of that river; ſkreened, on either hand, by wooded heights, and backed by wilder diſtances. Each of theſe views is worthy of the pencil. The former is grand; but the latter is more picturable, as a landſcape. The home views, on every ſide, are pleaſing. The ſurface finely broken; reſembling that in the environs of Bridport; but the features are larger, and the lines leſs abrupt.

The ſoil, of this midway of the ſwell, is a fertile well coloured loam; on a pale and ſtronger ſubſoil.

The

The whole country is inclosed; mostly in large fields, with coppice fences—cut down by the wind: a circumstance more favorable to the admirers of natural landscape, than to the husbandman.

No hedgerow timber: but a few groups of trees are scattered on the hills. The steep banks of the Oke, are chiefly hung with coppice wood.

The farm produce chiefly grass; with some little corn; and most of it still out!

The stock, observable from this station, are cattle and sheep. The former in herds, as if the farms were large. The sheep are above the middle size,—and mostly polled.

Nearer the summit of the hill, the land is colder, and the herbage coarse: abounding with Marsh Fleabane and other aquatic weeds. But the summit itself is again dry, sound, and tolerably well soiled.

A wide circle of views are seen, from an Object House (in ruins) near the summit. A very extensive view opens to the South East. But the horizon is too hazy to trace it to its farthest distance. To the South West, a strongly featured upland District;

large

large well turned cultivated ſwells, ſeparated, and the face of the country diverſified, by winding wooded vallies, in the beſt ſtyle of Kent or Hereſordſhire; with tall and ſtately towers of Churches ſcattered over the wide ſpreading ſcene.

On the upper ſtages of this eminence, and in deſcending its Weſtern declivity, I obſerved many young horſes; much of the Yorkſhire breed; but ſomewhat ſhorter and thicker.

Alſo ſome good North Devonſhire cows.

BIDDEFORD MARKET.

A few fat, and ſome ſtore cattle; with three or four heifers and calves. The heifers ſomewhat ſmall; but neat; and with remarkably fine bags! the moſt promiſing appearance of milk, that I have obſerved, in the Devonſhire breed of cattle.

A few ſheep, and two or three colts (weaned foals) in halters.

The Corn Market well filled with long two-buſhel bags; chiefly of wheat.

The

The ſhambles full of good mutton;—with a ſcanty ſhow of beef.

Salmon in conſiderable plenty; but no ſea fiſh!

The women's market well ſupplied.

Cart loads of country bread, expoſed in the market place, for ſale. A market article, this, which I have not before *obſerved.*

Upon the whole, the Market of Biddeford may be ſet down as very reſpectable.

STROLL UPON THE RISING GROUNDS, ON THE NORTH SIDE OF THE TOWN.

Theſe grounds are ſeparated from the hill on which the Town is ſituated, by a creek of marſhland, in its natural ſtate, as formed by the tide; excepting a plot of ſeven or eight acres, which is now embanking: an operation, which, if it were carried on, with *proper exertion*, could not fail to pay threefold for the money expended. If the men, who are employed upon it, it, may be conſidered as a ſample of the *Laborers* of North Devon, they exceed, in idleneſs, their Countrymen of the Weſt.

A low bank, thrown up acroſs theſe marſhlands, furniſhes, at once, a ſafe road, and gives effect to a tide mill, ſituated near one end of it.

A rich loamy ſoil to the very ſummit of this hill: a narrow ridge.

A good view of the Bay of Barnſtaple, and its finely diverſified coaſt: here, a flat ſhore; there ſteep lofty cliffs.

Some charming near views are ſeen from theſe grounds. Tapley (Mr. Cleveland's) a fine ſituation, is ſeen with advantage.

The entire environs are ſtudded with *houſes*: ſome of them ſubſtantial; others neat. Yet ſtill we find the Town itſelf a contraſt to Torrington. The influence even of half a ſcore families is not ſufficient to burniſh the appearance and manners of a ſmall ſeaport Town, in a remote ſituation.

General Remarks.

The climature of this District is evidently later, than that of West Devonshire: much of the corn, grown in it, is yet out!

There are few orchards in these environs. Several carts appear; but no waggons. Packhorses are chiefly prevalent.

The state of husbandry is on a par, with that of the rest of the County, I have yet seen; or somewhat superior: a laudable assiduity, in collecting and mixing manures, is singularly conspicuous.

On a general view of the District, at this season, it resembles South Devonshire, so much, with respect to natural characters, and Farm Management, that, in a register of their Rural Economy, they might well be considered as one and the same District; excepting an observable superiority in the breeds of cattle and horses, in this part of the County; and except a somewhat freer use of wheel carriages, here, than in the South Hams, and West Devonshire.

BIDDEFORD

TO

BARNSTAPLE.

(Eight miles.)

WEDNESDAY, 17 SEPTEMBER, 1794.

ANOTHER broken billowy Diſtrict: high rotund ſwells, ſeparated by deep narrow vallics.

The materials of theſe hills appear to be chiefly rotten ſlate, or ruſty ſlate-ſtone rubble, ſimilar to that of Weſt Devonſhire and Cornwall.

Creeks of marſhland branch out of the eſtuary of the Taw: the ſoil of theſe marſhlets is ſomewhat reddiſh. Now ſtocked with cattle. But they are at preſent in a rough unreclaimed ſtate, and appear to be highly improveable..

The road of ſtone, and remarkably good.

The ſtems of corn ſtacks thatched with reed.

Leave a ſweet woody dell, to the right.

A ſtuccoed barn: mud-wall plaiſtered.

A breed of remarkably tall white Pigs.

Roof heaps of lime and earth compoſt, on unbroken ſward. Q. For Wheat?

Paſs over a well-ſoiled upland country: the ſubſtratum earthy ſlate, up to the ſoil.

A few ſtone buildings obſervable.

High mound coppice hedges, full of growth.

The timber trees, *on this ſide of the County*, are remarkably ſhorn with the *Northweſt* wind.

The wide valley of the Taw opens to the view,—and the nature of the Country changes, from clean ſound land, to a cold aquatic ſoil: alder ſwamps, ruſhy incloſures, and rough furze grounds; with much oak wood. The coppices in general healthy; but the timber much injured by the coldneſs of the ſubſtratum, and the winds from the ſea. One wood compleatly ſtag-headed: a waſte of property to let it ſtand.

Meet ſeveral flocks of "Exmore" lambs; many

many hundreds; invariably horned; and, moſtly, even in carcaſe; on their way to the Northweſt of Devonſhire, and the North of Cornwall, to their winter paſture.

An inſtance of coppice wood, on a flat ſurface; as in Kent and Suſſex: the firſt inſtance of it, I have obſerved, in the Weſt of England.

Enter on the deſcent into the vale, or valley, of Barnſtaple.

A large field breaſt-plowed, and now burning.

Still a cold ſoiled, well timbered Diſtrict. Much furze-grown rough ground; which appears to be very capable of improvement.

See a heath-covered knoll, to the right. Good cows; moſtly of a dark blood-red colour.

Towards the foot of the hill, the land improves. A broad flat of meadows and marſhlands.

Good grazing cattle, in rich marſhes.

Some large houſes are ſeen, among the fine ſcenery, on the oppoſite banks of the valley.

The bridge of Barnftaple is fimilar to that of Biddeford.

GENERAL REMARKS.

The climature improves; no corn obfervable in the field, in this ftage.

The produce—arable crops, grafs, wood, and roughets of furze, and rubbifh.

Townfhips—apparently large.

The whole Country inclofed;—moftly, large fquare fields.

The farms apparently of a good fize.

The fences truly Danmonian.

The cattle, which appeared, are of a good fort. But not fuperior to what I expected to have feen, in this neighbourhood.

No Sheep obferved, in the inclofures:

Nor wheel carriages, on the road.

In the general ftate of hufbandry, nothing *new* ftruck me, in this paffage of country.

The moft obvious improvement, of which it appears to be capable, is that of draining, burning, and fallowing, the cold rough lands.

BARN-

BARNSTAPLE

AND ITS

ENVIRONS.

THE day inceſſantly rainy, and ill calculated for pedeſtrian examinations.

The Town is reſpectable. The ſtreets are wider and better laid out, than thoſe of old Towns generally are. Many of the houſes are ſubſtantially built of brick. But the covering, here, is of the ſame mean-looking ſlate, as that which is in uſe at Biddeford.

Leith carts and Highland ſledges (or implements very much reſembling them!) are ſeen in the ſtreets of Barnſtaple.

Some ſmall craft in the river, and in a creek which waſhes one ſide of the Town. And two ſmall veſſels on the Stocks.

Pilton, a pleaſant village, adjoins to Barnſtaple.

A bold Promontory, which riſes abruptly in the center of the broad valley, above the Town,—ſevering the Taw from the Brook of Pilton and its ſweetly winding woody Dell,—forms a ſtriking feature, among the aſſemblage of picturable ſcenes, which the environs of Barnſtaple *appear*, even through the dim medium of rain, to be capable of affording.

BARNSTAPLE

TO

SOUTH MOULTON.

(Eleven Miles.)

WEDNESDAY, 17 SEPTEMBER, 1794.

A RICH flat of meadows and marſh-lands, above the Town; nearly a mile wide: evidently formed by the tide and floods.

The Country, on either ſide, picturably broken, and well wooded.

Some fine Cows now in the meadows.

Sea

Sea ſand compoſt is here in uſe.

Paſs through Newport, a large village.

The Buildings chiefly Earth and Thatch; but ſome Brick, Stone, Slate, and Pantile, in uſe.

The breed of very tall white Pigs ſtill continues.

Meet more Exmore Lambs going Weſtward to their wintering grounds.

The day is ſet in for rain; yet the appearance of the Country is delightful beyond deſcription. Perhaps rain, as varniſh, mellows the Views.

The ſubſtratum, here, ſlatey rock; worn into hollow ways.

Lofty ſwells productive to their ſummits, as thoſe of the South Hams.

The prevailing ſubſoil, ſlatey rubble.

A valley opens to the left; richly ſoiled, well cultivated, and ſtocked with fine cattle.

Some large orchards in this valley.

Cloſe woody hedges, with ſome timber in them.

The roads in a ſhameful ſtate: evidently injured by the hedges. Why is not the Law enforced? In this Country, where woodlands abound, and where coals may be had at a reaſonable rate; no ſerious evil could ariſe were all the hedges in it ſhorn to their mounds.

Sea ſand composts are ſtill ſeen by the ſide of the road (5 miles from "Barum").

A ſmall waſte hillock appears to the right.

The ſubſtratum—a maſs of rock, broken into chequers,—and riſing to the ſoil.

Get a broad view of the rich and beautiful VALLEY OF SWIMBRIDGE.

A large flock of Sheep appear on its baſe.

Inſtance of Oats now green as Graſs! the ſecond inſtance obſerved?

A wide view opens to the Eaſt; but is curtailed by the hazeyneſs of the atmoſphere.

Rich graſsland, to the ſummits of the ſwells.

The Valley of the Taw opens, at ſome diſtance to the right: a wooded Diſtrict.

A fine back view of the Eſtuary and its banks: broad, but grand, and picturable.

An obvious improvement, in the line of road. The hill is croſſed, when its baſe might be traced nearly on the level.

The

The fields in this Country, as in the South of Devonſhire, appear to be large in proportion to the Farms.

A breed of ſmall ſheep; apparently with fine wool.

Rock and ſlate rubble riſe to the ſoil of rich graſsland.

Grazing Cattle, on the higher hills; as in the South Hams.

Meet a pair of wheels: the firſt from Biddeford.

The road improves.

A ſweet Country; but moſt difficult to be *ſeen!* A diſtant view, at length, opens to the Eaſt.

Black Limeſtone road: tolerably good.

Philley, Lord Forteſcue's noble place, breaks at once upon the eye: a finely wooded baſon. The Timber abundant, and ſeemingly well ſet out.

A herd of young cattle, and a flock of ſheep, in the grounds about the houſe.

The Farmery large; beſpeaking a ſuitable portion of demeſne in hand.

A very

A very deep quarry of black Limeſtone. Similar, in appearance, to the Chudleigh marble: but the color is leſs bright.

This capacious quarry is not leſs than fifty feet deep. The ſtones are brought up from the lower depths on horſeback; and the water raiſed by a horſe pump.

Paſs a ſtring of two-horſe carts, guided with reins, in the Cleveland manner! Has a colony of Clevelanders formerly ſettled in North Devonſhire, and brought with them their carts and horſes? See page 51.

Vile roads again: and in the neighbourhood of a great man's reſidence! But, perhaps, his Lordſhip's Lime Work is the principal cauſe of the evil. The color of the materials, and the ſtate in which they at preſent lie, give them every appearance of roads to Coal pits.

Still an incloſed, well ſoiled Country.

A ſtately Tower, proudly ſituated. North Moulton?

Mount a rich well turned ſwell, and enter the Town of South Moulton.

SOUTH

SOUTH MOULTON

AND ITS

ENVIRONS.

THURSDAY, 18 SEPTEMBER, 1794.

THE TOWN, which conſiſts of a ſpacious well built Market Place, ſurrounded with inferior ſtreets, caps a rotund hillock, ſituated among other hillocks of a ſimilar nature, and wearing ſimilar appearances; rich and beautiful in a ſuperior degree.

The ſoil a rich greazy loam.

The ſubſoil pale rubble, or rotten ſlate, or a kind of ſoft checkered rock.

Some wood in the vallies; but not one acre of unproductive land, to be ſeen, in the neighbourhood. One of the fineſt farming Diſtricts in the Kingdom.

Walked towards the Barton of Great Hill to view Mr. Trigg's Breed of Cattle; which is reckoned one of the firſt in this neighbourhood.

bourhood. And the Diſtrict of South Moulton is ſpoken of as the firſt, for the North Devonſhire breed.

Saw ſix of his Cows. All of them good. One of them ſuperior to the reſt: remarkable in the carcaſe; well loined, wide at the hips, and ſquare in the quarters; with a fine head and bone. The horns alſo fine, and ſhorter than ordinary. The color a lightiſh blood-red; the reſt darker, and moſtly with ſmokey faces. All of them low on their legs: a ſize between the Gloceſterſhire and the Herefordſhire.

The day is too tempeſtuous, to keep the field: and I have already gained a ſufficient idea of the North Devonſhire breed of Cattle. A farther examination might gratify; but could not inſtruct; they are evidently a ſuperior variety of the middle-horned breed. And are of courſe one of the firſt breeds of Cattle in the Iſland.

GENERAL

GENERAL OBSERVATIONS,

ON THE COUNTRY BETWEEN BIDDEFORD AND SOUTH MOULTON, INCLUDING THEIR ENVIRONS.

IN a general view of this Line of Country, ---whether we attend to the height or formation of its surface,---to its soil, its substrata (a short passage on the West of Barnstaple excepted), or their present produce; to the state of inclosure, the size or shape of fields, or the nature of their fences, ---to the species of arable crops (no trace of the bean crop or other article of pulse now observable); or the manner of producing them (so far as it appears at this season); or to the livestock or animals of labor (except as above excepted*)---it so perfectly resembles the District of South Devonshire, that they might be conceived to have once been united; and to have been forcibly separated, and thrown into their present

* See P. 64.

present situations, by the Mountain of Dartmore, in one of Nature's convulsive paroxisms, having broken them asunder, and placed itself in the breach.

SOUTH MOULTON

TO

DULVERTON.

(Thirteen Miles)

THURSDAY, 18 SEPTEMBER, 1794.

AT less than two miles from the Town, leave its fertile Environs.

A pretty but unproductive valley to the left: alders, rushes, and rough grounds.

Climb the side of this valley. The substratum close rock, up to the soil: no intervening rubble, or other earthy subsoil; the land lean, and the produce weak: a contrast to the neighbouring lands; though the *soils* appear to be similar.

Another rainy day, with a storm of wind.

Meet

Meet a *drove* of cart horfes; and a ftring of faddle horfes, on their way to the Fair of Barnftaple; the property of a Dorfetfhire Dealer.

Mount a rough furze-grown height, an extenfive Common,---and catch a broad view to the South: apparently, a cold infertile Diftrict.

Bend to the left, from the Tiverton road; and enter narrow woody lanes, barely pervious, by a carriage.

Break out of this pafs, into other Commons; and nearly approach the heaths of Exmore; a narrow valley only intervening.

Exmore, in this point of view, is without feature; appears as a flat, or at moft, a tamely billowy heath. Its hills fcarcely rife above the cultivated fwells that environ them. This fide of it, at leaft, has not a trait of the Mountain character.

Wind along the brink of the valley. The oppofite banks apparently well foiled and well cultivated; though they form the immediate fkirts or margin of the Moor.

Some wooded Dells branch out of the valley.

Sheep

Sheep on these Commons, similar to those of West Devonshire and Cornwall! part horned; part hornless.

See corn in arrish mows; or small field stacks.

Trace a ridge of cold land: a woodland soil; and leave a similar dip to the right.

Enter and skirt a wide fern-grown Common: large plots of fern now in swath. Also dwarf furze, and some heath. The soil deep and culturable.

Approach still nearer the Exmore Heaths: now crimsoned with blossoms; which brighten as the day clears up.

The soil of the Moor Skirts somewhat red.

Laid out in large square Danmonian Fields. Much of it in a state of arable land: a few Turneps.

The valley widens, and breaks into well soiled hillocks. The two parishes of East and West Anstey appear to be in a good state of culture. Several plowed fields; apparently clean fallows.

Meet strings of Lime Horses; from Bampton Lime Works.

Several

Several inſtances of good young Cattle, of the North Devon Breed.

Building Materials---Earth and Thatch: an entire ſuite of new Farm Buildings, juſt finiſhed, of theſe materials.

Loſe ſight of the Exmore Hills; but ſtill keep the brink of the valley; having enjoyed a tolerably level road for ſeven or eight miles!

Holly abounds in this cold ſituation: it is ſeen to mix frequently with the Alder.

Leave the high ground, and deſcend into the valley. Subſoil ſlatey rubble.

Stirring Wheat Fallows, with four oxen: the firſt oxen, and the firſt plow, I have *ſeen* at work, in North Devonſhire!

Narrow Wheat ridges, as in Weſt Devonſhire.

The road, of black Limeſtone, is narrow but well laid out,

Thick polled Sheep, as in the South Hams.

Inſtance of watering Graſsland: the firſt I have *obſerved*, in North Devonſhire.

"Dunſtone," and good Graſsland, as about Moulton.

 A Lime

A Lime kiln: black ſtone, lodged among "Dunſtone."

Some tolerably large Orchards; with low *Devonſhire* trees; though within the *County* of Somerſet.

Another Sea, or rather Bay, of rich Danmonian ſwells.

Approach DULVERTON; by another Gothic bridge.

DULVERTON

AND ITS

ENVIRONS.

THIS ſmall Market Town is ſituated in a deep narrow valley; chiefly near its baſe, but ſomewhat climbing up its Eaſtern bank. The Church conſpicuous and neat; and the place altogether, has a plain, neat, and pleaſing appearance: and immediately below the Town is a ſmall place, Pickſton, belonging to the Ackland family.

The approach from Moulton is ſingularly ſtriking. Pickſton, a plain dreſſed place, firſt

firſt meets the eye; and immediately the Town, equally unſuſpected, burſts abruptly into the ſequeſtered ſcene: a rich and beautiful Baſon, hemmed in on every ſide; the valley to the North being cloſed with ſteep winding banks hung with Coppice wood; and, on the other hand, the riſing grounds and woods of Pickſton forman impervious ſkreen; the Exmore Hills juſt ſhowing themſelves above the middle ground of the view; a meek, modeſt, lovely little picture.

Walk upon the Hill above the Town.

A charming view, from the midway of the ſteep, of the valley below (in this point of view alſo cloſed in as a baſon), including Pickſton.

Reach a deſerted place of view, on the ſummit of the hill; and catch a moſt intereſting detail of the winding valley of Dunſbrook; the eye tracing it within the wilds of Exmore: ſteep, narrow, and thickly wooded; with a ſlip or coomb, of water formed land, waving with the ſtream; a finely alpine ſcene.

At a ſharp bend of the valley, immediately under the eye, and facing a long reach, that points to the North Weſt, the Coppice wood is cut down, by the wind, in a very ſingular manner; even at this diſtance---twelve or fifteen miles---from the Sea. But the bleak air of Exmore may, alone, be equal to produce the effect.

The ſoil of this Eminence is dark-colored and fertile, to its higheſt ridge.

Large ſatting Wedders now grazing upon it.

Some fine Cows, on a neighbouring ſwell.

Whichever way the eye is turned, it meets with ſomething rich or beautiful. But perhaps its judgement has been warped by meeting with more than was expected. The ſtyle of ſcenery is ſingular. There is much in the ſituation of Dulverton that reminds me of Blair of Athol; though, in ſcenery, they ſomewhat differ.

DULVERTON

DULVERTON
TO
TIVERTON.

(Thirteen Miles)

THURSDAY, 18 SEPTEMBER, 1794.

PASS under Pickſton Houſe, a low white building, within a deer paddock.

Many ſheep obſervable in the baſon of Dulverton: all thick-carcaſed, and polled.

Obſerve ſeveral wheel carriages,---carts and waggons,---on this road, and in Dulverton: on their way to and from Minehead, and other parts of the Coaſt.

Three-wheeled barrows, drawn by horſes; uſed in ſetting about manure.

Beginning to ſow wheat. Shovel out the interfurrows; as in Weſt Devonſhire.

The valley contracts, and the tall impending trees, with which its ſides are hung, appear to close it, as below Blair *. But, breaking through this *pass*, a wide valley, diversified with bold rotund knolls, is entered.

Lime horses seen creeping up the steep sides of the hills.

More good Cows in the valley.

The road good, and the day fine.

The soil of this passage is redish;—the subsoil rubble, the lower stratum rock: seldom-failing criteria of fertile land.

Leave the valley, and surmount a rough furze-grown height.

A few large Beeches scattered over this District.

Catch a good back view of Exmore, and seem to leave it.

A wide view opens to the South West.

Still keep the hills; a well soiled, upland District.

See the Exe, at some distance, winding at the foot of a tall steep woody bank; a passage of natural scenery,---sketched with a broad free pencil.

Descend

* A Seat of the DUKE OF ATHOL, in the Perthshire Highlands.

Deſcend precipitouſly into another fertile and recluſe plot of Country;—the beautiful Environs of Bampton.

BAMPTON—a ſmall mean market town; overlooked by an extenſive Limework, whoſe ragged excavations and heaps of rubbiſh ſeem to conſpire with the town to disfigure this ſweetly deſigned paſſage of Nature. But the face of a Country cannot be disfigured to a better purpoſe, than that of contributing to its improvement. Theſe works are ſaid to have been carried on, time immemorial, for the purpoſes of huſbandry.

The ſtrata of theſe Quarries lie ſteeply ſhelving. The Limeſtone, in thick ſeams of large irregular blocks; divided by thin ſeams of rediſh baſe ſtone; and by thicker ſtrata of brown earth; ſome of it ſoft and light as ſoot! and ſoils the fingers as ſoot or oker; having every appearance of a valuable pigment. The workmen call it "rotten ſtone."

The ſtone, in general appearance, reſembles that of Chudleigh; darkly colored, and interſperſed with white veins; but the Bampton ſtone has a purpliſh caſt, and ſparkles with micaceous particles, and is of a looſer texture, than that of Chudleigh.

The rubbiſh of the Quarries is carried out on horſeback; and the ſtone drawn up to the kilns, in three wheeled HORSE BARROWS;—which, an old Laborer tells me, have been uſed, in this Country, beyond memory.

The conſtruction and dimenſions of one of theſe barrows are as follow: The form is that of the common old-faſhioned wheel-barrow of moſt Diſtricts. The ſides nearly upright, ſomewhat ſpreading outward, and projecting behind the body of the barrow; and are there ſhaped into handles; for the purpoſe of moving it, by hand; or adjuſting it readily to the required ſituation. The hind wheels are fitted upon a ſquare axle, which is placed under the hind part of the body of the implement; and which turns round with them, as that of the Highland, and Cumberland cart. The fore wheel has a drag chain adapted to it, to check the motion of the carriage in deſcent. The three are nearly of the ſame ſize and conſtruction: namely, each a circle of thick plank,

plank, about two feet diameter, and bound with iron. The width of the body of the barrow is three feet, behind, two feet ſix inches, before, and four feet long. The depth of the ſides, and of the head and tail boards, twelve inches. The headboard leans ſomewhat forward, over the fore wheel; which is rather ſmaller than the hind ones, and turns on iron ſpindles, inſerted in the part of the ſides which project before the body of the barrow; as in the ordinary wheelbarrow. The draft is by common crane-neck ſtaples, fixed on the outſide of the fore part of the implement, near the pivots of the fore wheel *.

The fuel of theſe Limeworks is Welch culm, fetched, by land, from Watchet, ſixteen miles.

Draw

* BAMPTON BARROW. This implement might be uſed with great advantage, on many occaſions; eſpecially in moving earth, or other heavy looſe materials, a ſhort diſtance. It is more manageable, by hand, than the Gurry Butt of Weſt Devonſhire, and carries a much greater load. I traced it from Dulverton to Tiverton; and ſaw one near Taunton. I have not obſerved it, in any other part of the Iſland.

Draw the kilns, with heartſhaped ſhovels, formed of parallel bars, as the gridiron; the interſpaces ſuffering the aſhes and ſmall lime to drop through; and thus cleaning the ſtone lime, at an eaſy expence of labor. The price of ſtone lime, three ſhillings the hogſhead;—of the aſhes, two ſhillings, for the uſe of the Maſon!

Several orchard grounds, in the neighbourhood of Bampton.

Aſcend a long ſteep hill, and catch another back view of Exmore, and of the finely diverſified environs of Bampton and Dulverton.

Reach a rough, improveable, red-ſoiled height; from which Dartmore, for the firſt time, is ſeen riſing to the view.

The Exe ſtill continues to wind among high upland ſwells, which riſe on either ſide of it: the ſurface gently billowy; the Downs of the Southern Counties, or the Wolds of Yorkſhire, in a ſtate of incloſure.

The Soil, Subſoil, and Road, red.

A dunged fallow: the firſt obſerved, in this journey.

Field

Field ſtacklets common.

Paſs between Beechen coppice-hedges.

The VALE OF EXETER burſts open, with fine effect. Alſo a broad view of the more Eaſtern confines of Devonſhire preſents itſelf.

Now, a rich Vale view, of the Bradnich quarter of the Vale of Exeter, is ſpread under the eye.

Deſcend, by a long broken ſteep, to TIVERTON.

REMARKS.

The elevation of this paſſage is very great, for a well-ſoiled cultivated Diſtrict. The higher lands are nearly equal in elevation to the Exmore hills; yet

The climature is forwarder than that of the North coaſt, whoſe lands lie lower: the harveſt, here, is entirely finiſhed.

The ſurface billowy, in the ſtricteſt ſenſe: no regular ridge and valley. The river and brooks ſeem to wind among the hills.

The

The ſoil, in general, is rich and productive, as that of Vale Diſtricts; except the very ſummits of a few of the higheſt hills.

The ſubſoil, of the beſt lands, is invariably a ſlatey rubble; the under ſtratum, a looſe rock, broken into checkers or long-cube pieces, of ſizes according to the depth at which they lie; enlarging in ſize as the depth encreaſes; until the rock becomes cloſe and firm. The *ſubſtance* of this rock, whether entire or broken, appears to be the ſame as that of Slate, but wanting its laminated *texture*.

FUR-

FURTHER

GENERAL REMARKS

ON

NORTH DEVONSHIRE *.

THE Inhabitants, throughout, appear to be civilized and intelligent; the lower claſs differing much, in theſe reſpects, from thoſe of the mining country.

Their fuel—wood and Welch coals.

Their employments—huſbandry, and the worſted manufactory.

The Farmers appear to be of the middle and lower claſſes: moſtly, plain, decent-looking, working Huſbandmen, of twenty to fifty or a hundred pounds a year. I ſaw few, if any, which appeared to be of the ſuperior order of Farmers.

The woodlands are moſtly in a ſtate of coppice.—Some timber; but not much large

* For former Remarks, ſee page 77.

large Ship timber obſerved; except between Okehampton and Torrington.

The Orchard grounds of this Diſtrict appear to be inconſiderable, compared with thoſe of the other Diſtricts of Devonſhire.

No Rabbit Warren fell under the eye; indeed the lands, paſſed through, are in general too good for that application.

To Apiaries, however, the goodneſs of the lands cannot be an objection; yet I obſerved few, if any Bees, in this large tract of country.

The ſtate of Huſbandry, from this curſory view of it, appears to be ſuperior to that of South Devonſhire; and on a par with that of the kingdom at large. In the management of Liveſtock, eſpecially Horſes, Cattle, and Swine, North Devonſhire, it is probable, has, for ſome length of time, paid more than ordinary attention.

DIS-

DISTRICT THE FIFTH.

THE

VALE OF EXETER.

THE information I obtained, reſpecting this highly favored Diſtrict, and its Rural Practices, aroſe in TRAVELLING repeatedly through its central parts, in different directions; in examining, at different times, the ENVIRONS of EXETER, TIVERTON, and HONITON; and in going over that part of the DRAKE ESTATE, which lies within its limits. The Weſtern parts of the Diſtrict, the neighbourhood of CREDITON, is the only part which has not engaged more or leſs of my attention.

As the materials, which I occaſionally gathered, lie ſcattered in my Journals, I will

will here collect them into the Register form; as being best calculated to give a comprehensive idea of this interesting passage of country, which deserves a more minute examination, than I have been able to bestow upon it. However, from what will here appear, we shall find it resemble so much the other parts of Devonshire, which have been more closely examined, that a minute detail is the less requisite.

A GENERAL

A

GENERAL VIEW

OF

THIS DISTRICT.

I. SITUATION. This natural Diſtrict is more accurately defined, than any other Diviſion of the WEST OF ENGLAND. It accompanies the Exe and its eſtuary, from the ſea to the Tiverton hills, juſt deſcribed, which form its Northern boundary. This boundary is continued, towards the Eaſt, by Black Down, to the Heights of Honiton; the South-Eaſt quarter being contracted, by a range of barren high lands, between the Otter and the Exe. The Weſt ſide of the eſtuary of the Exe is, in like manner, contracted, by Hall Down, and a continuation of the ſame range of Heights, to the North of Exeter; where the Vale ſpreads

 Weſt-

Weſtward, to the neighbourhood of Crediton. The Northern extreme of Dartmore, or the unproductive lands in its vicinity, with the range of hills firſt mentioned, define its more Weſtern boundary.

II. EXTENT. The irregularity of the outline, of this Vale Diſtrict, renders it difficult, to calculate its contents, with exactneſs. If I were to riſk a random eſtimate, it would be, that, including its marginal banks, and ſome unproductive hillocks which riſe in its area, it contains about two hundred ſquare miles of ſurface.

III. ELEVATION. This is by far the leaſt elevated extent of ſurface, in Devonſhire. It may be termed a Vale Diſtrict; eſpecially the central and more Southerly parts of it. It is overlooked by lands of much greater elevation, on almoſt every ſide.

IV. SURFACE. There are two modes of examining and judging of the ſurface of a Country, like that which is now under notice. Its more prominent features, and greater

greater variations, are beſt obſerved from the eminences which overlook it: its ſmaller inequalities, by travelling acroſs it.

I have had abundant opportunities of examining the Vale of Exeter, in both theſe ways. From Black Down, and other Eminences of the Eaſtern Confines,—from the Halldown Hills, on the oppoſite ſide,—from the Tiverton Hills on the North,—and moſt eſpecially from an inſulated Hillock, ſome mile or two to the North of Exeter (from whence almoſt every ſquare mile of its ſurface is commanded), I have ſeen its greater variations; and, by travelling between Honiton and Exeter; Honiton and Nutwell, on the Eaſtern banks of the eſtuary, below Topſham; between Nutwell and Exeter, by different roads; and between Exeter and Bradnich, Collumpton, &c. to Taunton; I have had opportunities of obſerving its minor inequalities.

On the whole, it may be ſaid of this Diſtrict, that although it partakes more of the character of a Vale, than any other part of the County, it is barely entitled to that diſtinction. Between Tiverton and Exeter, it is beſet with prominences of conſiderable magnitude, obliterating, in ſome points of view, the Vale character; and between Exeter and Collumpton, much billowy ſurface intervenes: nevertheleſs, round Ottery, the Clyſts, and along the Eaſtern bank of the eſtuary towards Exmouth, and in the environs of Exeter,—we find much true Vale country: deep rich ſoil, lying with a ſurface, ſufficiently elevated, and ſufficiently varied, to admit of mixed cultivation; with a portion of low flat lands, adapted to the production of herbage only.

V. CLIMATURE. The frequency of rain, which renders Weſt Devonſhire uncomfortable to live in, and, in a wet ſeaſon, ungenial to Agriculture, is much leſs experienced in the Vale of Exeter. The paſſing vapours that are ſufficiently buoyant, to elude the attractive powers of the more Weſterly mountains, travel undiſturbed over this paſſage of depreſſed ſurface; whoſe climature appears, by the opportunities I have had of obſerving it, whether in the Spring,

Spring, or in the Harveſt months, to be forwarder, than that of any other part of the WEST OF ENGLAND, which has particularly engaged my attention.

The winters of this, as well as of the more Weſtern Diſtricts, are mild, compared with thoſe of the central and Northern parts of the Iſland. In the neighbourhood of Exeter, Graſs may be ſaid to grow freely, through the winter months; at leaſt, in moderate winters.

VI. WATERS. The EXE, and its fine ESTUARY below Topſham, are its chief waters. But two principal branches of the Exe, divaricating Eaſt and Weſt, and a portion of the OTTER, with their numerous branchlets, water the interior of the Vale. At Tiverton, the Exe has barely acquired the River character. And even at Exeter, it ranks low among the Rivers of the Iſland.

VII. SOIL. This varies exceedingly, and ſhows the Diſtrict, it covers, to be formed with fragments of various origin.

 This

This diverſity and intermixture of ſoils will beſt appear, in detail, as they fell under my obſervation.

HONITON TO EXETER. The ſoil various: much deep ſtrong good land. Part brown; part ſtrongly tinged with red. The firſt red ſoil obſerved, in entering the Weſt of England.

ENVIRONS OF EXETER. The ſoil round the Town is a rediſh, deep loam, of an extraordinary quality. To the North of the Town, it varies in productiveneſs, with the ſubſtrata. Where the rock does not riſe too near the ſurface, it is productive to the ſummits of the higher ſwells. On the South, between Exeter and Topſham, a riſing ground, of ſome extent, exhibits arable land of the firſt quality: Wheat, Beans, and Flax, luxuriating on ſome parts of it; other portions of it, being of a lighter weaker quality. Much of the red ſoil, in the neighbourhood of Exeter, is of a ſtrong, argilaceous, binding quality; and, as ſuch, differs eſſentially from the ordinary ſiliceous ſoil of the County.

EXETER

EXETER TO NUTWELL (by Heavytree and Bishop's Clyst). The soil and subsoil inclined to red, intermixed with a small quantity of gravel; the whole hardening, in some places, into a sort of pudding stone; which is used for ordinary buildings.

ENVIRONS OF NUTWELL *. The soil various: some strong good red land; much dark, pebbly loam, of a tolerable quality; some light sandy soil; and other still poorer, black, and moorlike. At the feet, and hanging on the sides of the marginal swells, above Woodbury, a cold weak woodland soil is prevalent.

EXETER TOWARDS TAUNTON. The hills, in general, light turnep and Barley land. In the intervening passages of Vale, a strong red loam is prevalent;—good wheat and bean soil. About Bradnich, a rich valley of grassland.

ENVIRONS of TIVERTON. The soil, in general, red, and much of it of a superior quality: towards Maiden Down, through

* The residence of the late SIR FRANCIS DRAKE, now of LORD HEATHFIELD.

Halberton, three or four miles from Tiverton, is a passage of red-soiled rich Vale country.

VIII. SUBSOIL. It might be thought superfluous to detail the remarks on this subject, which I made in different parts of the Vale: let it therefore suffice to say, that the lands of the Vale of Exeter, as those of other Districts, are characterized by their respective substrata, rather than by their surface soils: that the strong red soils cover strata of clay or loam of the same color: that the strong brown soils are likewise incumbent on brick earth, of a kindred color; that the rich productive lands, round Exeter, towards Tiverton, and in various parts of the area of the Vale, have a peculiar kind of earthy gravel for their basis; and in some places, as on the banks of the Exe, a cleaner gravel is observable. On the West side of the Vale, some of the higher lands have a sort of slate rock rising to the soil. But the prevailing subsoil of the high grounds, which rise in the area of the Vale, is a red sand. And

And in an inſtance, between Tiverton and Maiden Down, a variegated ſubſtratum is ſeen; compoſed of thin layers of red and white loam and ſand; reſembling what is obſervable in Glouceſterſhire, and under the red lands of Nottinghamſhire. Theſe circumſtances plainly ſhow, that the Vale of Exeter has been formed from various materials, and of courſe exhibits a variety of lands.

General Remark.

This intermixture of lands is ſeen, in an intereſting point of view, from the inſulated hillock, already mentioned, in the neighbourhood of Exeter (Stoke Hill I think it is called).

The deep rich Vale lands are thickly ſet with Hedgerow Elms, pruned up to poles, and riſing in cloſe order, as we ſee them in the Vales of Gloceſterſhire, and on the rich deep lands in the neighbourhood of the Metropolis! Has this ſpecies of produce, and this peculiarity of practice, riſen ſpon-

ſpontaneouſly out of the nature of the lands? or has the tree, and the method of treating it, been imported from the Continent, eſtabliſhed on the banks of the Thames, and from thence tranſplanted to thoſe of the Severn and the Exe?

IX. On the POLITICAL DIVISIONS of this Diſtrict, I find few remarks; except what relates to the ſizes of TOWNSHIPS;—which appear to be ſmaller, than what I have obſerved in the other parts of Devonſhire: a circumſtantial evidence, this, amongothers that will preſently be adduced, that the fertile Vale under notice was early *cultivated*, and thereby acquired an early population.

X. PUBLIC WORKS. The only INLAND NAVIGATION, which this Diſtrict at preſent enjoys, is that of the Eſtuary of the Exe, to Topſham; with an artificial Navigation, from thence to Exeter. And, perhaps, the only CANAL that could be proſecuted with profit, to the County at large, would be one from Exeter, by Crediton,

diton, to Okehampton, there to join the one proposed, between Biddeford and Plymouth *. And even this I suggest with diffidence, from my not having sufficiently traced the ground, in detail. The *Line* is, in every respect, what could be wished. If this triple Canal should be executed, Devonshire might, with good reason on her side, boast of her acquired, as well as of her natural advantages. Possessed of such a public work, she would stand unrivalled in facility of internal transfer: there would scarcely be a farm in the County, situated at more than one day's journey of a team from water carriage;—an accommodation, whether in bringing in manures, or carrying off produce, which no other County, I believe, can claim; and which, in a Country where wheel carriages are, in some cases, difficult to use, would be an advantage to the LANDED INTEREST, scarcely to be calculated.

The ROADS of the Vale are most remarkable for their closeness; narrow lanes, beset with mounds, and overhung with trees,

* See Page 39.

trees. This charge, however, does not lie, invariably. The more public Roads are, in general, well formed and well kept: the barrel gently convex, and the materials (moſtly ſtone—ſome gravel), properly reduced.

The STATE OF INCLOSURE is the ſame, here, as in the other Diſtricts of the County. The appropriated lands are univerſally incloſed: a few rough ſummits of hills, apparently commonable lands, remain open.

This State of Incloſure is probably of long ſtanding; and, from the ſmallneſs of the fields, obſervable in many parts of the Vale; eſpecially round Exeter and on the Eaſtern banks of the Eſtuary, it is reaſonable to ſuppoſe that thoſe parts, at leaſt, were early incloſed. What ſerves to corroborate this idea, the mounds of the hedges are lower here, than in the Ham Diſtricts; and are, in general, furniſhed with Timber Trees.

XI. The PRESENT PRODUCTIONS of the Lands of the Vale are chiefly ARABLE CROPS and HERBAGE; with a profuſion

profuſion of HEDGEWOODS; and ſome ORCHARD GROUNDS; but with very little WOODLAND, in the area of the Vale; not even in the more hilly parts of it.

Nevertheleſs, the Diſtrict, I underſtand, does not ſupply itſelf fully with grain; at leaſt, not with WHEAT; which is imported, occaſionally; and chiefly, I believe, from the Iſle of Wight. But the Country is populous. The Serge Manufactory employs many hands throughout the Diſtrict, and finally concenters at Exeter. Yet, of DAIRY PRODUCE, the Vale is enabled to ſend ſome ſupply to the Metropolis.

XII. Of the preſent STATE OF SOCIETY, in this Diſtrict, I am prepared to ſay but little.

The TOWNS, in general, are populous, cheerful, reſpectably built, and finely ſituated. The ſituation of Tiverton is ſingularly fine.

The COUNTRY HABITATIONS are generally mean in their appearance, from the nature of the materials of which they are almoſt univerſally conſtructed; namely,

red

red earth and thatch. The neatneſs of the latter, however, is ſuch as to render this ſpecies of covering more tolerable and leſs improvident, here, than it is in countries where ſtraw is beaten to pieces with the flail, and laid on with leſs dexterity, than is the "reed" of the Weſt of England. Earthen walls, rough caſt, and covered with a reed roof, form a neat and comfortable habitation.

The EMPLOYMENTS of the Inhabitants are thoſe of *Huſbandry*, and the ſame branch of the *Woolen Manufacture* which prevails throughout the County: SISTER EMPLOYMENTS, which ought to prevail, more or leſs, in every Diſtrict of the Iſland.

XIII. Of the FACE of this fair COUNTRY it were impoſſible to ſay too many fine things. But, as its goodly features might loſe much of their force in my own deſcription, I will briefly ſet it down at what its *happy* Inhabitants believe and aſſert it to be—"the richeſt fineſt Country in the world."

THE

THE RURAL ECONOMY OF *THIS DISTRICT.*

MANAGEMENT OF ESTATES.

THE only particulars which ſtruck me forcibly, relative to this ſubject, are

I. Laying out Farm Lands.
II. Farm Buildings.
III. Hedgerows.

I. DISTRIBUTION OF FARM LANDS. There needs not better evidence of the firſt Laying out of Lands, in this Diſtrict, being different from that of South Devonſhire, than the ſmallneſs of Fields, and the intermixture of Farm Lands, obſervable in the Vale: at leaſt in that part of of it which I had the beſt opportunity of examining; namely, the Eaſtern banks of the Eſtuary; which, in theſe particulars, might vie with Eaſt Norfolk.

Whether this intermixture of ſmall fields has ariſen from the lands being diſtributed, originally, among ſmall hand-labor huſbandmen, or from their having been once in a ſtate of common arable fields, as in other parts of the Kingdom, and have been kept in that intermixed ſtate, by the nature of life-leaſe-hold, is a point which, probably, might now be difficult to aſcertain.

Where theſe lands ſtill remain under life-leaſe-hold, it is difficult to do away the evil; but, where they are free from that tenure, the impropriety of ſuffering them to remain in ſo unprofitable a ſtate, reſts with the Proprietors and Managers of Eſtates.

II. Of the FARM BUILDINGS of the Vale, little is required to be ſaid. They are, in general, without plan, and meanly built: earth and ſtraw being the chief materials. Even the farm yard fences

are

are of "cobb:" in ſome inſtances raiſed ten or more feet high, with ſolding doors, wide enough to admit laden pack horſes; and with ſheds, perhaps, on the inſide: thus forming comfortable ſtraw yards, at a moderate expence.

The favorite material of theſe walls appears to be the ſtrong red loam mixed with gravel; which has been mentioned, and which acquires, in drying, a ſtonelike hardneſs. "If kept dry, it will ſtand for ever."

This material of building (earth of various ſorts under the general name of cobb) has been uſed, here, time immemorial. Barns and dwelling houſes, of almoſt every ſize, are built with it. The walls from fourteen inch to two feet thick; the flues of chimneys being carried up with the gables, as in building with ſtones or bricks.

III. HEDGEROWS. In this reſpect, too, the incloſures of the rich deep lands of the Vale reſemble the wood-bound Pightles of Eaſt Norſolk.

The Elms of the Hedges have been already noticed. Oak Pollards, and, in some parts, Oak Timber Trees, stand thick on the Hedge banks, or grow out of their sides, or at their bases; with Coppice wood rising between them, as in Kent, and other Districts.

I mention this circumstance the rather, as it forms one of the few distinctions, which mark this Eastern District, from North and South Devonshire *.

WOODLANDS.

ON this subject, nothing of importance struck me, except what relates to the MANAGEMENT OF HEDGEWOODS.

The COPPICE WOOD is treated, as in West Devonshire; the Oak stubwood being peeled on the stem.

And

* It is in a manner needless to remark, that the GATEWAYS of Devonshire are adapted to Horse-and-Crooks, rather than to Wheel Carriages. Even where the latter are in partial use, seven or eight feet is the usual width. GATE POSTS, within the reach of Dartmore, are commonly of Moorstone.

And in the Management of HEDGEROW TIMBER, the only particular, which is noticeable, is that of lopping, not only Elms, but Oaks, to bare ſtems! a practice which is not common to Hedgerows, only; but which I have ſeen extended, in this Diſtrict, for the firſt time, to Grove Timber! Oak Woods!!

A practice ſo deſtructive of private property, and public benefit, can only have ariſen in a ſcarcity of fuel, or in the rapine of tenants, and the neglect of thoſe who ſhould reſtrain them. Indeed, I would hope that the practice is not univerſal; at leaſt with reſpect to Wood Timber; but is confined to the eſtate which I more particularly examined.

The practice of pruning off the ſide boughs of Hedgerow Elms is a venial crime; provided it be not deferred too long from the laſt cutting. In the more valuable applications of the Elm, knottineſs of texture is a deſirable quality. But in moſt, or all, the uſes to which the Oak is applied, a cleanneſs of grain is its beſt recommendation.

AGRICULTURE.

I. FARMS. From the ſize of Farmeries, and the appearance of FARMERS, this Diſtrict reſembles the reſt of the County, in the SIZE of its Farms.

II. BEASTS OF LABOR. In this reſpect, too, the Vale of Exeter is truly Danmonian. OXEN are uſed in plowing; PACK HORSES in carriages of every kind; even to the gates, and within the ſtreets of Exeter. I have ſeen, in its immediate environs, dung ſetting about with "horſe and potts *." In this inſtance, three horſes, with a man to fill and two boys to drive, formed the ſett. The diſtance fifty to a hundred yards. The diſpatch far from inconſiderable.

III. IMPLEMENTS.

* See Vol. I. P. 122.

III. IMPLEMENTS. Still we find ourselves within the limits of Danmonia. The PLOW, here, is more truly heraldic, even than in West Devonshire. The body longer, and the beam shorter: the end of the beam merely shooting before the point of the share!

IV. PLAN OF MANAGEMENT. In the ARABLE CROPS of the Vale, we find a deviation from those of the more Western Districts:—arising, no doubt, from an alteration in the quality of the soil. On the strong cold lands, in the area of the Vale, *Beans* are a common crop; and, on the richer deeper soil, *Flax* is not unusually grown. And, perhaps, in this part of the County, a greater proportion of Cows are kept for the BUTTER DAIRY. But, in other respects, I have detected no obvious marks, in the outlines of Management, which distinguish this from the more Western Districts of Devonshire.

V. MANURE. The same roof shaped heaps of LIME COMPOST, that are common

 in

in South Devonſhire, are obſervable in the Vale of Exeter. The upper parts of the Vale are ſupplied with Lime, from the borders of Somerſetſhire: the central and Southern parts are ſupplied, by water, with ſtones, which are burnt at Exeter, and on the banks of the Eſtuary, after the manner of Weſt Devonſhire.

I have ſeen no traces of the SHEEP FOLD, in this or any other part of the County.

VI. WHEAT is here grown on narrow ridges, generally running diagonally acroſs the ſlope, as in Weſt Devonſhire, &c.

VII. All the BEAN CROPS, that I obſerved, were raiſed in the random or broad caſt manner.

VIII. TURNEPS. The HOING of Turneps is coming into practice, in the Vale. I obſerved, in different parts of it, clean good crops.

IX. GRASSLAND. On the Management of Graſsland, nothing ſtriking, or remarkable,

remarkable, occurred to me, in this Diſtrict; except an inſtance or two of ſmall parcels, which lie in a rough, unproductive ſtate; apparently for want of being properly freed from ſuperfluous moiſture.

X. ORCHARDS. Many ſmall Garden Orchards are ſcattered, in every part of the Vale. In the Environs of Tiverton, I obſerved ſome full ſized Orchard Grounds. And the Villages round Exeter are en-wooded, with Apple Trees; which are ſtill Danmonian: but, as the borders of Somerſetſhire are approached, the ſtems increaſe in length; as will be more particularly noticed, in the VALE OF TAUNTON.

XI. CATTLE. This being a Dairy, rather than a Breeding Diſtrict, a mixture of breeds may be expected. Nevertheleſs, in the more remote parts of the Vale, I have obſerved different inſtances of fine Cattle, of the pure North Devonſhire ſort.

In the neighbourhood of Exeter, many Alderney, or "French Cows" are ſeen;

and a mongrel ſort, betwen that and the Devonſhire breed, are not uncommon.

XII. The DAIRY. The produce of the Dairy, here, as in Weſt Devonſhire, is BUTTER and SKIM-MILK CHEESE.

This ſpecies of Farm Produce has increaſed, of late years; the butter, even of this extreme part of the Iſland, being now ſent, in greater or leſs quantity, to the London Market.

Nevertheleſs, the CLOUTING OF CREAM, I underſtand, ſtill remains the prevalent practice of the Vale; in which, however, ſome "RAW-CREAM DAIRIES" are already eſtabliſhed: and, as the practice of raiſing cream, or ſuffering it to riſe, in the natural way, has gained poſſeſſion of the DAIRY DISTRICT (which will preſently be deſcribed), on the Eaſtern banks of the Vale, there will be little riſque in predicting, that it will require no great length of time, to extend itſelf over the area. How long it will afterwards take it, to climb over the Weſtern banks, into South Devonſhire, is much more difficult to foreſee.

XIII. What

XIII. What SWINE I have obſerved, in the Vale, are of the ſame tall white ſort, which appears to be common to the County.

XIV. SHEEP. The Sheep which are REARED in the Vale, are chiefly, I believe, of the HOUSE-LAMB BREED.

But the more ordinary ſtock of the ſmaller Farmers are bred on the Heights about Tiverton; and are the ſame variouſly headed race, which is common to all the high lands of Devonſhire and Cornwall.

On the rich grazing lands, below Exeter, I have remarked a large polled breed; ſimilar to that which has been noticed, about Totneſs. So commonly do Soils invite congenial Stock.

DISTRICT

DISTRICT THE SIXTH.

THE

DAIRY DISTRICT

OF

WEST DORSETSHIRE,

&c. &c.

Introductory Remarks.

THE paſſage of country, to which I have given this appellative diſtinction, is at once NATURAL and AGRICULTURAL. Natural, as poſſeſſing a peculiarity, as well as a uniformity of ſtyle, in the formation of its ſurface;—agricultural, as having the ſame leading object, in its plan of Rural Management.

Nevertheleſs, I was led to an examination of it, by circumſtances more fortuitous, than thoſe which attended the ſurveys of ſome of of the other Diſtricts, noticed in theſe Volumes.

In my firſt journey, into the WEST OF ENGLAND, being ſtruck with the appearance of the country, about Bridport, I ſtopt a few days to examine it; and went over it, ſome miles round, on either ſide: thus gaining a competent knowledge of the Eaſtern part of the Diſtrict, and a general idea of its Rural practices. In paſſing, repeatedly, between Bridport and Honiton, I have had opportunities of ſeeing ſomething of the Center of the Diſtrict. And, in travelling between Crewkern and Chard, and afterwards taking a deliberate view of the Drake Eſtate, lying in the Valley of Yarcombe, I compaſſed the Northern margin, and ſaw much of its Weſtern extremity: thus gaining a comprehenſive idea of the whole Diſtrict; except its South-Weſtern quarter.

But, notwithſtanding the information I had collected, reſpecting the paſſage of country here brought forward, I might, in forming this public Regiſter, have paſſed it, as an intermediate Diſtrict, had it not con-

constituted a striking part of that extraordinary tract, of which these Volumes have hitherto been treating, and of which I am desirous to render my account as full as possible.

In attempting to give a comprehensive view of this Division of the West of England, I will briefly digest the particulars that struck me, in the cursory views which I have had of it; and first of the

DISTRICT.

I. SITUATION. Its boundaries are the lower flatter Vale lands of Dorsetshire, and Somersetshire, on the North *. The Vale of Exeter, on the West. The Chalk Hills

* The indeterminate boundary, on the Somersetshire side, may be caught from the following remarks, made between Crewkern and Chard.

CREWKERN to CHARD.

Leave the Limestone lands, at Crewkern.

Ascend, by a sandy hollow way, a furze grown Common, with a gravelly subsoil.

Ascend

IV. SURFACE. By the formation of its surface, this District is most strongly marked; exhibiting the Danmonian style, in all its purity.

Immediately upon the coast, the hills are many of them rotund, and fertile to their summits; but, farther from the Sea, they are mostly flattened on the top, and comparatively infertile with the wide winding vallies, which seem to worm their way in among them; displaying the most broken and *troubled* surface. Still farther towards the Northern margin, especially towards the Western extreme, the ground breaks into more regular ridges and vallies; branching out, in the ordinary manner of mountain surfaces.

The wider Vallies, that have fallen under my notice, are the Valley or Bason of Beaminster; the Valley, or, as it is called, the Vale, of Marshwood; the Valley of Yarcombe *, and that of Upottery: each of them,

* The VALLEY OF YARCOMBE. This Valley contains part of three Parishes, lying, I believe, in three Counties:

them, except the last, containing several hundred acres of valuable land.

V. CLIMATURE. In the lower lands of this District, even in its more Northern vallies, the seasons are early. In 1791, Haymaking was at its height, in the neighbourhood of Bridport and Beaminster, the beginning of July; and, in 1794, Raygrass was ready to shoot into head, in the Valley of Yarcombe, the first of May. I should conceive it to be, on a par of years, ten days or a fortnight before West Devonshire.

VI. WATERS. Each Branch Valley of the Northern margin has its rivulet or brook; which, collecting, form the upper branch of the Otter, the Axe, and the Brook or River of Bridport: the Axe receiving the principal part of the waters of the District.

VII. SOILS.

Counties: namely, Membury, in Dorsetshire; Whitstanton, in Somersetshire: and Yarcombe, in Devonshire: —the last comprizing the principal part of its lands.

VII. SOILS. These vary, in different parts of the District. In the Bridport quarter,—the lower lands are mostly of a superior quality—deep rich loams—throwing out full crops of Wheat, Beans, Flax, and Hemp; and, in this part of the District, the sides and even the summits of the swells and hillocks are many of them well soiled; the best a limestone loam; others of a lighter sandy nature.

But, in the Valley of Yarcombe, and apparently in the neighbouring Vallies, much of the soil is a strong red loam, lying on a cool basis,—Wheat, Beans, and Oak, land.

The soil of the higher hills, throughout this District, is a sandy loam, intermixed with a singular species of stone, a base kind of flint; a species of soil and accompaniment, which are common to the higher less fertile hills of East Devonshire, and are extended to the Halldown Heights, on the West side of the Vale of Exeter; and which, the flints at least, are peculiar perhaps to this part of the Island: I have not observed them in any other.

VIII. SUBSOILS. These are various, as the soils, the passage of country under notice resembling the Vale of Exeter, in this respect. The cool red soils have a strong clayey loam for their base; the rich lands in the environs of Bridport, have either a lighter loam, or a sort of flinty gravel, beneath them: the hills are of sand, intermixed with flints, with here and there a mass of limestone.

IX. FOSSILS. The most useful Fossil production, that fell under my notice in this District, is LIMESTONE; which is raised, not in the neighbourhood of Bridport only, but more or less in other parts of it. Beside being burnt into Lime, it is used as a walling material, as well as for paving Slabs, Drain Bridges, and Stiles; large Slabs of it being not unfrequently set onedge for this purpose. It is also used as a road material. It appears as a mass of conglutinated shells; resembling much, in general appearance, the Sussex marble: a species of Limestone dug out of the strong lands

lands of the Wild of Suſſex; whereas, this is found on the dry ſummits of hills.

On ſome of the Northern Heights, detached maſſes of CHALK are found;—fragments, probably, of the neighbouring hills. White Down, between Chard and Crewkerne, appears to be chiefly compoſed of Chalk; and is the moſt Weſtern collection of that Foſſil, which I have obſerved; or which, probably, is found, in this Iſland.

X. ROADS. The Roads, in the more recluſe Vallies, are nearly in a ſtate of Nature: the antient Horſe paths of the Foreſt ſtate: crooked, narrow, numerous, and full of ſloughs.

XI. STATE OF INCLOSURE. The lower grounds are wholly incloſed; the hills, at preſent, are open; but they ſhow evident marks of their having been, heretoſore, in a ſtate of incloſure and cultivation! diſcovering ſtrong lines, which, on the wide Commons of Yarcombe and the neighbouring Pariſhes, ſtill remain perfectly legible;

gible; and which are not yet obliterated, on the higher more barren ſummits, in the neighbourhood of Bridport.

Tradition, in this Eaſtern Diſtrict, as well as in the Weſt of Devonſhire, ſpeaks of theſe open neglected lands, as having once been *inhabited*. But this ingenious Hiſtorian aſſigns different reaſons, for their being abandoned to the neglect, in which we now find them. On the Weſtern ſide of the County, we are told, it was owing to a decreaſed population. But, on the Eaſtern, to a widely differing circumſtance. Here, the hills were *firſt* inhabited; by reaſon of the Vallies being, in the early ſtages of ſociety in this Country, ſo full of Wolves, as to be rendered uninhabitable, by the Human Species. In proceſs of time, however, the latter crept down the ſides of the hills; clearing off the wood, as they deſcended; until at length the Wolves were driven away, or deſtroyed; the Vallies taken poſſeſſion of; and the hills, in conſequence, given up, for a more fertile ſoil, and a more genial climature.

This

This marvellous tale of tradition, whatever may have given rise to it *, seems altogether unnecessary, to explain the phenomenon under notice; as it may be accounted for in a more simple and reasonable way; there being nothing different, in the present appearances of these Commons, from those of the Commons of North Devonshire, that are actually, at this time, undergoing the very operations, which, in all human probability, moulded the faces of those of East Devonshire into their present form; and which, heretofore, left similar vestiges of inclosure and cultivation, on the surfaces of some of the commonable lands of West Devonshire †. The most striking difference between the appearances observable on the Commons of Yarcombe, and on those of Buckland, is, that the lines

* TRADITION, when it reaches not farther than a few generations, is entitled to every respect, and is frequently good authority. On perilous events, as of war or pestilence, it is able to go much farther back, than it is respecting the ordinary and quiet operations of Agriculture.

† See Vol. I. P. 32.

on the former are much ſtronger; ſome of the ſtill mouldering hedge mounds having no appearance of being more than a century old; ſome of them, perhaps, are of more modern date: indeed, incroachments, of a ſimilar nature, are made at the preſent time.

There can be little doubt, I think, of the truth of the poſition, that it was once the prevailing practice of Devonſhire, to CULTIVATE ITS COMMONABLE LANDS, in a manner ſimilar to what we have ſeen practiſed, not only on public Commons, but in private Incloſures, at this time *.

It is reaſonable to ſuppoſe, that, in early times, the *Aſhes* of the ſward or coarſer covering, were depended on, as manure: and that, afterwards, *Lime* was uſed, as an additional ſtimulus. And it may be allowable to conjecture, that, through the means of theſe two powerful ſtimulants,—without returning any part of the produce, thus extracted, to the ſoil, — it at length became ſo much exhauſted, as no longer to repay the expence of cultivation. What cor-

* See Vol. I. P. 149. Alſo Vol. II. P. 48.

corroborates this idea is, that the only part in which I have obſerved the practice continued, to the preſent day, is that in which Lime is moſt difficult to procure; and where it may not yet have been obtained in ſufficient quantity, to lower the lands to the laſt ſtage of exhauſtion.

Having proceeded thus far, I muſt mention, here (though ſomewhat out of place), a circumſtance relating to the COMMON RIGHTS of Eaſt Devonſhire: I ſpeak more particularly of the Manor of Yarcombe; whoſe Commons belong excluſively to the Lord of the ſoil, and are ſtocked (without ſtint) by his own tenants, only. The "lands," as they are emphatically called, of other Freeholders, within the manor, have no right of Commonage! A cuſtom of manors which may have eluded my reſearches in other parts of the County.

Should it be ſaid, that this circumſtance favors the ſtory of the Wolves, for that theſe lands were private property of their reſpective Lords, and were thrown up for the uſe of their own tenants only, I will not gainſay it. I have, perhaps, already done more than my duty; and I leave it to the Antiquary, whose bent leads him to topographical enquiries, to determine the point.

Therefore, returning to what more immediately relates to the subject matter of this Register, I will finally observe, that, whatever may have been the circumstances which led to the inclosure of the Vallies under notice, they were made from the unreclaimed forest state; without the intervention of common fields* or stinted pastures; judging, I mean, from their present appearances; which resemble those of the Inclosures of Kent, Herefordshire, and other Districts; which have been, undoubtedly, inclosed from a state of unreclaimed woodland. The hedgerows are crooked, and furnished with timber; and the banks raised, in *imitation* of those of Devonshire; but are much lower than the

alto-

* It is to be observed, however, that, to the East of Bridport, I saw some faint traces of common arable fields: but in the area or the Western parts of the District, I observed no appearances of that sort.

altogether artificial mounds of the more Weſtern part of the County.

XII. The PRESENT PRODUCTIONS of the Soils of this Diſtrict are WOOD (chiefly of Hedgerows,—not much detached Woodland),—ARABLE CROPS, FRUIT TREES, and GRASS;—the laſt being the moſt prevalent produce of the incloſed lands. The Hills are overgrown with DWARF FURZE, HEATH, and COARSE HERBAGE; a few of the more barren parts of them being occupied chiefly by heath.

XIII. The TOWNS of this Diſtrict are BRIDPORT on the Eaſt, AXMINSTER near the center, HONITON on the Weſt, CREWKERNE and CHARD on the North, with different Sea Ports on the South.

XIV. VILLAGES. In this particular, the Diſtrict under view is ſtrictly Danmonian: the Villages, that have fallen under my eye, are inconſiderable; the farm houſe, and cottages being happily ſcattered over the areas of the Townſhips: a circumſtance

cumſtance more or leſs obſervable, perhaps, in every part of the kingdom, where incloſures have been made from a ſtate of Woodland, or of Paſturage: cloſe arrangements of houſes, in the form of Villages, being moſt obſervable, in Common-Field Diſtricts *.

XV. HABITATIONS. The BUILDING MATERIALS, here, are various. Stones of different ſorts are in uſe; but earthen walls are, nevertheleſs, prevalent; and, on the whole, the habitations of this Eaſtern Diſtrict are much inferior to thoſe of Weſt Devonſhire; which far excels the reſt of the County, in this particular.

XVI. The PRESENT APPEARANCE of the Face of this Country may be conceived,

* The LAYING OUT OF TOWNSHIPS, and their PRESENT STATE OF INCLOSURE, are ſubjects ſo very intereſting to a mind employed in Agricultural Reſearches, that no apology can be wanting for the Remarks that are interſperſed in theſe Volumes, reſpecting them; as no other Department of the Iſland furniſhes ſo many ſtriking facts, relating to theſe ſubjects, as the WEST OF ENGLAND.

ceived, from what has been said, respecting its Surface, its Productions, its State of Inclosure, and the Distribution and Style of its Habitations.

Viewed from some elevated points, where the barren or infertile summits of the hills only are seen, it has all the appearance of a Mountain District.

But, in travelling through it, and still more in penetrating its recluser parts, the most striking transitions are produced, and compositions the most picturable are caught. It is observable, however, that the prevailing characteristic of the views of this passage of Country is Beauty, rather than picturesque Effect; differing much, in this respect, from the wilder scenery of the West of Devonshire.

In Circles of Views, this passage of Country abounds. The Summit of the Knoll, the Brink of the Sea Cliff, on the West side of the Harbor of Bridport, is an interesting point; commanding Land and Sea Views of the first cast. On Beaminster Down, one of the broadest and richest circles of scenery, this Island affords, is seen

ſeen with every advantage. In variety, extent, and richneſs, conſidered jointly, I know nothing that equals it. To the Eaſt, the ſoft billowy ſurface of the Chalk Hills of Dorſetſhire, even to their farther extreme. To the Weſt, the more rugged mountain ſummits of Devonſhire, with Dartmore (I believe) riſing in the fartheſt diſtance. To the North, the rich Vales of Somerſetſhire, backed by the Quantoc and Mendip Hills, with a portion of the Briſtol Channel breaking in between them. To the South, the ſingularly broken and beautiful ſurface, in the Environs of Bridport; the varied ſummits of the hills giving feature and additional effect to the Bay of Bridport; ſpreading its ample ſurface immediately under the eye; its Weſtern Coaſt being finely broken and varied, by ragged promontories, and bold cliffs; and its Eaſtern terminated, by the Iſle of Portland; with mackrel ſkiffs playing on the ſurface of the Bay, and with veſſels of burden plowing their way acroſs it.

THE

THE

AGRICULTURE

OF

THIS DISTRICT.

THE leading Object, in viewing it, especially its Western quarter, being that of catching OBVIOUS IMPROVEMENTS, in the MANAGEMENT OF AN ESTATE, rather than to register the minutiæ of its AGRICULTURE, I am the less prepared to enter into a detail of its practices. I shall therefore confine my remarks to a few general heads.

I. FARMS. The distinguishing character of Farms, in the interior of the District, is Grassland. There are many which have very little, if any, arable land; being strictly DAIRY FARMS.

In

In SIZE, the Farms of this Eastern District are conformable to those of the rest of the County; being mostly of the lower class. But, here, it is not uncommon for one man to hold two or three distinct Farms: stocking them with cows, and letting them out to dairymen: a practice however which admits not of commendation; and which will be renoticed.

II. FARMERS. Even in the most recluse part of the District, I met with some intelligent men. And although the rust of prejudice may not yet be sufficiently worn away, the late memorable change, in the management of the dairy, shows demonstrably, that the spirit of improvement is awake, and augurs much for the benefit of the Country.

III. BEASTS OF LABOR. In the interior of the District, OXEN are in use; but, in the Eastern quarter CART HORSES prevail.

IV. IMPLEMENTS.

IV. IMPLEMENTS. The only thing that ſtruck me, as excellent or peculiar, in the conſtruction of the Farming Utenſils of this Diſtrict, relates to the YOKE; whoſe draft iron, or ſtaple, is inſerted, not perpendicularly, as it uſually is; but diagonally; entering the lower angle of the hind part of the Yoke, ſhooting upward and forward to the oppoſite angle; where it is keyed, in the uſual manner. This prevents the bend of the bow from bearing too hard againſt the throat of the Ox, and is theoretically good. How it operates, in other reſpects, in practice, I had not an opportunity of obſerving.

V. PLAN OF MANAGEMENT. In the general outline of practice, obſervable in the more Weſtern parts of this Diſtrict, we find little which ſpecifically differs from that of the County at large. The OBJECTS are nearly the ſame, and the means uſed in obtaining them ſimilar. The difference lies chiefly with the proportional quantity of each ſpecies of produce. In Eaſt, as in Weſt Devonſhire, the objects are permanent graſs,

graſs, arable crops, and temporary leys: part of the graſs, in both Diſtricts, being applied to dairy cows, for butter and ſkim cheeſe. But the proportion of Graſsland, and the proportional number of cows, is much greater here, than in the Weſtern parts of the County. Of the lower grounds of the Valley of Yarcombe, four fifths, perhaps, are in a ſtate of graſs, permanent or temporary; and this is chiefly depaſtured by cows; the number of working cattle being few, and the ſheep and young cattle chiefly confined to the hills, and upper grounds.

The ARABLE CROPS of the interior of the Diſtrict are chiefly *Wheat*, and *Oats*; no *Beans!* and but little *Barley*.

The SUCCESSION is ſimilar to that of Weſt Devonſhire: ley ground, partially fallowed for wheat, with one or two crops of oats; graſs ſeeds being ſown with the laſt crop. Some take oats, wheat, oats; agreeably to the practice of the Midland Diſtrict; whoſe ſoil and ſubſoil are very ſimilar.

In

In the more Eaftern parts of the Diftrict, there are fhades of difference obfervable in the Plan of Management: which, probably, partakes more or lefs of that of the Vales of Dorfetfhire, and the rich low lands of Somerfetfhire, from which this part of the Diftrict, now under view, is feparated by a narrow ridge of hill, only.

But what marks the Rural Management of the Environs of Bridport moft evidently, is the culture of *hemp* and *flax*,—to fupply the confumption of a MANUFACTORY of SAILCLOTH and CORDAGE (from the cable of a man of war, to the fineft packing thread), which has long been carried on, there: giving employment to the female villagers of the neighbourhood; and, of courfe, operating as a mutual benefit to Agriculture and Commerce. A mutual good, however, which can only fubfift, in a rich-foiled Diftrict.

VI. MANURES. LIME is more or lefs in ufe, throughout the Diftrict: being burnt, from ftone found within it, with Welch culm; at leaft in the Bridport quarter.

 Formerly,

Formerly, much "MARL" has been uſed, in the valley of Yarcombe; which exhibits "marl pits" of conſiderable capacity, and old enough to have produced Oaks of conſiderable ſize; perfectly reſembling the "marl pits," and the "marl" of the Midland Counties: namely, a red clayey loam, without the leaſt proportion of calcareous matter in its compoſition! and, what is noticeable, the marl of this Diſtrict, as that of the Midland Counties, is now giving way to lime: the change, if one may judge from general appearances, having taken place about the ſame period of time!

In the Bridport quarter, I obſerved the SHEEPFOLD, in more than one inſtance; agreeably to the Dorſetſhire practice.

VII. GRASSLAND. Notwithſtanding this may be conſidered as the main object of the Diſtrict under view, I obſerved nothing praiſeworthy in its Management. In the Valley of Yarcombe, where the ſoil is tenacious, and the ſubſoil retentive, the Graſslands, whether permanent or temporary, are injured by ſuperfluous moiſture:

an

an injury which is not ſo much owing to a want of draining, ſubterraneouſly, as from their lying too flat, to ſhoot off, with proper effect, the ſuperficial waters. The natural conſequence is, much of the ſurface is over-run with aquatic weeds and the coarſer graſſes, when it ought to be occupied by nutritious and more profitable herbage.

It is to be obſerved, that the Spring WATERS of this Diſtrict are of an ameliorative quality, and that they are here, as in Weſt Devonſhire, partially, and inaccurately, led over the Graſslands.

VIII. ORCHARDS are common, in every part of the Diſtrict. I bring them forward, here, merely to ſay of them, what may be readily conceived, that, with reſpect to the ſtature of the trees, and the order in which they are arranged, they form a mean between the Orchards of Devonſhire and thoſe of Somerſetſhire. The ſtems are, here, ſomewhat taller, than in Weſt Devonſhire, but are conſiderably ſhort of the Engliſh ſtandard. And, in the cloſeneſs of arrangement, they ſtill more reſemble the Devonſhire Orchard. I ſpeak more particularly of thoſe of the Valley of Yarcomb *.

IX. THE DAIRY. This has been, time immemorial, a Dairy Diſtrict. Formerly, its produce was CHEESE, made from the neat milk; probably of the Somerſetſhire kind, ſold under the name of Bridgewater Cheeſe; ſome of which I have met with of a very ſuperior quality. The Valley of Yarcombe was noted for its produce, which was known in the Vale of Exeter, by the name of Membury Cheeſe. Indeed, its ſoil and herbage are ſuch, as never fail to produce fine Cheeſe, if properly manufactured. It is naturally a Cheeſe Diſtrict.

Nevertheleſs, of late years, its produce has been changed to BUTTER, for the London

* In approaching theſe Hills, from the Eaſtward, the Orchards of Chard were the firſt that ſtruck me, as partaking of the Devonſhire Orchard. The ſtems ſhorter than thoſe of Dorſetſhire and Somerſetſhire; but tall enough for young Cattle to paſture beneath the Trees.

London market; to which it is ſent in tubs, as from the North of England: a change which has been brought about, by the powerful influence of the London prices, compared with thoſe of the Country.

The SIZES OF DAIRIES, judging from what fell under my own obſervation, riſe to thirty or forty Cows. I ſaw one of near ſorty.

The BREED OF COWS, employed in theſe Dairies, is that of the WEST OF ENGLAND; namely, the well formed, clean, middle-horned breed, which is common to the Counties of Somerſet, Devon, and Cornwall. In the neighbourhood of Bridport, I ſaw a tolerably good Dairy of Cows, of a mixed breed; apparently a croſs between the middle and the long horned breeds.

Formerly, the Cows uſed in theſe Dairies were chiefly REARED, in the Country; but, of late years, Butter has borne ſo profitable a price, as to induce the Farmers to forego the rearing, and to PURCHASE their Cows: a practice which, if it ſhould continue, will ſoon introduce a mixture of ſtock.

Of the DAIRY MANAGEMENT, of the Diſtrict under view, I can ſay little: I collected nothing on the minutia of practice worth regiſtering. Its preſent practice can ſcarcely be ſaid to be, as yet, *eſtabliſhed.* It was not, therefore, an object; even had I had leiſure to attend to it. To regiſter the minutiæ of the Dairy Management, ſo as to render the detail intelligible and uſeful, is a tedious and irkſome taſk; and requires, not only time, but a ſpecies of opportunity, which did not occur to me, in this Diſtrict.

Many of theſe Dairies are LET TO DAIRY-MEN, at a certain rent for each Cow; the Farmer keeping up the ſtock, and ſupplying them with paſturage and winter food; and finding a dwelling as well as a dairy houſe, for the renter. It is common for opulent men to hold a plurality of farms, and to let them out to under tenants, in this way: a practice which is injurious to an eſtate; as tending to let down the buildings and the fences of farms, thus occupied by under tenants; who have not ſo permanent an intereſt, in keeping them up, as a leſſee, or firſt tenant, who makes the place his reſidence,

reſidence, and expects to occupy the premiſes for a length of time; and who is himſelf liable for dilapidations.

X. SHEEP. I obſerved, in the Bridport quarter, ſome fine flocks of DORSETSHIRE EWES: kept as breeding flocks; ſimilar to thoſe of the Vale of Exeter, and Weſt Devonſhire, which have been already ſpoken of. The Sheep of the higher hills are of the ſame mountain ſort, which occupy the other hills of Devonſhire and Cornwall.

SOME

HINTS

FOR THE

IMPROVEMENT

OF

THIS DISTRICT.

IT has been mentioned, that my chief intention, in going over it, especially its Northwestern quarter, was that of endeavoring to point out the probable means of its Improvement. And although my examinations, and the result of them, were mostly of a private nature; some of the Remarks, they gave rise to, may, nevertheless, bear the public eye, and may be more or less useful, to those who have property in the District, and who are desirous to improve its condition. Nor may the suggestions, here thrown out, be altogether inapplicable to other Districts.

The

The few subjects of Improvement which I can bring forward, here, with propriety, are,

I. The HILLS, or COMMONABLE LANDS. Something has been already said respecting the PRESENT STATE of these lands; so far as relates to their soil, and the marks of cultivation which appear on their surfaces.

The SOILS, however, are various in quality. Some of these hills are covered with a loamy soil, of sufficient depth and texture to admit of profitable cultivation *: while others are nearly destitute of mold. The latter, very fortunately, is by far the smaller proportion.

The PRESENT PRODUCE has been mentioned, as being furze, heath, and the coarser grasses: interspersed, however, with patches of sward.

The

* At the head of the Valley of Yarcombe, cultivation and permanent Inclosures climb up the side—there a gentle slope hanging to the North—and spread over the top of the hill. And some of the soil of the Common appears to be of a quality, similar to that of the cultivated Inclosures.

The PRESENT STOCK is an inferior kind of Sheep; and young Cattle.

The MEANS OF IMPROVEMENT appear, to me, to be those which I have suggested, above, for the improvement of DARTMORE *.

The first step is to separate the culturable from the unculturable lands;—to cut off the steep ragged brows of the hills, for PLANTING. And the next, to inclose the flatted tops of the hills, for CULTIVATION; or for open SHEEP WALK, or RABBIT WARREN; agreeably to the soil and surface, and conformably with the Proposals already offered †.

II. HEDGEROWS. Among the various Improvements of which the LOWER GROUNDS, VALLEY LANDS, or "BOTTOMS," as they are called, are capable, none strikes the eye more forcibly, than that of its HEDGEROW TIMBER; which is, at present, in a state of neglect. The same unpardonable practice of lopping Oak Timber

* See P. 29.

† See as above.

Timber Trees, ſo ſhamefully prevalent in the Vale of Exeter, is extended, in ſome degree at leaſt, to this Diſtrict. The ſoil of theſe Valley lands is peculiarly ſuitable for the growth of Oak Timber; and, on the broad hedge banks, which interſect them, Ship Timber of the firſt quality might be raiſed, in great abundance, with little injury to the Occupiers of the lands, compared with the advantages which would therefrom accrue to the Proprietors and the Public. Yet we ſee theſe valuable nurſeries, in many parts deſtitute, or very deficient, with reſpect to this ineſtimable article of produce: owing, principally or wholly, to neglect, or a want of ſkill, in the Management of Eſtates. The COPPICE WOOD of theſe Hedgerows being reaped by the Tenants, they have an intereſt in deſtroying, and preventing the growth, of TIMBER TREES: a circumſtance which calls for double diligence, on the part of thoſe who have the ſuperintendance of Eſtates. There is, evidently, ſufficient room, in the wide Hedgerows of theſe lands, to grow an abundance of fuel, for the

the Tenants, and a valuable ſupply of Timber, for the Landlord, and the Public.

The means of Improvement are evident. Take down the trees, that are irrecoverably maimed, or which are ſtunted, or fully grown, and *number* thoſe, which are proper to be left ſtanding. Train up the young ſtands, or timberlings, ſo as to give them length of ſtem; not more to improve them as Timber Trees, than to prevent their doing unneceſſary injury to the crops on either ſide, and to the Coppice wood, which ſhall hereafter riſe beneath them. And ſet out, in vacant ſpaces, at every fall of Coppice wood, ſuch promiſing ſhoots, as ſeldom fail to riſe among Coppice wood, growing on a ſoil ſo favorable to the Oak, as that of the Valley Lands which are now under conſideration.

The laſt is a buſineſs which requires particular circumſpection. It cannot, for obvious reaſons, be left to a Tenant or his workmen, with ſafety; at leaſt not to Tenants in general. The only way, in which it can be done with a certainty of ſucceſs, is to ſend round an experienced

and

and faithful Woodman, previously to the cutting season, to set out, and distinguish with paint, or other conspicuous and permanent mark, the plants which are proper to be left for standards.

In this District,—where the ordinary Woods are usually cut out, in winter, leaving the Oak standing, until the barking season, agreeably to the Danmonian practice,—there would seem to be a favorable time for marking the standards, between these operations. But when it is considered, that the seedling plants, which ought always to be chosen where a choice offers itself, are frequently of inferior size to the sapling shoots from the stubs, and generally too inconsiderable to be left for peeling, such interval of time is too late. We may, therefore, without hesitation or hazard, give it in opinion, that every OAKLAND ESTATE, having wide woody Hedgerows, should have an established regulation, requiring its tenants to give due notice of their intentions, previously to the cutting of their Hedgewoods; in order that the proper plants, they contain, may be marked

for

for ſtandards; they being allowed a full compenſation for the wood thus marked, as well as for the attention and care which may be requiſite, in preſerving them from injury: giving due encouragement to the tenants, who encourage the growth of Timber upon their reſpective farms;—and treating with neglect, thoſe who are negligent of its preſervation.

For Remarks on Training Hedgerow Timber, and its Effects on Arable Crops, ſee PLANTING and RURAL ORNAMENT, Vol. I. Pages 56 and 96.

III. PLAN OF FARM MANAGEMENT. Some alteration, in the arable department of Management, ſeems to be wanted. The temporary leys are moſtly foul, weak, and thin of herbage; owing, doubtleſs, to the practice of taking two or three grain crops, in ſucceſſion, and laying the land down in a ſtate of exhauſtion, as well as foul, and out of tilth. Perhaps taking a crop of beans, in rows well cleaned, between the wheat and the oat crop, might be found doubly beneficial; as introducing

a ſpecies

a ſpecies of produce, new to the ſoil; and ſerving to prepare it for the reception of the graſs ſeeds, by a fallow crop. In caſes where the ſoil is very foul, a whole year's fallow is, of courſe, requiſite.

IV. In the MANAGEMENT of the SOIL, two or three Improvements are obvious. Much UNDERDRAINING is wanted; not only in the meadows or lower lands; but on the riſing grounds and hangs of the hills. Stones are plentiful; and ſod drains might be found to anſwer on the ſtronger lands.

Another Improvement, which preſents itſelf, in the Management of the Soil, relates to the method of LAYING IT DOWN TO GRASS.

In Weſt Devonſhire, where the ſubſoil is abſorbent, and the ſoil friable and firm, it is perfectly right to lay it down, as flat and ſmooth as poſſible. But, here, where the ſoil is tenacious, and the ſubſoil retentive, and much of it kept in continual ſurcharge, by the waters pent up beneath it, the practice is in a degree abſurd. Nevertheleſs, the

the practice of these two distant Districts, with respect to the depositing, or forming the surface of their soils, with the plow, to receive the given crops, is precisely the same. For wheat, the soil is gathered up into narrow ridges; and is laid flat, for every other crop.

The Improvement which strikes me, as proper to be proposed for this District, is that of keeping the land in ridges, of half a statute rod in width, for every crop; or of preserving the present narrower ridges for wheat, and throwing two of them together, for beans, oats, and ley herbage: being ever mindful to form the surfaces of the ridges gently convex, to shoot off the superfluous rain water which falls on them; with deep narrow interfurrows, to receive the water; and with cross trenches, to convey it away, to the neighbouring ditches and common shores: a principle of Management, which is applicable to all cool retentive soils, in the Island.

V. MANURES. In a remote situation, like that which is now more particularly

under

under notice, every experiment and expedient ſhould be uſed, to meliorate the condition of its lands, and to make up for the loſs, they annually ſuſtain, by the produce carried off, without any foreign ſupply or return for ſuch exhauſtion. Lime appears to be the only extraneous, or factitious Manure, at preſent in uſe: a Manure whoſe operation is generally weak, on cool, coheſive lands.

In the RURAL ECONOMY of YORKSHIRE, I ventured to ſuggeſt, as a probable means of meliorating ſtrong coheſive ſoils, the burning of their ſurfaces;—not more for the aſhes, as a Manure, than for the cinders, or BURNT CLAY, which ſuch a proceſs neceſſarily produces, as a means of improving the contexture of ſuch coheſive ſoils *. And I have lately been informed, that the burning of the clay of drains, and ſpreading it over the ſtrong coheſive lands of Somerſetſhire, is now practiſed, with great advantage. Theſe ſimple and cheap operations are, at leaſt, ſubjects of experiment, in every Diſtrict, whoſe lands are of a cloſe retentive nature.

* See YORK. ECON. Vol. I. Page 313.

The lands, now immediately under consideration, have another probable means of Improvement within their reach; and which can rarely be commanded, by lands of a similar nature. I mean the BLACK MOORY EARTH of the heaths, which inclose and overlook them. There is doubtless much earth of this kind, which lies at present useless on the hills, and which cannot, there, be turned to so useful a purpose, as, in much probability, it may, in the Vallies: applying it, either in a simply digested state;—or in compost with lime; or in the state of coal, or of ashes;—as a short course of experiments, attentively conducted, could not fail to determine.

DISTRICT THE SEVENTH.

THE

VALE OF TAUNTON,

AND ITS

ENVIRONS;

TOGETHER WITH

CURSORY REMARKS

IN A JOURNEY THROUGH

SOMERSETSHIRE.

IN September 1791, on my way from West Devonſhire to Suſſex, I ſtopt ſome days at TAUNTON; to look round its fine Environs; and to get a general view of the Natural Characters, and ſome inſight into the Rural Management, of this celebrated Paſſage of Country. I, then, not only

 examined

examined the Area of the VALE, on either side, but ascended the QUANTOC and the BLACKDOWN HILLS, which over look it; and went into one of the SEDGEMORES, which mark Somersetshire so discriminately, from the rest of the Island.

I have, since, had repeated occasions to travel through the Vale: and, in the autumn of 1794, on leaving Devonshire, I renewed my attention; continuing my Remarks THROUGH THE COUNTY, in the line between Tiverton and the Devizes.

In making out this sketch, I find it most convenient to myself, and I believe it will be found most advantageous to the Reader, as being most perspicuous, to keep these Passages distinct: treating of the Vale, as the main subject; and joining the rest, as appendices.

THE

VALE OF TAUNTON.

THE SITUATION of this ſertile Vale or Diſtrict, is in the Weſtern Quarter of Somerſetſhire. Its NATURAL BOUNDARIES are, on the North, the Quantoc Hills, which ſeparate it from the Vale of Bridgewater: on the South, the Blackdown Hills, which ſever it, in a ſimilar manner, from the Vale of Exeter:—and, on the Weſt, the Skirts of Exmore and the broken hilly Diſtrict of the Coaſt. On the Eaſt, it is leſs accurately defined;—the riſing grounds of Curry, and the extenſive marſh of South Sedgemore, may be conſidered as its natural boundary.

Its EXTENT is ſmall. It is barely entitled to the diſtinction which is here given it, and which it not uncommonly bears; though, in natural characters, its dimensions apart, it is, in the strict sense, a *Vale District*. One hundred square miles, I apprehend, would contain the whole of its more valuable lands.

The ELEVATION of its Area, above the sea's surface, is, even at present, inconsiderable; yet is sufficient to keep it dry and healthy. Nor does any part of it, except its lower extreme, appear to have ever been liable to the tide, or collected floods: it contains none of such level marshes, or "moors," as are scattered in the central and Southern parts of Somersetshire.

In SURFACE, as has been intimated, this District takes the Vale character. Its area is diversified with rising grounds, and interspersed with low meadowy lands. The banks, on either side, rise to a great height. On the South side, the foot of Blackdown shelves smoothly, though somewhat steeply, into the Vale; but, on the North, the Quantoc Hills rise abruptly, and with a more broken and strongly featured front. From Cotherston Lodge, which crowns a prominent knoll, that juts out from these hills, the entire surface of the

the Vale is commanded. It is closed, to the West, by a crowd of hillocks,—in tumult wild assembled: a genuine passage of that singular species of surface, which is common to the Western extreme of the Island; and which may be said to terminate, or rather to commence, here.

The CLIMATURE of this Vale might be prejudged, from its situation. The bases of high extended hills are generally cool; and backward, with respect to seasons:—especially if they face the North; and still more especially, if the substrata are of a cohesive retentive nature; as are those of the South side of the Vale of Taunton. In the second week of September 1791, much barley was still unharvested, and some uncut.

The SOILS of this, as of many other contracted Vale Districts, vary in quality, with the hills which form them. Much of the North side of the Vale of Taunton is a deep rich sand—a carrot soil: while the opposite side is chiefly the same strong red loam, which we have found in the Valley of Yarcombe, and in the Vale of Exeter;

 and

and alſo, in ſmall plots, in the South Hams, and in North Devonſhire.

The SUBSOILS are ſtill more various. In the area of the Vale, a Gravel is ſeen: under the rich red ſands of Biſhop's Lydiard, a concrete ſubſtance of the ſame color, and of various degrees of hardneſs, prevails. This concretion, in ſome places, takes the nature of rock; which, on being expoſed to the air, acquires a great degree of hardneſs, and is uſed as a building material. Under the ſtrong red ſoils, of the oppoſite ſide of the Vale, a deep loam, of a ſimilar nature, is found: and, under this, ſubſtrata of white ſandy ſubſtance, hardening in ſome inſtances into a kind of ſtone, is ſeen interlayered with red loam; an accompaniment, perhaps, which is common to all the ſtrong red lands of the Iſland.

The RIVER of the Vale is the TONE, or TAUN,—which is rendered NAVIGABLE to Taunton. The freightage is chiefly, Welch COALS, for fuel, and CULM, for burning Lime.

The chief PRODUCTION of this fertile Diſtrict is, at preſent, CORN. There is is very little GRASS obſervable; unleſs near the Towns; and by the ſides of the Tone, and its branches. And, even from the commanding point of Cotherſton, not more than two or three ſmall plots of WOODLAND are ſeen, in the area of the Vale. The HEDGEROWS, however, are full of wood; and, when viewed from the oppoſite banks, a greater degree of woodineſs appears.

The whole is in a STATE OF INCLOSURE; with FIELDS of various form and ſize.

FENCES. In the Vale of Taunton, we trace, by broken ſteps, the decline and termination of the DANMONIAN FENCE.

In the more Weſtern and central parts of the area of the Vale, the prevailing Fence reſembles that of the Valley of Yarcombe, and the lower grounds of the Vale of Exeter: namely, a low broad bank, loaded with coppice wood, and hedgerow timber trees: the former moſtly Oak; the latter Elms, ſhorn of their boughs, as in the ordinary practice of the kingdom.

But, in paſſing down the Vale, the HAW-

THORN HEDGE begins, by degrees, to mix with the coppice mounds, and, before the Eastern extremity is reached, becomes the prevailing Fence.

In the MANAGEMENT OF FARMS, the Vale of Taunton differs, in some respects, from the DANMONIAN HUSBANDRY; especially in the outline or PLAN OF MANAGEMENT. It is properly an ARABLE DISTRICT: the TEMPORARY LEY, which is common to Devonshire, scarcely appears to extend into this Vale. In the second week of September, half the District, as seen from the hills, was PLOWED GROUND, or TURNEPS! the rest appeared to be PERMANENT GRASS, with the CORN, then unharvested, and STUBBLES unbroken up.

Nevertheless, in MINUTIAL PRACTICES, particularly in the management of Lime, the burning of Beat, and the sowing of Wheat, the Vale pursues the Devonshire method.

The CROPS are *Wheat*, *Barley*, *Oats*, and *Beans*, the last more especially, on the stronger lands of the South side of the Vale.

ORCHARDS.

ORCHARDS. The height of Orchard trees, as of Hedges, undergoes a change in this Diſtrict. In travelling, between Exeter and Taunton, the ſtem of the Apple tree is ſeen to lengthen towards Somerſetſhire; but not in uniform progreſſion: And, in paſſing from Tiverton, into the Vale, ſimilar appearances are ſeen. The firſt full-ſtemmed *Engliſh* Orchard was obſerved, in the neighbourhood of Wellington.

But as this and other particulars, relating to the remarkable tranſition,—obſervable in Rural Practices, on leaving the Weſtern Peninſula, or extreme part of the Iſland,—will appear in the following JOURNAL, it is unneceſſary to enter farther, in this place, on the particular management of the Vale of Taunton.

THE

THE

QUANTOC HILLS.

THESE form a narrow range of Mountain Heights, which rise near the junction of the Parret and the Tone, below Taunton, and lead, in a Northwest direction, towards the Coast of the Irish sea, or Bristol Channel; dividing the low fertile lands of the Vale of Taunton, from those of the Vale of Bridgewater.

Their ELEVATION, with respect to the adjoining lands, is considerable; though their positive height, above the tide, is not great. They are, however, too high, and too mountainlike, in their general aspect, to be merely deemed upland; yet not of sufficient importance to be styled mountain.

The SURFACE of these hills, or rather chain of hills, is greatly diversified. They resemble, in surface, soil, and present produce, the hills of East Devonshire; and, like those, have been heretofore cultivated (in whole or in part): the vallies or breaks, between

between them, being now in a ſtate of cultivation.

The SOIL of the extended ſummit, to the Eaſt of Cotherſton Lodge, appears to be of a nature that would pay for cultivation; being now chiefly covered with graſs and the upland ſedges. But, to the Weſtward, the ſoil appears to be more barren, and much of the produce heath.

There being evident traces of Limeſtone on theſe hills, their IMPROVEMENT, in much probability, might be rendered very profitable, to individuals.

The inſulate ſituation of theſe Hills renders them highly intereſting, to thoſe who admire the ample ſcenery of Nature. The Mendip Hills, and the principal part of Somerſetſhire which lies to the South of them; the Hills of Wiltſhire and Dorſetſhire; Beaminſter Down, with the other prominent Hills of Eaſt Devonſhire, terminating with Black Down; diſtant Hills, in Devonſhire; Exmore, and the Hillocks of the Coaſt; with the Briſtol Channel and its Holms, backed by the Welch Mountains; ſpread out wide to the view.

THE

THE

BLACK-DOWN HILLS.

IT has been ſaid, that theſe Hills form the Southern bank of the Vale of Taunton, and ſeparate it from the Vale of Exeter: and, in like manner, they divide the Counties of Somerſet and Devon. They are a continuation of the Axminſter Hills; forming their Northweſtern extremity.

In ELEVATION, they exceed everything in their neighbourhood; equally overtopping the Quantoc and the Axminſter Hills.

In ſurface, they reſemble the reſt of the mountain heights of this extreme of the Iſland; namely flat, or ſwelling; divided by wide open Dells, or ſhallower Dips; and partially ſevered, by deep rich Vallies or "Troughs"—as they are called—of cultivated lands. The extreme point, to the Weſt, forms a bold Promontory; wearing, on on its Northweſtern brow, a mountain appearance.

The SOIL of the ſummit is of an inferior quality; of a black moory nature: and ſtrewed with the ſame baſe kind of *Flints*, that are obſervable on the other hills of Eaſt Devonſhire; and this without any traces of *Chalk*: an unuſual circumſtance, worthy of the Naturaliſt's attention.

The STOCK of theſe mountain heights are young cattle of the Weſt of England breed, and moſt of them neat: with the ſame aukward, half-horned breed of Sheep, that are common to all the wild lands of this extremity of the Iſland.

On the Northern hang,—about the mid-way,—of theſe hills, are quarries of LIMESTONE, found in a ſingular ſtate.

The quality of the Stone is evidently that of the Clayſtone of Glouceſterſhire, of Leiceſterſhire, and of the Vale of Belvoir; but inſtead of being depoſited in regular ſtrata, it is found in detached fragments, bedded, promiſcuouſly, in pale-colored earth; ſimilar to that with which it is interlayered, in the inſtances above mentioned;

tioned;—as if the strata of Stone had been broken to pieces, while the earthy matter was in a plastic state, and the mass had been blended, by some violent agitation.

The color of the Stone is blue, internally, and white, towards the surface; and burns to a somewhat sulphur-colored Lime; resembling that of Barrow, in Leicestershire *.

Further Remarks on the Limestone of West Somersetshire.

I afterwards examined the Limeworks and quarries of the Hills, which bound the Vale of Taunton to the East, and which are entirely detached from the Blackdown and Axminster Hills.

Here, the same Stone is found, in regular unbroken strata; as they appear in the quarries of Glocestershire, Leicestershire, &c. but with a very striking difference respecting their situation. In the places abovementioned, they are lodged beneath the surface of low flat Vale lands; whereas, in

* See Mid. Econ. Vol. I. P. 28.

in the inſtance under notice, they break out of the face of a lofty and ſteep hill.

Nevertheleſs, ſuch is the impervious and retentive quality of theſe ſtrata, that the land which lies over them, even in this elevated ſituation, and cloſe upon the brink of a precipice, which probably has heretofore been the waterworn cliff of an eſtuary or arm of the ſea, is cold and ungenial, as that which covers their watery bed, in the low grounds of the Vale of Glouceſter. The ſurface, in many places, is occupied by Coltsfoot. A field, cloſe upon the brink of the cliff which overlooks the marſh, or Sedgemore, that will preſently be noticed, was under fallow for Wheat, at the time I was upon theſe Hills (in Sept. 1791); and, from the *complection* of the ſoil, it appeared to be barely worth the labor of cultivation.

How much more depends on the quality of the ſubſtratum, than on that of the ſoil itſelf: the very ſoil, here under notice, if incumbent on an abſorbent ſubſoil, would be worth three or four times its preſent value.

SOUTH SEDGEMORE.

FROM the eminence juſt mentioned, I had a favorable opportunity of gaining a general view of this rich Level of marſh-lands. And, by riding a few miles within its area, paſſing through its herds and flocks, and converſing with thoſe who were attending to them,—I had a ſimilar opportunity of obtaining the particulars of information, which a curſory view required.

The natural boundaries of theſe marſhes are the Limeſtone Heights, abovementioned, on the South and South-Eaſt; on the Weſt, the broken baſe of the Eaſtern extremity of the Quantoc Hills, and the narrowed *mouth* of the Vale of Taunton. On the North, the Parret and the Tone are conſidered as the boundary of the "Moor" immediately under conſideration; their junction forming the extreme point to the North. But lands of a ſimilar nature

nature are ſeen to ſtretch away beyond that point, to the North-Weſt.

In the view from the hills, there appears to be an EXTENT of theſe lands ten or twelve miles in length, and ſome miles in width, under the eye. But the outline is extremely irregular.

The ELEVATION of theſe lands (the part I examined at leaſt) is ſuch as to ſecure them, at preſent, from the tide; nor did I learn that land floods incommode them, in any conſiderable degree.

Their SURFACE is level as that of the water, which, with moral certainty, once occupied the ſpace they now fill. If we calculate on the rapid increaſe of earthy matter, at the mouths of rivers, whoſe waters are collected from rich arable lands; —and on the decreaſing depth of the Sea; which, though perhaps not equal to what ſome modern Writers conjecture, has probably been conſiderable, during the laſt millennium of time;—it is reaſonable to ſuppoſe, that ſince the firſt ſettlement of this Iſland, the Sea rolled its rapid tides within the area now under contemplation: and the rapidity of the tides, in the eſtuary of the Parret, as of the Severn, accounts more fully for the rapid increaſe of land; occaſioned by the ſilt forced up, by the "Boar" or Eagre, which is common to the rivers of the Severn Sea *.

The preſent name of the marſhes of Somerſetſhire, is a ſufficient evidence, to prove, that, at the time it was aſſigned them, the reclaim was not compleated: that they were, at the time it was applied, in

* This ſtriking natural effect, I have repeatedly obſerved, on the banks of the Severn, near Glocefter; where, at certain times of the tide, and moſt eſpecially during a ſtrong Weſterly wind, a body of water, ſome few feet in depth, ruſhes impetuouſly up the Channel of the river; gliding, as it were, upon the deſcending waters; ruſhing out at the more abrupt bends, and daſhing its ſpray to a very great height, on every obſtruction; attended by ſounds, which may ſometimes be heard to a conſiderable diſtance.

This effect is probably cauſed, by the form and ſituation of the Briſtol Channel; which receives the tide, from the Atlantic, by a wide opening, and contracts towards the mouths of the rivers that are thus affected.

The narrowing eſtuary of the Humber, produces a ſimilar effect.

in a ſtate of *Fen*; not in that of firm, dry *Marſhlands*, as we now find them.

The SOIL of this marſh is a red loam, of conſiderable ſtrength and tenacity; reſembling, with great exactneſs, that of the Iſle of Alney, and the other marſh or meadow lands of the Severn *; except in the deeper tinge of red which the ſoil of South Sedgemore has received, from a greater mixture of colored water, which the red ſoils of the Vale of Taunton, and the North Eaſtern baſe of the Blackdown hills, have furniſhed.

The HERBAGE is ſingularly fine: apparently the Dogstail (*Cynoſurus Criſtatus*), Raygraſs, and White Clover; with, however, ſome plots of thiſtles, on the drier parts, and ſtripes of ſilver weed (*Potentilla Anſerina*) on the ſides of the drains, and more ſwampy places.

Hence, this extent of marſhes may be conſidered as land of the firſt quality: fit for every purpoſe of permanent graſsland.

 The

* For farther Remarks on the formation of Marſh and Meadow lands, ſee the RURAL ECONOMY of GLOCESTERSHIRE, Vol. I. P. 179.

The STOCK which it bore, at the time I was over it, were Horses, Cattle, Sheep, and Geese.

Of the *Horses*, I saw nothing which struck me as requiring notice.

The *Cattle* consisted chiefly of young growing stock—mostly two or three years old. With, however, many Cows; some of them apparently in milk, or recently thrown up. The condition of most of these Cattle was good; many of them were full of flesh; though the grass was short, as that of Sheep and Geese Commons usually is found. Aged Cattle, I understood, are brought forward on these commonable lands, to be finished with aftergrass.

The *Sheep* were chiefly or wholly of the horned breed; and had been put upon these lands, for the purpose of fatting. In a favorable year, it seems, they get tolerably fat. But much drought bakes those clayey lands, and much rain renders them too wet for Sheep.

The myriads of *Geese* are incalculable, The whole are subjected to the operation of of "pulling." They are now (13 September) covered with down, only. The operation, I was informed, is repeated several times, in the course of the summer; and found very profitable. They are kept on the "Moor," all winter. In long-continued frost and snow, they are fed, and, generally, I was told, with Beans.

Remarks.

FROM this cursory view, of these unappropriated lands, they appear to be of some considerable value, in their present commonable state. But viewing them as being, naturally, grazing and mowing grounds of a superior quality; and seeing the uncertainty of seasons in this climate; there can be little doubt of their being capable of affording much greater profit, to individuals, and to the Community, in a state of appropriation and division.

The prompt objection to the alteration is that of giving a check to the rearing of Cattle; and, some will add, to the rearing of Geese. The last, however, is not an object of sufficient importance, either in RURAL, or POLITICAL ECONOMY, to weigh, as an argument, on this subject;—though the feathers may be entitled to their full weight. And, with respect to the former, it may be said, that it cannot be good policy to suffer lands to lie in an under-productive state; by way of forcing the propagation of any particular species of animals; to the detriment of the aggregate produce of the Country.

CURSORY

CURSORY REMARKS

IN A JOURNEY THROUGH

SOMERSETSHIRE*.

TIVERTON TO TAUNTON.

(Twentyone Miles.)

FRIDAY, 19 SEPTEMBER, 1794.

LEAVE the charming environs of Tiverton: the finest situation in Devonshire; and one of the first in the Island.

Meet many lime carts, from the works on the borders of Somersetshire. The lime mostly in bags; some in bulk.

Pack-

* In continuation of that through NORTH DEVONSHIRE. I must again apologize for the *nakedness* of these remarks.

Packhorſes laden with hay, in truſſes.

A view of the rich environs of Bradnich opens: backed by the hills of Eaſt Devonſhire.

Paſs through a rich plot of country, round Halberton (three miles). The ſubſoil red grouty gravel; as near Hatherley.

Some fields of fine turneps; beautifully clean.

The road good: now mending, with flinty gravel, or broken flints.

More good turneps; near Sampford.

A variegated ſubſoil: red and white.

Enter flat furzegrown commons, and leave the rich Diſtrict of Tiverton.

The Blackdown hills, with mountain features, appear in front, and at hand.

Meet more lime carts, and ſome waggons: the laſt of the Weſt of England conſtruction.

Inſtance of mowing dwarf furze: a ſecond workman following, with a rake, to form the ſwaths into faggots.

Paſs a young plantation of foreſt trees, of different ſpecies; put in among dwarf furze: the firſt inſtance of planting (excepting

cepting the Scotch firs near Hatherley) obſerved in this journey of near a hundred miles!

Pits of red gravel, by the ſide of a good road.

The ſubſoil—a ſeam of waterworn gravel, and rough pebbles.

Leave the Vale of Exeter.

Join the Exeter road (nine miles), and enter Maiden Down: a wide furzegrown common: the depreſſed ridge which ſeparates the Vales of Exeter and Taunton.

A broad view of Somerſetſhire breaks upon the eye: the Vale of Taunton, backed by the Quantoc hills.

Obſerve ſmall and very neat cattle, on the commons.

A deep white ſandy ſubſtratum, and heavy ſandy roads.

Some good oxen of the *Somerſetſhire* breed. Not ſo *clean* as the beſt of the North Devonſhire.

More beautifully clean turneps.

Sandy road, and hollow way: the ſubſtratum red ſandy rock.

A tall

A tall Engliſh orchard! (near Wellington) the ſtems five or ſix feet high.

Inſtance of burning Beat, in the Devonſhire manner.

Weſtcountry waggons prevail: no infection.

A fallow laid up, in ribs and trenches.

Poor village huts.

Six oxen ſtirring a fallow of ſtrong red land,

Meet a ſtring of culm carts; on their way, from the Taunton Navigation, to the Limeworks.

Some neat clean young cattle.

Dip into a cloſe wood-bound flat: high hedges and hedgerow timber; as in Eaſt Norfolk.

The hedgebanks lower; but ſtill wide, and partake of the Devonſhire coppice hedges.

Devonſhire tools in uſe, here. The pointed ſhovel, common.

Paſs ſeveral pieces of good clean turneps.

Hedge trees univerſally lopped.

A few

A few ſingle Hawthorn hedges begin to appear.

Several inſtances of ſtubble turneps.

Some thick polled ſheep.

Lime compoſt, on headlands, as in Devonſhire.

Inſtance of bean ſtubble, or the "arriſh" of ſome other pulſe, dunged for wheat.

Some good Somerſetſhire oxen: dark blood red..

Subſoil variegated: ſtreaks of red and white.

Healthy, tallſtemed, Engliſh orchards.

Leave the red land: the ſoil and ſubſoil, now, of a light brown color.

Obſerve ſmall mountain ſheep; partially horned; as thoſe of Okehampton.

Much hedgerow timber; moſtly Elm.

A dairy of good cows.

Charming road; with a high broad ſoot-path. A London-like approach to

TAUNTON;—a large, well built, handſome town: the tower of the Church of St. Mary is ſingularly tall and beautiful.

THE MARKET OF TAUNTON.

THE Market Place of Taunton is one of the firſt in the Kingdom; whether as to ſize, neatneſs, or accommodations: a triangular incloſure, fitted up with ſtreets of covered ſtalls, for butchers meat, and furniſhed with ſpacious colonnades, for corn, poultry, &c. and one for cheeſe, bacon, and other articles,—which are ſold, *retail*, by farmers' wives and daughters: an unuſual, but a very *political* way of bringing theſe articles, at once, to the conſumer; without the intervention of mere dealers.

The Corn Market, here, as in Norfolk, is held in the afternoon; beginning about three o'clock. Much corn in the market, in narrow two buſhel bags; each ſeller having a tray, to ſhoot part of a bag into, that its quality may be the better ſeen. Obſerved no ſamples; but underſtand that much is ſold through their medium *.

TAUNTON

* Theſe Remarks, on the Market of Taunton, were chiefly made in 1791.

TAUNTON

TO

SOMERTON.

(Eighteen Miles.)

SATURDAY, 20 SEPTEMBER, 1794.

THE Country, for the firſt two miles, is nearly flat: then ſomewhat ſwelling: a rich fine country.

Hawthorn hedges common.

Many ſtubble turneps: ſome of them promiſing.

Much arable land: ſoil moſtly a ſtrong red loam.

Many wheat ſtubbles turned under: an evidence of the forward ſtate of huſbandry.

Arriſh mows common, in this part of Somerſetſhire.

Inſtance of an Ox cart, with the yoke hung to the pole, by means of a wooden bow, inſtead of an iron ring. Doubtleſs the

the primitive method. Beautifully ſimple; but liable to accidents.

Miſletoe obſervable in the orchards!

The plow of Somerſetſhire has a long but well turned moldboard; with a wreſt, ſtanding ſomewhat high: and with a ladder-piece behind, which ſteadies a long, ſlender, right handle, ſhooting forward to the beam.

Leave a plot of vale land, to the right.

The under ſtratum appears in ſeams of red earth, and a ſort of white ſtoney ſubſtance.

Wheat ſtubbles in narrow ridges, as throughout Devonſhire.

Many fallows, for wheat, are ſeen.

Act of Parliament hedges, againſt the road. The firſt, probably, of any extent, from the Landsend.

Still many hedgerow Elms.

Inſtance of paring and burning.

A large field orchard going to decay.

Paſs ſome good young cattle.

The pointed ſhovel ſtill in uſe.

Croſs a dip of cold weak land (five miles).

A rainy

A rainy ſtormy morning. How convenient is a carriage, and how productive of information! A tablet full of intereſting facts, in travelling five or ſix miles; notwithſtanding the unfavorableneſs of the morning. A traveller on horſeback could not look up: nor if anything met his eye, could he note it, with conveniency *.

Ox carts (wains or coops) common.

Inſtance of a young field orchard (at North Curry). The plants tall, and ſet out at good diſtances, in the beſt Herefordſhire manner.

A quarry of blue building ſtone.

Many orchard grounds.

A newly planted quickſet hedge.

Many neat young cattle.

The ſoil and ſubſoil ſtill red.

Good limeſtone road †.

 Aſcend

* This remark applies to TRAVELLING. In examining a particular Diſtrict or STATION, RIDING ON HORSEBACK is preferable to a carriage; and WALKING, infinitely preferable to either.

† A ſingular method of breaking road materials, eſpecially the baſe flints, that have been repeatedly mentioned, is

Aſcend the limeſtone heights *.

Carts and waggons, at the lime kilns: no pack horſes.

A good back view of the Vale of Taunton.

A broad view of South Sedgemore,—covered with cattle, ſheep, and geeſe; and, over it, a view of the Poldown and Mendip hills.

Some good horned lambs.

Thin limeſtone land; and more lime kilns.

A rich looking valley of land opens to the right.

Inſtance of a field orchard, in a ſtate of arable culture, as in Herefordſhire.

A Sedgemore, or Marſh, of ſome extent, is ſeen to the right.

Swing plows univerſal.

More field orchards.

The hedges of the road cropped.

A herd

is obſervable in this Country: a one-handed hammer being uſed, by a workman ſitting: a method which, it is aſſerted, is more expeditious, than the ordinary one of uſing the ſledge hammer.

* See Page 176.

A herd of tall thin white pigs.

Continue upon cold limeſtone heights.

Paſs Burton Pynſent.

A neat farmery, and large farm.

Clean fallows, and good clover.

Farm hedges kept down to fence height.

Four heavy horſes plowing broken ground.

Six oxen employed in the ſame operation; with heavy long ſwing plows.

A full hedgerow of apple trees; as about Bromyard in Herefordſhire.

Paſs through Curry Rival.

Strong cold land: wheat, beans, and clover.

See large flocks of horned ſheep; of a breed ſimilar to that of Dorſetſhire and Eaſt Devonſhire.

Leave the limeſtone heights, and deſcend towards Langport.

A wide Vale Diſtrict opens to the right.

A naked Chiltern Country, in front, and to the left.

Six oxen at plow, and four at harrow: all in yoke: alſo two at plow, with two horſes before them; as in the South Hams

 of

of Devonſhire; and as formerly in Yorkſhire.

See Ham Hill, or Hamdown Hill; a broken prominent, ſtriking object.

Flat-roofed hayricks, as in Cleveland.

Croſs the Parret, at LANGPORT,—a mean market town. A Navigation and Coal Yard.

Pantiles in uſe, as a covering.

Enter a common field: the firſt from the Landsend.

Foul bad huſbandry: couch and thiſtles.

The ſubſoil limeſtone gravel; yet the land appears to be cold and weak.

Flocks of ſheep now in theſe open fields.

Another flat of marſhes appear to the right.

In front, a wide range of limeſtone *Downs*. Large depreſſed ſwells of arable lands, with ſhallow graſſy dips between them: part in open common fields,—part incloſed.

A windmill appears: the firſt in this journey.

Large flocks of ſheep, in the open fields.

A ſheep fold: the firſt.

An

An open naked Cambridgeſhire-like Country.

Catch a diſtant view of the Dorſetſhire hills.

Many good cart horſes, on the road.

Large limeſtone flags—or coarſe marble ſlabs—raiſed near the road.

The plow team—four horſes, at length.

The tops of the ſwells are dry—ſtone to the ſurface: but the ſides appear cold and weak.

Foul thiſtly common fields.

A roughly broken paſſage, to the left.

A large ſheep fold.

Somerton appears in a broad flat; or ſhallow baſon; with riſing grounds on every ſide.

A large field of rough old graſsland: *appropriated waſte.*

An ox waggon, partially loaded with ſtraw, and thatched: doubtleſs, a harveſt waggon, thus ſet by for the next ſeaſon.

Enter SOMERTON,—another mean market town: the ſuburbs in ruins.

SOMERTON AND ITS ENVIRONS.

A DECAYING Place: the remains, probably, of a good Town: now, evidently, in neglect.

The building materials limestone and thatch. The stones neatly formed, as in the Vale of Pickering.

Below the Town, towards the East, the environs are beautifully broken. A valley of rich marsh land, overlooked by bold wooded knolls.

Large good oxen, and good, horned wedders, now grazing in the marshes.

SOMERTON TO SHIPTON MALLET.

(Fifteen Miles.)

SATURDAY, 20 SEPTEMBER, 1794.

CROSS the meadowy valley, and wind among the rugged hillocks, which form its Northern bank.

A flock

A flock of very neat, horned ewes:—in the beſt *Dorſetſhire* form.

Aſcend a thin ſoiled limeſtone ſwell.

The Valley re-opens, to the right.

Paſs a dairy of indifferent cows.

The ſoil encreaſes in ſtrength.

Small fields and hedgerow elms: evidences of deep well ſoiled land; but unuſual in elevated ſituations.

The Country now more open; and a fine Valley is diſcloſed to the left.

A remarkable line of road; on a well ſoiled ridge, with a rich Vale Diſtrict, on either hand: the Vallies of Somerton and Glaſtonbury.

The conical hillock, near Glaſtonbury, ſurmounted by a tower, is a ſtriking object, in this point of view.

Strong wheat ſtubbles, on theſe uplands.

A fallow for wheat, now folding.

Marble quarries on either ſide of the road. Many men at work; and teams waiting. Moſtly raiſed in large ſlabs, ſix or eight inches thick, and ſeveral feet in dimenſions. Lie horizontally, and near the ſurface of level ground. Men employed in poliſhing them. The color a blue grey.

Village buildings of ſtone and pantile.

Some orchards, on this cool ſoil. But the ſubſtratum is calcareous.

The Valley or Vale of Glaſtonbury, backed by the Mendip Hills, ſpreads wide beneath the eye.

Enter cold-ſoiled common fields (five miles).

Beans a prevailing crop.

The ſoil a cold crumbling clay; like that over the clayſtone of the Vale of Glouceſter.

Reach the point of the cold-ſoiled ridge; and deſcend into the VALE OF GLASTONBURY *.

Croſs the river Brent, at Lydford.

A parcel of ill formed cows, moſtly black.

Cold Vale land—at preſent bare of herbage.

The

* This is a difficult paſſage of country to claſs. It is more than a *Valley*; yet wants ſomething of the *Vale* character. However, below the part, here croſſed, it ſeems to ſpread wider, and to acquire a variety of outline and diverſity of ſurface. I denominate it of Glaſtonbury, as it contains that antient place.

The mile ſtones ſhamefully defaced; but how eaſy to remedy the defect, with paint.

Marble ſtiles and fences common.

Elm trees and pollards, ſcattered over graſs incloſures.

Still a cold flat Vale Diſtrict. The fields blue, with Devilsbit (*Scabioſa ſucciſa*).

The graſs incloſures interſected with ſurface drains. A very cold plot of country: weak and languid, even at this ſeaſon of the year. Adapted to the cheeſe dairy, and the rearing of cattle.

Some lean cows: but of a better breed than the laſt.

Many pollards in the hedges.

A plot of woodland, well timbered: much of the land of this Vale is well adapted to oak timber. The hedgerows, at leaſt, ought to be filled with it.

The whole in a ſtate of graſs: no arable land ſeen from the road.

Another dairy of ſmall ill-formed cows.

Hayſtacks in the field; as in the dairy Diſtricts of Yorkſhire.

The land improves: ſtill wholly in graſs.

A well-

A well ſoiled riſing ground, in front; wholly covered with graſs.

A large dairy of cows, of the middle-horned breed; but not of the *Devonſhire* variety.

Hayſtacks capped, only, with thatch; as in the Yorkſhire practice.

Some roomy good cows: variouſly colored?

Arrive at the foot of the hill: the Vale is ſome three or four miles wide.

The road acroſs it is a ſtraight line. Q. Roman?

Another dairy of many colored cows.

Reach the upper ſtages of the ſteep;—and enjoy the views:—extenſive, rich, and picturable.

Good graſsland upon theſe hills; and ſtocked with good cows.

From the ſummit of the hill, an entire circle of views are commanded: a wide ſea of graſslands: the hills and the Vale equally green.

The ſubſoil, of this fertile upland, is limeſtone gravel, in thin layers, between loam.

Some

Some very good cows, on these hills.

Another Vale opens to the left: a fine, strongly featured country.

A large Marsh or Sedgemore appears to the left.

Observe several *sheet cows:* are they natives of Somersetshire * ?

Many good sheep,—of the Dorsetshire, or West of England breed. They appear to be common to Dorsetshire, East Devonshire, and this part of Somersetshire.

A rick-frame loaded with straw, and thatched as a roof.

Meet a load of *Somersetshire* "reed:" differing from that of *Devonshire*; as having the ears cut off: consisting of clean straight unbruised stems only.

Descend into another Valley of grassland; narrower, but better soiled, than the last.

Limestone still raised by the side of the road:

* This singular variety, which is observable in Gentlemen's grounds, in different parts of the Island, is given by color, chiefly or wholly. A SHEET COW resembles a red cow of North Devonshire, or West Somersetshire, with a white sheet thrown over her barrel; her head, neck, shoulders, and hind parts, being uncovered.

road: thick ſtrata of brown earth between the ſeams of ſtone; differing from the blue marble.

Inſtance of underdraining, with flat ſtones ſet up, in the form of the letter V, inverted.

Aſcend another range of graſsland ſwells.

Stone fence walls, on theſe uplands: the firſt, from the weſtward, in this line of road. Some, in courſes of dry ſtones, alternately with other courſes, laid in earth mortar.

Inſtance of unbitten aftergraſs; the firſt obſerved, in this ſtage:—a dairy country.

Good horned wedders, in theſe graſs grounds.

Leave a rich graſſy hillock, to the right.

The valley of Shipton opens prettily:---rich graſsland, beautifully ſurfaced; but disfigured with ſtone fences.

SHIPTON
AND ITS
ENVIRONS.

A SMALL Market Town; ſituated near the head of a fine valley.

The church ſtately, and in a good ſtyle of architecture. Several neat houſes: a ſeat of the woollen manufacture.

On the North ſide of the valley, are ſome bold hillocks, compoſed wholly of maſſes of limeſtone, covered with a rich deep ſoil. The rock remarkably ſtrong: very different from the blue marble, before noticed. This, in general appearance, reſembles more the ſtone of St. Vincent's rock, near Briſtol.

A limekiln and large quarries;—ſeemingly of long ſtanding.

Aſhen pollards ſcattered over theſe graſslands; chiefly by the ſides of ſtone walls: a practice I have elſewhere obſerved, on well ſoiled limeſtone lands.

Some conſiderable dairies of good cows, in theſe environs.

SHIPTON

SHIPTON MALLET
TO
FROME.

(Twelve Miles)

SUNDAY, 21 SEPTEMBER, 1794.

CROSS the valley above the town: the water a mere rivulet. No appearance of mills of manufacture.

A shameful road toll: and this where materials are so abundant.

Pass a dairy of twenty or thirty good cows.

A large flock of sheep, on a thinsoiled hillock to the right.

Rise another grassy height: the soil redish; the subsoil limestone gravel.

A foul wheat stubble; and an attempt at turneps. Dairy men are bad arable farmers.

More

More large light-colored cows; alſo a few calves: the firſt obſerved in this cow Diſtrict!

More finch-backed, Glocеſterſhire-like cows: with ſome mixed-breed heifers: how little young ſtock appears.

A wide view, to the right, backed by the broken heights of Stourton.

Still graſsland and aſhen pollards: with ſome ſtone fences; but more thorn hedges.

Paſs ſome large dairy farm.

A herd of good Weſt of England cows: a ſingle inſtance.

A limeſtone quarry: a ſtrong rediſh rock: the ſoil over it red, and of good depth.

Leave the limeſtone graſsland Country.

Enter a weakſoiled arable Diſtrict: the *ſoil* ſtill red: in appearance, the ſame as that which covers the limeſtone rock.

The ſoil ſtill weaker: ſandy and wet.

A ſtrongly featured country to the right; about Stourton.

A wide Vale Diſtrict opens, in front. The fertile Vale of Trowbridge: ſkreened, on the right, by the Wiltſhire Downs; and,

Round rodden cow cribs, as in Glocestershire.

A ſmall orchard or two.

Large dairy grounds, intermixed with arable incloſures.

A flock of good Wiltſhire ewes.

Croſs a ſweetly wooded dell.

The ſubſtratum, on the weſt ſide, red ſhattered rock; on the eaſt ſide, pale ſoft rubble: diſtinct maſſes of materials.

Village Buildings — ſtone pantiles and thatch; with ſome heavy ſtone-ſlates.

Paſs a large farmery, on the right.

A paſſage of fine graſsland.

Good ſtone road, between cropped hedges.

Enter FROME: a large well built place; in a fine ſituation. Several neat boxes, in its environs: the town likewiſe neat; though a manufacturing place: — Leeds, without its coals and dirt. The Warminſter and Longleat Hills, are good objects from theſe environs.

FROME
TO
DEVIZES.

(Twenty Miles)

SUNDAY, 21 SEPTEMBER, 1794.

MORE deep loam on limeſtone: with mixed cultivation: graſs and arable.

Stone walls, in the environs of Frome, as of Shipton: ugly, it is true; but effectual againſt hedgebreakers. Both of them are manufacturing towns; and, of courſe, inhabited, by the diſſolute and daring.

A large dairy of longiſh-horned cows: apparently of a mixed breed.

A rich, clean country (two miles).

The name of the village, on a board, at the entrance of "Beckington:" a liberal act, in thoſe who placed it there.

A large

A large dairy of mixed cows.

The road hedges legally kept.

Field hay ricks ſtill common.

Three full-bred longhorned cows: the firſt.

Deep clayey ſubſoil (four miles).

Single-wheeled plows, with winding wooden moldboards.

A recent incloſure, from a ſtate of common.

The land a deep loam. The quickſets guarded with two lines of dead hedgework.

A flat, yet apparently, dry country.

Enter WILTSHIRE.

A cold flat vale paſſage.

Farm houſes—of timber and brick pannels; with weatherboarded barns; as in the Southern Counties.

Riſe a dryer, betterſoiled ſwell of land: Stocked with large herds of cows.

Fat cart horſes, at graſs (Sunday).

A view of North Wiltſhire opens, in front.

Longhorned Cows, and Weſt of England Oxen.

Paſs through TROWBRIDGE; a fair town, finely ſituated. Many good houſes. The principal ſtreet is remarkably neat. Seated on a clean ſwell of rich land; over-looking a ſweetly wooded baſon, backed by the Wiltſhire Hills.

Catch a broad and extenſive view of the Vale of North Wiltſhire.

The road hedges univerſally ſhorn.

Inſtance of high graſsland ridges, as in Glocesterſhire and North Wiltſhire: the firſt obſerved in this journey.

Some large orchard grounds.

Bad roads: ſoft limeſtone is among the worſt of road materials.

Many hedgerow Elms.

Singlewheel plows, in common uſe.

Some very foul bad farming:

And a large incloſure of rough anthilly land: left, in this waſteful ſtate,—as if to keep the arable lands in countenance.

Gates, with four bars, and ſhouldered hartrees, univerſal, acroſs this Vale.

Twenty full-bred longhorned cows.

A fine Vale Diſtrict: rich *waves* of graſs-land (3 miles from Trowbridge).

More

More rich grasslands; stocked with longhorned cows: now apparently in full possession.

Many hedgerow Elms: some of them large.

A compleat dairy country (three to four miles). A small goose and pig common: how much like many passages of the Vales of Glocestershire.

A good longhorned bull; and some heifers.

See, in a quarry, fine loam, three feet deep, on limestone!

Some patches of field potatoes.

A wide extent of Elm-wooded Vale, to the right.

Many good Wiltshire sheep.

The base, or unbroken area, of the Vale terminates. Ascend the fair hillock of Seend:---charming situation! rich and beautiful views, from every point: three or four habitable houses scattered on the hill: elegant village!

Cross a dip of rich arable land: strong dark brown soil. Wheat and beans; but no clover!

Aſcend the firſt ſtage of the Wiltſhire Hills, to DEVIZES; a large and reſpectable market town; finely ſituated.

From its environs, catch a broad view of the rich and extenſive Vale of Trowbridge; backed by the riſing grounds of Somerſetſhire, and diſtanced by the Mendip Hills;—tracing back, with the eye, a principal part of this day's journey.

A GENERAL

A

GENERAL VIEW

OF THE

MORE SOUTHERN PARTS

OF

SOMERSETSHIRE.

THE Line of Country, which passed more immediately under the eye, in this journey, varies much, in Natural Characters, and Rural Management; separating, analytically, into

The Vale of Taunton;

The inclosed Limestone Heights, between the Tone and the Parret;

The open-Field District, or Limestone Downs, between Langport and Somerton:

The strong arable Lands, on Limestone, between the Brook of Somerton and the Brent;

The Vale of Glastonbury;

P 4 The

The rich Grafsland Limeftone Heights, on either fide of Shipton Mallet; terminating in

The Vale of Trowbridge.

The ELEVATION of this Line of Country is inconfiderable; unlefs towards its Eaftern extremity. The tide flows, or has heretofore flowed, within much of thefe Southern parts of Somerfetfhire; extenfive flats of marfhes being feen on either hand. About Shipton, and thence towards Frome, the ground rifes, but not confiderably, and the waters which fall on it divide; part of them paffing weftward to the Bay of Bridgewater; the reft falling into the branches of the Avon.

The SURFACE is fingularly diverfified; the hills frequently rife abruptly, from wide flat vallies; or extenfive tracts of marfhes, which fpread their broad level furfaces between them; giving them, in fome points of view, and through a humid atmofphere, the appearance of Iflands.

The CLIMATURE is probably forward. Every appearance of harveft had paffed away.

The

The WATERS,---SOILS,---SUBSOILS,---and FOSSILS, are detailed in the Journal; and it may be needleſs to remark, here, that, between the Vales of Taunton and Trowbridge (both of which have evidently been formed, with heterogeneous materials), the Country is a continued chain of LIMESTONE hills; or that the nature of the ſtone is ſtrikingly different; conſiſting of two diſtinct ſpecies of Limeſtone; which doubtleſs have had ſeparate origins; the wide Valley of Glaſtonbury appearing to divide them.

The INLAND NAVIGATIONS, obſerved, are thoſe of Taunton and Langport. Few parts of this Iſland are better adapted to navigable Canals, than this part of Somerſetſhire: and ſurely, the Brent and the Avon, ſeeing the Coals, the Limeſtone, and the Manufacture, which lie between them, might be joined with advantage.

The STATE OF INCLOSURE appears in the detail: the entire Country is incloſed; except the moors or common marſhes, and the paſſage of open common fields, between Langport and Somerton.

The

The PRODUCTIONS may likewiſe be gathered from the detail. To the Weſt of the Valley of Glaſtonbury, *arable crops* are prevalent: in that Vale, and to the Eaſt of it, *graſsland* is the almoſt only produce, even to the confines of the County, and through the whole of the Vale of Trowbridge: an extent of graſsland Country, which is rarely met with; eſpecially where the ſurface is greatly diverſified. Of *woodland*, this Line of Country, the Vales which terminate it excepted, may be ſaid to be deſtitute: and the *hedgerow wood* is inconſiderable; the fuel being chiefly, perhaps, *peats* of the fens and marſhes.

VILLAGE and FARM BUILDINGS are wholly of ſtone, covered with thatch, tiles, or a heavy kind of ſlate. Left the mud wall, in the Vale of Taunton; and met the half-timber building, and weather-boarding, in the Vale of Trowbridge.

A BROAD CLOTH MANUFACTURE, of conſiderable extent, I believe, is carried on, in the Eaſtern parts of this Line of Country. But, in travelling it, few traces of ſuch a manufacture appear. The manufacturing Diſtricts

Diſtricts of Yorkſhire, and Lancaſhire,—more eſpecially thoſe of the woolen manufactures, are marked by their dirt and miſery: companions, however, which, it would appear, in travelling through Somerſetſhire and Wiltſhire, are not eſſentially neceſſary to the WOOLEN MANUFACTURE: the moſt NATURAL, as well as the moſt POLITICAL, branch of Manufacture, this Iſland can encourage.

The FARMS, or parcels of land in the occupation of individuals, appear to be ſmall; eſpecially the arable farms, on the Weſt ſide of the County, where the life-leaſe tenure is prevalent, and extends, I believe, more or leſs throughout the county of Somerſet, and within that of Wilts. On the Eaſt ſide of the County, there appears to be ſome dairy farms of a greater magnitude.

BEASTS of LABOR. On the arable ſide of the County, Oxen are prevalent, and freely uſed, in all the ordinary works of huſbandry; but, in the dairy country, and on the borders of Wiltſhire, a leſs *profitable*

race

race of animals (for the Public at least) is, I fear, in common use *.

The CATTLE of Somersetshire are various. The West of England breed are confined to the Western and Southern parts of the County; the Vale of Glastonbury appearing;

* TAX ON HORSES. In these days of famine and taxation,—what political blindness must that be, which suffers the produce of the Country to be consumed, by animals that make no return to the magazine of human food; nor make any adequate recompense to the Community, for the expence they are hourly creating. Animals that are preying on the sustinence which is wanted to suppress the cravings of the species. Animals for whose support the Country may be said to be now paying sums incalculable. And, surely, they ought to be made accountable for an adequate part of the debt they are lavishly incurring.

A tax of one Guinea, a year (on every horse, whether used in husbandry or otherwise), for the first three years, with an additional tax of one Guinea, a year, every third year, so long as sound policy shall see right (thus allowing time for the rearing of cattle), will raise an immense revenue; will lessen, essentially, the consumption of grain; and throw into the markets an abundant increase of animal food.

For Remarks, and Calculations, on the comparative Effect of Horses and Cattle, as Beasts of Draft in Husbandry, see the RURAL ECONOMY of the MIDLAND COUNTIES, Vol. I. Page 470.

appearing, in the Line of Country travelled through in this journey, to be the Northern boundary of this breed. The cows of the dairy Diſtrict are probably bought in; many of them have the marks of the Gloceſterſhire breed; while others wear appearances of the middle-horned breed of the North of Yorkſhire:---light colored, and irregularly pied: a variety of color in the middle-horned breed, which I did not expect to have met with, in Somerſetſhire. Knowing that the long-horned breed have been for a length of time eſtabliſhed in North Wiltſhire, and the red breed in the Vale of Taunton, I expected to have found a mixture of theſe two breeds, rather than a diſtinct variety.

The SHEEP of Somerſetſhire have not been leſs the ſubject of ſurprize, than its cattle. I did not expect to find what in Smithfield is emphatically called "horned ſheep,"---and much leſs the *Dorſetſhire* variety of that ſort,---inhabiting, as a native breed, any part of Somerſetſhire. But perhaps they are moſt prevalent, in Somerſetſhire,

ſetſhire, as in Devonſhire, on the Dorſetſhire ſide of the County.

Of SWINE, Somerſetſhire appears ſtill to perſevere in the old white breed; which may be ſaid to be in full poſſeſſion of the more Weſtern Counties.

Of BEES I *obſerved* but one ſolitary hive! In the long Line of Country, between Cornwall and Wiltſhire, I do not recollect to have *ſeen* more than half a dozen of thoſe induſtrious families! --- whoſe labors are clear gain to a Country,---who contribute to the National ſtock without diminiſhing any other article of its produce.

A RETROSPECTIVE

A

RETROSPECTIVE VIEW

OF THE

WEST OF ENGLAND.

FROM the foregoing Examinations, it is evident, that the Point of Land, which is the more immediate ſubject of theſe Volumes, forms a NATURAL DEPARTMENT of this Kingdom; and that it was, heretofore (and ſtill indeed may be ſaid to remain), a PENINSULA,---partially cut off, by inlets of the Bays of Bridgewater and Bridport, from the main body of the Iſland.

It is equally evident, from theſe ſurveys, that the Department now in view is, at preſent, under a courſe of RURAL MANAGEMENT which differs, in many reſpects, from

from that of the Iſland at large; and whoſe baſis, it is highly probable, has had a ſeparate origin.

Judging from the modern practice of colonization, it is reaſonable to ſuppoſe, that the Bays, Inlets, and Eſtuaries of Rivers, in this Iſland, were the firſt ſettled; and that, as inhabitants encreaſed, cultivation, by progreſſive ſteps, approached the higher lands; climbing, in the courſe of time, to the interior heights.

Admitting that Cornwall and Devonſhire were early colonized, and the whole of them by the ſame people; and that, afterward, a colony of a different race, took poſſeſſion of the inlets of the Bay of Bridgewater, and the rich and ample ſhores, which, at that time, they doubtleſs afforded, the differences that are now obſervable, in the Rural Practices of their deſcendants, may be, with leſs difficulty, reconciled.

On this principle of colonization, the Vale of Taunton,—had the time of ſettlement (or invaſion) been the ſame,—would naturally

naturally have belonged to the ſettlers (or invaders) of the Bay of Bridgewater; but admitting, what will not I believe be doubted, that the Vale of Exeter was priorly poſſeſſed, and that its inhabitants had overtopped the depreſſed ridge which divides theſe Vales, before their Northern neighbours had approached it, the VALE OF TAUNTON would, in courſe, fall into the hands of the firſt ſettlers; and the ſame circumſtances would naturally attend the range of heights, and their Northeaſtern ſkirts, which form what I have here named the DAIRY DISTRICT.

In proceſs of time, and when the entire Country became ſubject to the ſame Government, a mixture of practices would take place, and the two eſtabliſhed ſyſtems of Management would mix, and blend with each other, in the manner in which we find them, at the preſent day.

The Practices which, now, more particularly diſtinguiſh what, for the ſake of perſpicuity, I have denominated the DANMONIAN HUSBANDRY,---will appear in

 the

the following detail: some particulars of which, however, are common to the four most Western Counties; as if they had once been politically united; with customs distinct from those of the rest of the Island: the particulars, here alluded to, relating to matters of *Policy*, rather than to *Agriculture*.

The CULTIVATION OF COMMONABLE LANDS is, I believe, peculiar to this extremity of the Island.

The LIFE-LEASEHOLD TENURE, though not peculiar to the West of England, is the most prevalent within it.

The uniform prevalency of SMALL FARMS mark it, in a similar manner.

The singular MANAGEMENT OF COPPICE WOOD, which has been described, is common, and perhaps peculiar, to the Department in view.

The extraordinary FENCES of this part of the Island mark it most discriminately— common and peculiar to the Peninsula! even to this day!!

EARTHEN WALLS, though not peculiar to the West of England, is in no other quarter

quarter of the Iſland, carried up ſo high, and ſo ſubſtantially, as in this.

The circumſtance of having no fixed places of hiring, or ſtated times of changing, FARM SERVANTS, is, I believe, peculiar to the more Weſtern Counties.

The practice of putting out the children of paupers to farmers, as APPRENTICES IN HUSBANDRY, is, as an eſtabliſhed cuſtom likewiſe, peculiar to this part of the Iſland.

That of performing CARRIAGE ON HORSEBACK, may now be ſaid to belong to this extreme part of the Iſland, only. Even in the Highlands of Scotland, it is in a manner laid aſide.

Many or moſt of the IMPLEMENTS and TOOLS of this Peninſula are peculiar to it.

The practice of BURNING BEAT (by velling, harrowing, &c.), for wheat and turneps, is likewiſe peculiar to this Peninſula.

In the MANAGEMENT OF LIME—as in ſeparating the ſtones and aſhes; mixing it with earth; as well as the manner of ſpreading it on the land,---this part of the Iſland differs widely from the reſt.

In the HARVEST MANAGEMENT, we meet with many ſingular traits of practice. The Arriſh Mow appears to be common to the Peninſula,---even to its outſkirts.

HOUSING STACKS, by hand, though petty, is peculiar. And WINNOWING, in the open air, though once, doubtleſs, the univerſal practice, is now peculiar to Devonſhire and Cornwall; I mean, as the prevailing practice of an extenſive, well ſoiled, cultivated Country.

The method of THRASHING WHEAT, without bruiſing the ſtraw, is peculiar to the more Weſtern Counties: with, however, a notable difference that has been mentioned *.

In the Management of particular Crops, the SOWING OF WHEAT is the moſt remarkable. But the CULTURE OF TURNEPS may, at this day, be conſidered as almoſt equally extraordinary.

The TEMPORARY LEY, of five or ſix years, though not peculiar to this Peninſula;

* See Page 203.

ſula; yet marks it, very diſcriminately, from the other Weſtern and Southern Counties.

WATERING THE SLOPES OF HILLS, though not uncommon, at preſent; yet, a century ago, it was probably confined to this point of the Iſland; and is, at this time, nowhere elſe ſo prevalent.

By its ORCHARD GROUNDS, this Department of the Iſland is moſt diſcriminately marked.

By the purity of its Breed of CATTLE, which though not *ſpecifically* peculiar to this Department, are evidently a diſtinct *Variety*; which, in all human probability, have deſcended, lineally, and without admixture, from the native breed.

The fatting of GRASS CALVES, though not peculiar to this part of the Iſland, being likewiſe common in Norfolk, may nevertheleſs be conſidered as a diſtinct practice; as, in the interſpace of two hundred miles, which ſeparates them, I have not obſerved it, in the ordinary practice of Farmers.

 The

The ſingular method of RAISING CREAM, which is practiſed in this Country, may be called its own.

The BLEEDING of grown CATTLE, for the SLAUGHTER, I have not met with, out of this Department.

The practice of keeping SWINE to two or three years old, and the method of fatting them, are peculiar to this Country. That of boiling their food, and of letting all the females remain in a ſtate of fecundity, may likewiſe be mentioned as peculiarities.

The Mountain SHEEP of this part of the Iſland, appear to be peculiar to it. Thoſe of the Mendip Hills I have not had an opportunity of examining.

In the SHEPHERDING of ſheep, we have ſeen ſome ſtriking traits of practice.

And the practice of SHEARING ſheep, without previouſly WASHING their wool, is at preſent peculiar to a part of this Peninſula.

In this detail of peculiarities, we find many which cannot owe their origin to the

firſt

first civilized possessors. But what strikes us most forcibly, in examining it, is, that in the lapse of centuries, its Rural Practices should not have assimilated, more freely, with those of the Island at large.

MINUTES

IN

WEST DEVONSHIRE.

INTRODUCTORY REMARKS.

THE EXTEMPORARY OBSERVATIONS, that are here offered, may be conſidered as a continuation of thoſe, which occurred in my PRACTICE, in SURREY, in NORFOLK, and in the MIDLAND DISTRICT.

If theſe which I am now offering, and with the ſame ſacrifice of feelings that has ever attended my publication of extemporary Memoranda, have any claim to peculiarity of character, it conſiſts in their pointing

pointing out the regular approach to the Field of Improvement, and the requisite cautions observable, in entering it; so as to be able to pass through it, with safety and advantage.

In this aggregate capacity, it is presumed, they may be found useful to those who are desirous to enter a field, in which foresight and circumspection are, in a superior degree, requisite. Their Individual claims I presume not to adjust.

MINUTES.

I.

1791. JULY 14th. FROM PLYMOUTH to BUCKLAND PLACE. Three or four miles from the Town of Plymouth, the fertile inclosed lands of its environs terminate; the traveller entering, apparently, the outskirts of Dartmore. To the right, wild furze-grown Commons and wooded Vallies are seen; to the left, upland Inclosures. In distance,—the ragged Tors of Dartmore on the one hand, the Cornish Mountains on the other: the scenery truly mountainous; the Valley of the Tamer, and a cultivated dip to the right, being overlooked, and in a great measure hid from the view. DISTRICT.

About seven miles from Plymouth, the Valley of the Tavey opens; and the road, extremely unlevel, dips down to BUCKLAND BUCKLAND PLACE.

1. LAND PLACE; ſituated ſomewhat below the midway of the ſlope; at the head of a "Coomb," or inferior Valley; in this caſe ſhallow, and ſpreading wide as it deſcends.

BUCKLAND PLACE.

The ſituation is naturally recluſe, and is now rendered truly ſo, by long neglect. The remains of the Priory is the preſent habitation; and has been a reſidence of the FAMILY OF DRAKE, from the time of the CIRCUMNAVIGATOR, who purchaſed it.

Some half century ago, much planting has been done, round the ſite of the Monaſtery; and, during the laſt twenty or thirty years, ſcarcely a bough has been touched. The tower of the Priory, with a monaſtic barn of extraordinary ſize, and with various Gothic buildings, the remaining Offices of the Monaſtery, are ſeen (in the immediate approach through a grove of trees which fill the head of the Valley with a ſullen gloom), as in a foreſt, far diſtant from the haunts of men.

2. JULY

2.

2.

JULY 14. Rode over the DEMESNE LANDS of BUCKLAND PLACE. The buildings are beſet on every ſide with tall groves (and ſome of them overhung with large-grown trees, which are injurious to their roofs, and liable to cruſh them in their fall), except on the lower ſide, to the Weſt, where the Valley is choaked up with fruit trees, for ſome diſtance below the houſe; which is thus involved continually in a damp and ſtagnant air; unfit for men or animals to breathe. An over ſtocked rookery, which occupies a conſiderable part of theſe groves, is rendered, by this cloſe atmoſphere, offenſive in the extreme.

BUCKLAND FARM.

But, burſting from this gloom, one of the firſt farms in the Iſland is entered. It contains near eight hundred acres of land: lying on every ſide of the houſe; but

chiefly

2. BUCKLAND FARM. chiefly below it. Almoſt five hundred acres (including hedges, &c.) are in cultivation; the reſt in old woodlands, groves, and orchard grounds.

Near thirty acres of the lower grounds of the Valley, over which a principal part of the cultivated lands are ſpread, have long been imperfectly watered, by a rill that riſes in the uppermoſt part of the farm, and falls down the Valley into the Tavey; which forms the Weſtern boundary of the farm, for more than a mile.

The upper part of the Valley of the Tavey is a ſteepſided dell; hung with wood on either ſide; having a narrow meadowy bottom. The very Wye and its banks! winding in the moſt picturable manner; with here and there a rugged rock riſing above the coppice wood; its limits, with reſpect to this farm, cloſing, in a narrow ſecluded part, with a ſalmon weir, thrown acroſs the river; forming a cataract of no mean effect. The lower part of the Valley is more open; the river terminating, within ſight from the lovely ſwelling grounds of this *monaſtic demeſne*, in a winding eſtuary;

ary; which is there margined with ſteep banks,—feathered to the water, with the woods of Mariſtowe.

2. BUCKLAND FARM.

3.

DISTRICT.

JULY 15. Rode into CORNWALL; by Dinham Bridge, Beer-alſton, Calſtock Paſſage (Ferry), Calſtock Church—New Bridge—acroſs the Heath—and back by Dinham Bridge.

A moſt *romantic* ride! How much the ſcenery of this Diſtrict reſembles that of Monmouthſhire, &c.: ſteep wooded banks of rivers; here broken and rugged, there ſhowing a ſteeper face of rock. The heaths, on the Corniſh ſide of the Tamer, ſtrewed with blocks and fragments of granite, add to the ſavageneſs of the ſcenery, whether viewed at hand or in diſtance. And the inhabitants appear as rude and uncultivated as their Country: the Ferryman

at

3. DISTRICT. at Calstock is in the lowest stage of civilization.

The Valley of the Tavey, at the height here crossed, is a mere dingle, wooded down to the river. But that of the Tamer, opposite and below Calstock, is open, well soiled, and set with orchards; the river, here, beginning to expand into an estuary; the tide flowing some mile or two above the Village of Calstock. Nevertheless, its windings are most abrupt and striking; the antient mansion of Curteel marking one of its bends, in the happiest manner.

LIMEKILNS. The upper part of the estuary is set with limekilns on either side; for the use of the Country near and above them; the stones and culm being brought up in small vessels *. The cultivated country is, now, everywhere studded with lime heaps.

SALMON WEIR. Immediately above the tide's way is a Salmon Weir; and, above this, the wild savage scenery just described; in the midst [illegible] of [illegible]

* Observed two dinner kettles boiling on the top of one of these kilns. If the nature of the fuel requires that the fire should burn outwardly, this is a frugal practice. If not, it is an extravagant way of dressing dinners.

of which, near Newbridge, is a copper mine, now working. 3.

HORSES.

In this part of the ride, at the foot of Hingſtone, one of the higheſt of the Weſtern mountains, I obſerved two Corniſh mares and foals, the ſmalleſt I have ſeen; the mares not more, I apprehend, than eleven hands high. Young cattle, and even oxen, are ſeen on theſe heaths. But no ſheep appeared in any part of this morning's ſtroll.

CLIMATE.

The climature, even of the Vallies, is later than that of Eaſt Devonſhire. Wheats are ſtill green. On the Upper lands much graſs is yet unmown! but evidently receiving great injury by ſtanding.

PRODUCE.

The produce is corn, graſs, heath, and wood; the two latter covering, in this rude broken ride, much the largeſt proportion of ſurface.

4.

JULY 16. Rode to the SKIRTS OF THE DARTMORE HILLS; over Roborough Down, to Mavey, Walkhamton, &c. *

Roborough Down, with the chain of rough Commons which reach from hence to near Plymouth, forming an oblong depressed swell, has every appearance of being a fragment of the Dartmore Mountain †; from which it is separated by an irregular Valley, containing three or four townships of cultivated land. Some of this land is of a very

* In company with Mr. STAPLETON of BUCKLAND: a man to whose superior intelligence I owe much: a man who, with fourscore years of experience, possesses an activity of body and mind, which many men, of half his years, would be happy to enjoy.

† It has been observed, however, that the prevailing stone of these Downs is very different, in composition and texture, from the quartzose granite of Dartmore and the Cornish Mountains; between which this swell is situated: affording an interesting subject to the Geologist.

a very ſuperior quality; one conſiderable plot of it letting at forty or fifty ſhillings an acre, in this bleak and humid climate, and in this remote ſituation. 4. SOIL.

The more central parts of this Valley now contain ſome fine crops of wheat, and much tolerable barley. But the ſoil grows weaker, and leſs productive, as the Hills of Dartmore are approached.

SHEEP. The Sheep on the ſkirts of the hills are moſtly polled; but ſome individuals are horned: they are very uneven as to carcaſe: ſome of them, nevertheleſs, are not in a bad form.

CATTLE. The Cattle, ſeen in this morning's ride, are everywhere clean, and moſtly of good frame. Chiefly of a dark red color; a few of them with white Glouceſterſhire ſpines. The ſize that of Gloceſterſhire, and Weſt Suſſex.

PLOW TEAM. The Plow Team is chiefly Oxen. Saw ſix good ones in a Team, in light work; yet did not perform, even that, with due effect. One of the pairs, with a proper plow, in good hands, would make much better work.

4.
NAMES OF HUNDREDS.

It may be remarked, that the Hundred, or ſubdiviſion of the County, which includes a conſiderable part of the Diſtrict of Weſt Devonſhire, takes its name, or is underſtood to have taken its name, from the Common which I croſſed and repaſſed, this morning; or from ſome Town or Village which gave name to the Common; and of which there are at preſent no traces *.

In this ſtroll, I croſſed repeatedly the ARTIFICIAL BROOK, which waters the Town

* This correſponds with the tradition of Eaſt Devonſhire. (See page 132.) It is probable, however, that the Down, at leaſt, received its name from an extraordinary pile of rock, or large ſtones, the remains of which ſtill form a ſtriking object, on the face of theſe wild lands: bearing ſome reſemblance to the Tors of the Mountains. In the provincial dialect of the Diſtrict, *Roo*, is ſtill commonly uſed for *rough*; and *Burrow* is the ordinary name of a *heap*, whether of earth or ſtones (a combination which is ſtill ſtrictly preſerved in pronunciation). Under this rough pile of rocks, which may, heretofore, have been more conſiderable than it is at preſent, the huts of the firſt ſettlers may have been raiſed; or Druidical Aſſemblies have been held.

The etymons of the names of HUNDREDS, or DIVISIONS OF COUNTIES, are moſt difficult; and the Antiquary, at leaſt, is intereſted in their elucidation.

Town of Plymouth, and which is taken out of a ſmall river, in one of the Vallies of Dartmore. It is a treaſure, not only to Plymouth, but to the long range of dry uplands, through which it paſſes. This public good owes its valuable exiſtence to one of the Drake family: namely, the Grandfather of the preſent Sir Francis Drake. He not only furniſhed the water, from his own manor, but alſo the plan; and, in difficult caſes, directed the execution.

4. PLYMOUTH LEAT.

5.

JULY 27. Yeſterday, rode to TAMERTON, on the Eaſtern banks of the Tamer; diverſifying the road through this extraordinary paſſage of country.

DISTRICT.

The ſurface is broken in a moſt remarkable manner. The Stroudwater hills of Gloceſterſhire are not more diverſified.

5\.
DISTRICT.

But a ſtill more extraordinary feature, of this little Diſtrict is formed, by bays, creeks, and inlets, of the eſtuary of the Tamer, winding in among the wooded hillocks, in a manner which I have nowhere elſe obſerved, in this Iſland; but in perfect reſemblance of the ordinary ſcenery, of the more broken margins, of the Weſt India and Bahama Iſlands.

Nevertheleſs, the ſoil, where the Vallies have any width, is of a good quality; and even the tops of ſome of the ſwells are good arable land: ſo that, notwithſtanding the Country, in ſome points of view, appears to be covered with wood, from the quantity which hangs on its ſteeper acclivities, it contains a conſiderable proportion of cultivated ſurface.

SURVEYING A DISTRICT.

The Crops, and the Syſtem of Management, are the ſame as thoſe which I have obſerved, in my former rides; ſo ſoon is the general outline of Management caught!

TAMERTON FAIR.

A Fair held yeſterday, at the ſweetly ſequeſtered Village of Tamerton Foliot, gave me an opportunity of ſeeing ſomething more of the Liveſtock of the Diſtrict.

The

The Cattle—provincially "Bullocks"—were mostly of the West Devonshire, &c. breed: namely, bred on the East and West banks of the Tamer: they are in general clean, well framed, and not ill fleshed: but there were few in a fit state to be *handled*. 5.

CATTLE.

GRAZING.

Half a score remarkably fine oxen, eight or nine years old, of a size and form for anything which is required of oxen, stood as fat bullocks, for the butcher; but were barely forward enough for oil cakes, or other forcing food. If *fattened*, they would weigh eighty or ninety stones (of 14lb.) a bullock.

CATTLE.

BREEDING.

Also two "Barnstaple heifers"—in a beautiful form, and as soft as moles, at two years old! and for this reason they were brought, here, to be sold to the butcher. What an error in practice! an error, I understand, which is prevalent through the Country: there are two on *this* Barton, I find, in the same predicament. Those which are of a nature to fat at two years old, are *murdered!* those which will not, are kept to breed from!

5. CATTLE. A few ſhorthorned and polled cattle were ſhown: different Gentlemen, it ſeems, having introduced them into this County. But they are fortunately diſliked by the farmers; who prefer their own breed; and, prejudice apart, they have good reaſon for their partiality; their own being a much more eligible breed for a thinſoiled Diſtrict. Their great defect is in milk, and perhaps this defect may have induced the Gentlemen of the County to bring in the Holderneſs breed; and, if they are kept merely for the dairy, no miſchief may enſue.

SHEEP. The Sheep were moſtly mountaineers—provincially "Moor Sheep:" thin, ſcraggy, illformed creatures.

FAIRS. The Fairs of this Country begin about eight o'clock, and laſt till about twelve.

6.

JULY 29. Hitherto, I have been looking round me, and aſcertaining facts. PRELIMINARIES OF IMPROVEMENT.

1. I have traverſed the Country, for a few miles on every ſide, and have gained a general idea of its outline of management.

2. I have ſtudied a map of this noble Farm; traced its outlines; and ſurveyed, repeatedly, every field and parcel of it.

3. I have aſcertained its preſent produce, or ſtate of occupancy, by analyſing, claſſing, and reuniting its various parts: thus bringing into one view the exact quantity of

Culturable lands,
Orchard grounds,
Planted groves,
Natural woodlands,
Hedges, lanes, &c. &c. &c.

4. I have tabled the SUCCESSION, or ſtate of occupancy of each individual field in cultivation,—during the LAST FOUR YEARS.

5. In

6. PRELIMINARIES OF IMPROVEMENT.

5. In the margin of this table, I have noted the ſpecies and quantity of MANURE which each field has received, during that period; the term of the miniſtry of the preſent "Hine."

6. I have regiſtered the ARRANGEMENT, tabled the crops and fallows, of THE PRESENT YEAR; ſo as to ſhow, *firſt*, the number, name, ſize, and crop of each field; arranged according to their reſpective numbers in the map, which correſpond with their natural ſituation in the farm: *ſecondly*, the fields, arranged agreeably to their reſpective crops; thus coming at the aggregate quantity of each; and, *thirdly*, the totals of theſe aggregates, to prove the truth of the analyſis *.

7. A table of the LIVESTOCK, now on the farm.

8. The quantity of MANURE IN STORE.

9. The

* This method I ſtruck out, during my practice in Surrey (ſee MINUTES OF AGRICULTURE IN SURREY), and have invariably followed it, in the different parts of the Iſland, in which I have practiſed.

9. The IMPLEMENTS, &c. at present in use.

6. PRELIMINARIES OF IMPROVEMENT.

10. The WORKPEOPLE now employed.

Until these particulars be ascertained, and spread out before the eye, so as to be referred to, in the most extemporary way, no man should presume to give orders, or suggest improvements, in husbandry. Nor, then, until he has considered well

The genius of the Country; and

The locality of the given farm, as to markets, water carriage, &c. &c.; also

Its natural characteristics, of fitness for corn or grass, dairying or grazing, &c. &c. taken collectively as a farm; as well as

The aspect, soil, subsoil, and state of tillage, of its several parts.

But, having duly informed himself in these requisites; and having assiduously caught, and preserved, the hints for improvement, which first impressions may have furnished him with, any man, having previously an adequate knowledge of the general subject, both in theory and practice, may venture to begin, with cautious step, to enter upon its improvement: being how-

6. PRELIMINARIES OF IMPROVEMENT. however, even then, careful not to derange the eſtabliſhed machine of management; until one, which is preferable, be ready to replace it: beginning with its more glaring improprieties and defects, as they occur fairly in the courſe of management; at once, to ſave unneceſſary expence, and to prevent unneceſſary alarm.

7.

TILLAGE. JULY 29. The lands of this farm are evidently much out of tilth. The young leys are overrun with fern, and thoſe of three or four years old are bare of graſs. But no wonder; they have been moſtly leyed, I find, agreeably to the cuſtom of the Country, after three ſucceſſive crops of grain; for which not more than three or four plowings are uſually given!

PLOW. Indeed, were more to be aſſigned them, the Plow of the Country would be inadequate to the taſk of cleaning them. It is the

the worſt Swing Plow I have ſeen. The beam ſhort and clumſy, and the body long and illformed, without a riſe or wreſt, to force open the furrow; the mold-board being ſet high above the keel or ſoal of the Plow; which operates, in looſe ground, as the Kentiſh Turnwreſt Plow; making a mark only, not opening a furrow *. 7. PLOW.

A foul piece of ground, intended for Wheat, but which I wiſh to cleanſe thoroughly, for Barley the enſuing Spring, by way of making a beginning in the great work of purgation, I ſaw tantalized by this ineffective implement.

IMPROVEMENT OF PLOWS.

However, by fixing a wreſt in the uſual place, below the mold-board (the work of a few minutes), it cleared its way, and effected more in going once over the ground, than the ſame Implement, without this ſimple addition, would have done in going over

* The DEVONSHIRE PLOW reſembles much, in general appearance, the Plow of the Herald and the Sign Painter: a circumſtantial evidence, that it has heretofore been prevalent in the Kingdom; or that the Heraldic Figures of this Country, and the Plow of Devonſhire, are equally of Norman extraction.

7. IMPROVEMENT OF PLOWS.

over it almoſt any number of times; and this without vexing the Plowman, or alarming the Country, with "a new-faſhioned Plow."

Being deſirous, however, to get the Implement into a better form, and to adapt it to two Oxen or two Horſes, I have embraced an incident, to gain a pretence for conſtructing a Plow, ſuitable to that purpoſe. A ſmall plot of ground, which is ſo much encumbered with trees, that a team cannot work in it, and which has in conſequence been "hand beaten" and "hacked over," to free it from the foul ſtate in which it has long lain, was nevertheleſs capable of being plowed, with a ſmall Plow, and a ſingle Horſe.

In conſtructing this little Implement, I ſuffered the Plow-wright to purſue his own beaten track, with reſpect to principal pieces and general conſtruction; deviating chiefly in the proportion of the ſeveral parts; making the beam proportionally longer and the body of the Plow ſhorter, than in the Plow of the Country: adding, however, a wreſt, and endeavouring to give the

mold-

mold-board the proper caſt. It fully anſwers the intended purpoſe; and bids fair to ſuperſede the introduction of the Yorkſhire Plow, for two Oxen or Horſes. It has, indeed, one main advantage over any alien Plow: it is ſet to work and regulated, as the ordinary Plow of the Country; is indeed a Devonſhire Sewl; and as ſuch it is held.

7. IMPROVEMENT OF PLOWS.

A PRINCIPLE OF IMPROVEMENT.

Seeing this, it ſtrikes me, that a ſimilar kind of ſucceſs may be obtained, in any Diſtrict, by adopting the general conſtruction of the faſhionable Plow of the Country, whether it be the Wheel, the Foot, or the Swing Plow; only altering the proportions, and giving the OPERATIVE PARTS the requiſite caſt.

June, 1795. Men, who have never attempted to introduce improvements in Agriculture, may conſider theſe ſacrifices, to the prejudices of eſtabliſhed cuſtoms, unneceſſary and trifling; but thoſe who have had experience, in this nice matter, will ſee their propriety.

JULY

8.

SALMON WEIR.

JULY 31. The SALMON FISHERY of the Tavey is appendant to this eſtate. The WEIR, which has been mentioned, is a work of conſiderable magnitude and expence. It conſiſts of a ſtrong dam or breaſtwork, ten or twelve feet high, thrown acroſs the river, in a part where two projecting rocks ſerve happily as buttreſſes to the maſonry; which is built ſomewhat compaſſing or archwiſe (but not regularly nor ſufficiently), to reſiſt the preſſure and force of the waters, in times of flood; when they are collected, by the ſlopes of the Dartmore Hills, and ſent down with extraordinary impetuoſity. At one end of the dam, is a "weir houſe" or TRAP; on the principle of the Vermin trap, whoſe entrance is outwardly large, but contracted inwardly, ſo as to elude or prevent the eſcape of the animal which has taken it. It is remarkable,

remarkable, however, with reſpect to ſalmon, that although the entrance is by no means ſo narrow as to prevent even the largeſt from returning, it is believed that there is no inſtance of thoſe which have once entered, quitting their confinement, though they may have remained in it ſeveral days. A circumſtance, perhaps, which can only be accounted for, in the natural propenſity, or inſtinct, which directs them againſt the ſtream, and will not ſuffer them to give up any advantage which they may have gained; the aſcent into the trap being an effort of difficulty: in this caſe perhaps too great.

8. SALMON WEIR.

On the higher ſide of the trap (which is ſome twelve or fifteen feet ſquare on the inſide), oppoſite to the entrance, is an opening or ſluice in the ſtone work,—or rather the rock,—as a paſſage for the water. This opening has two lifting floodgates: the one cloſe, to ſhut out, occaſionally, the whole of the water; the other a grate, to ſuffer the water to paſs, and at the ſame time to prevent fiſh of any conſiderable ſize from eſcaping. When the trap is ſet, the

8. SALMON WEIR. close gate is drawn up, with an iron crow: thus suffering the water to pass through the house. On the contrary, to take the fish which have entered, the close gate is let down, and the trap is presently left in a manner dry.

It is observable, that the narrowed entrance of the trap is judiciously placed, somewhat above the floor; so that before the salmon are seriously alarmed by the fall of the water, it has sunk below the mouth of the trap, and their retreat the more effectually cut off; for by following the water, near the floor, they are led away beneath the tunnel: which, like the open floodgate, &c. is made of strong wooden bars, open enough to permit the passage of the water, but not that of the fish.

The top or covering of the trap is a floor of planks, nearly level with the top of the weir; on the lower side of which the trap is, of course, situated.

Some days ago, when the water was unusually low—provincially and not improperly "small"—the whole river passed through the weir house. But the recent rains

8. SALMON WEIR.

rains have ſwoln it to a tenſold ſize. The water now pours over the weir, in a denſe, broad ſheet; ſmooth, and glaſſy above; but furrowing as it deſcends; and producing, in its fall, a white foaming whirlpool; the regularity of the fall being broken, on one ſide, by the torrent, ruſhing down the ſteep deſcent from the ſluice, and, on the other, by the margin of the river burſting its way over the native rock,—a pleaſing object is produced; while the extreme recluſeneſs of the ſituation, — the wild coppice wood on the one hand, and the high grown, impending timber on the other, —add to the picturable effect of the ſcene: which, in a mild evening after rain, is ſtill heightened, and rendered more intereſting, by the animating and beautiful accompaniment of ſalmon, diſplaying ſetes of futile agility;---throwing themſelves far out of the water, in endeavouring to ſurmount the cataract; or ſtruggling, with more fatal zeal, to reach the treacherous hold, from whence there is no return.

RIVER FISH.

The ſpecies of fiſh taken at this weir are ſalmon, ſalmon peel — provincially

8. "pail," and, at some certain seasons, a few trouts.

NET FISHING.

But the principal part of the produce of this fishery is taken by NET FISHING. The river, for near a mile below the weir, is broken into rapids and pools, some of them very deep. Seven or eight of these pools are adapted to the seine or draw net, which is drawn once, or twice a day, by four men: with horses to carry the net, and the fish caught; and with dogs to convey the end of the rope across the water, where it is too deep or inconvenient to be forded.

The fishing season commences, in *this* river (the Tavey), the middle or latter end of February (but on the Tamer not until several weeks afterward!), and closes in October or November; when the weir is thrown open, and the fish, afterward, suffered to go up to spawn.

Presently after a flood, and when salmon are abundant, ten or twelve are frequently taken at a draught; sometimes more; upwards of a hundred, it is said, were once drawn to shore.

No

No wonder that a fishery thus productive, and lying at a distance from any habitation, should be liable to the depredations of POACHERS: especially as the river forms the boundary of a mining parish, notorious for its pilferers. They have been known to come down in bodies, like the game poachers of Norfolk; bidding ten or a dozen men defiance. 8. FISH POACHERS.

The net poaching is done, chiefly, in the night; while the river abounds with fresh water. But, in the day time, when the water is dead and clear, the poachers are not inactive; then using the spear, which they throw with dexterity; and, by this practice, are known to carry off numbers.

Nor does daylight deter them, wholly, from net fishing, when the water is favorable and fish in plenty. Yesterday, in passing, with the Hine and his son, through the meadows which margin the river, a party of three or four net poachers were discovered. They fled, on our approach; taking refuge among the underwood of the opposite banks; leaving behind them a net which has doubtless cost them the profits of many a month's illicit practice.

9.

REMARKS ON RAIN.

AUGUST 1. The RAINS of this Country take a ſingular appearance: at leaſt, have done ſo, in the commencement of the heavy ſhowers, which have followed each other with little intermiſſion, during ſeveral days paſt. They come on, in a ſort of miſt, or fine rain: not of uniform denſity; but driving before the wind, in perpendicular laminæ, with void interſpaces; reſembling more, in their proportions and general appearance, combs of honey in the hive, than any other object I can bring to my mind.

Theſe rains are brought by the Southweſt wind; are the produce of clouds arriving from the ſea, and, being laid hold of by the high lands of this Diſtrict, are checked in their courſe, and overtaken by thoſe which follow; thus becoming more and more denſe, until the heavieſt rain is brought on.

On this theory, which is verified by fact, Cornwall and this Weſtern and inter-mountainous

mountainous Diſtrict of Devonſhire, receive more rain than the Vale of Exeter; and this a greater quantity, than the more central Diſtricts of the Iſland. 9. REMARKS ON RAIN.

I have repeatedly obſerved the high lands of Maker and Mountedgecumbe, which riſe full to the view, from the higher grounds of this demeſne, arreſting a cloud on its arrival from the channel; appearing to hold faſt its lower limb, while the upper parts ſeemed eagerly haſtening to the Dartmore Mountains; and while the ſurrounding Country was enjoying the fineſt weather.

The ſingular appearance, remarked above, may perhaps be accounted for, in its being the firſt ſtage of precipitation of the vapors which previouſly formed the unbroken cloud, or uniform miſt. The vertical poſition of the laminæ apart, the appearance very much reſembles that of the firſt breaking of the cloud, produced by ſolutions of calcareous matter and fixed alkali; into the flocks which form, and follow each other to the bottom of the flaſk.

10.

DISTRICT. AUGUST 3. Rode to the VIRTUOUS LADY; a mine, ſituated on the banks of the Tavey, a few miles northward of this place, amidſt the wildeſt ſcenery which ſteep-ſided vallies, rocks, woods, and bleak heaths, can well give.

ORCHARDS. Not one new or intereſting idea, in the Rural Economy of Weſt Devonſhire, ſtruck me, in this ſtroll; except that of paring off and ſubverting, apparently with a Breaſt Plow, the "ſpine" or rough ſod of an orchard: not with a view of burning it; but for the purpoſe of letting it rot, as a "dreſſing" or manure to the roots of the trees! a practice, I underſtand, which is not unuſual. In this caſe, the orchard is rocky; many ſtones, or points of rock, appearing above the ſurface.

Inverting the ſward may not operate more as a manure, than as, by checking the vegetation of the graſs and weeds, it may give

give additional air, moiſture, and freedom to the fibrils of the roots of the fruit trees. 10. ORCHARDS.

Nothing, indeed, could well effect this purpoſe better. For the inverted turf being laid flat, and evenly over the ſurface, the ſhoots from the roots which are not deſtroyed by the cutting, may be ſmothered, or checked, by the covering.

11.

AUGUST 7. I have, at length, got a WHIP-REIN PLOW fully into its work, in the field. See MIN. 7. PLOWING.

The firſt day, the horſes were led. The ſecond driven, with reins; by a youth, walking at the ſide of the plow; as much to make the horſes tractable, and render the new operation leſs irkſome to the plowman, as to teach the young man the uſe of the reins, in harrowing; which is here two perſons work; even though but one horſe were employed.

This,

11. PLOWING. This, the third day, the horſes are become tractable; and the plowman is guiding and driving them himſelf: making, with two ſorry rips, and the light plow above deſcribed, as good work, as ſix oxen are making, in the ſame field, and the ſame work, with the clumſy tool of the Country.

INTRODUCING WHIP REINS. IN FUTURE,—let two plowmen aſſiſt in the introduction of whip reins, holding and driving alternately: thus, while the horſes are rendered manageable, the plowmen will learn the uſe of the reins.

12.

COPPICE HEDGES. AUGUST 8. A great defect and inconveniency of the MOUND COPPICE FENCES of this Diſtrict, I ſee, is their being liable to be torn down by ſtock, whether cattle or ſheep, ſcraping away the baſe of the mound, and letting down the ſides, perhaps in wide ſhoots. The ſoil thus ſhot down is a ſtep to greater miſchief; and, if not ſtopt, a paſſage is made, acroſs the mound.

To

To prevent these mischiefs, many "hedges" of the District, and particularly of this estate, have been faced with stone:—the ordinary slate rock of the country; mostly set on-edge, or rather on-end; which, by the people of the Country, is considered as preferable to laying them horizontally, in the mason's manner. Most of the fences of this farm have been faced with stone, on both sides; at an expence, from first to last, equal perhaps to the fee simple value of the land. For, as the roots in the body of the mound swell, the facing is of course bulged out, and is at length thrown down; thus leaving the fence, if not timely repaired, in a worse state than those which have been left free for blackthorns, and other brushwood, to grow and defend the sides of the banks. 12.

COPPICE HEDGES.

Where this brushwood has got hold, and outlived the overhanging, and drip, of widespreading coppice wood, growing on the top of the mound, the sides are secure; for being cropped and stunted by pasturing stock, they have grown, in many parts, thick and impervious: and it is extraordinary,

12. COPPICE HEDGES. traordinary, that the idea of planting or encouraging ſuch bruſhwood, and ſtriking off the overhanging topwood, to prevent its being checked in its growth, ſhould not have taken place; inſtead of that of facing the ſides with ſtones; fetcht, perhaps, ſome diſtance on horſeback.

GUARDING HEDGE MOUNDS. Seeing the evident propriety of this treatment, I have been applying it to a hedge, of three or four years growth, from the laſt cutting; as a ſpecimen, or pattern, for the remainder of ſuch as will admit of its application.

The blackthorns and other ſhrubs, which grow at the foot of the mound, and on its ſides, I have endeavoured to ſpread, over the face of the mound; faſtening them, there, with hooked pins, as fruit trees to a wall: firſt clearing the brambles and weeds which grew before and behind them; and, afterward, trimming off the looſe ſpray on the face of the whole: whether thorn, furze, bramble, or briar. Finally, with a long handled hook, ſtriking off the over-hanging boughs of the coppice wood; leaving a regular face, as even as the live ſtuff,

ſtuff, at preſent, will admit of: not perpendicular; but leaning ſomewhat inward, towards the middle of the fence; ſo as to give every twig, from the bottom to the top, light, air, and headroom. 12. GUARDING HEDGE MOUNDS.

An advantage of this operation, beſide that of putting the fence in the way of improvement, is that of freeing the borders from weeds and brambles, and from the drip and ſhade of outhanging boughs.

13.

AUGUST 11. Rode to the head of "PLYMOUTH LEAT."* PLYMOUTH BROOK.

This ARTIFICIAL BROOK is taken out of the river MEW, towards its ſource; at the foot of Sheepſtor Tor; in a wild mountain dell.

I expected

* *Leat*, *Latt*, or *Lake*, as it is ſometimes pronounced, is perhaps a corruption of *Lead* or Conductor; being applied, I believe, to any artificial channel for conducting water.

13. PLYMOUTH BROOK. I expected to have found an accurate gauge, to regulate the quantity of water; agreeably to the act of parliament, under which it is taken. But in this I was disappointed. The Mew, itself, is there but a moderately sized brook. Across it a weir or dam is formed, of large rough stones, with which the bed of the brook is thickly strewed. A paltry, ill shapen, wooden frame or floodgate, with a gully underneath it (through which most of the water passes), receives about half the waters of the Mew; now lower than usual, but not at their lowest. In the dam is another floodgate; lying lower than that of the made brook, to draw off the water from this, during repairs.

The channel of the Leat differs, in dimensions, according to the ground it is led over. Across open plain ground, it is ten or twelve feet wide, with flat sloping banks; the water running six or eight inches deep, according to the descent; which is generally sufficient to make it ripple gently over the pebbles, with which its bottom is strewed, forming a living stream, a lovely brook.

The

The chief difficulty, in executing this valuable work, was in carrying it round the point of an almoſt perpendicular rock; where a wooden aqueduct was firſt conſtructed; but where a more ſubſtantial Channel has ſince been formed, with maſonry. 13. PLYMOUTH BROOK.

MILL LEATS. It is obſervable that the mill of Mavey, ſituated beneath this brook, and fed by the ſame ſource, the Mew,—and about whoſe waters, for want of accurate and ſubſtantial regulators, a perpetual contention is kept up,---is fed by an artificial channel, perfectly reſembling the Leat under deſcription. The mill of Milton, near this place, is ſupplied with water, in a ſimilar manner. And, it is highly probable, theſe Mill Leats furniſhed the deſigner with the idea of the Plymouth Brook *.

MADE BROOKS. Whatever fortunate thought gave riſe to it, its utility is great: not only in ſupplying a populous town with water; but in watering

* In ſome part of the Mill Leat of Mavey, a ſtone, I was told, is placed, with the date, 1600, upon it. The artificial Brook, or New River, of London was executed about 1610.

13. MADE BROOKS. watering a chain of uplands, fifteen or twenty miles in extent. The gratification experienced in falling in, abruptly, as frequently happens, with so ample a stream, in places where such an object is the least expected, yet where it is most wanted, is of a singular and superior kind.

How many situations, in this Island, wanting such relief, might have it in a similar way.

Where a sufficient quantity of water can be had at the source, much of the cost might be repaid, by letting off branches, to the adjacent country.

Upon Roborough Down, a rill is taken out of the Plymouth Brook, for the use of a Gentleman, who lives some two miles off, close by the banks of the Tamer! This rill not only supplies his house, but furnishes water to pasturing stock, in its way.

In this case, the quantity of water is accurately regulated, by a perforated stone, set on edge, in a sort of stone trough; the aperture circular, and about three and a half inches diameter: furnishing a sufficient supply,

ſupply, if frugally managed, for a hamlet or village. 13.

MADE BROOKS.

But the ancient rights of WATER MILLS are bars to improvements of this nature, as well as to the watering of lands: rights, however, which might, *now*, be alienated without exceſſive inconvenience to the community; windmills and ſteam engines rendering them no longer *neceſſary*; though, in ſome ſituations, a few might ſtill be uſeful.

14.

AUGUST 12. Rode to PLYMPTON, in the SOUTH HAMS of Devonſhire.

DISTRICT.

The ſcenery about Plymbridge is ſweetly recluſe; forming a happy contraſt to the open view from Lord Boringdon's arches; from whence Plymouth Sound and Harbour, with the intereſting ſcenery which ſurrounds them, are ſeen immediately under the eye.

14. DISTRICT. A broad view of the South Hams is alſo commanded from this proud point.

The Country immediately below it, about Ridgeway and the Plymptons, is ſingularly broken; yet moſt of it well ſoiled.

PLYMPTON FAIR. A Fair, of ſome repute, led me to Plympton, this morning. But it fell ſhort of my expectation. About a hundred and fifty head of cattle, chiefly cows and calves; with a few half-fat oxen, and leſs than half-fat cows. Alſo a few pens of ſheep; moſtly poor thin-carcaſed animals. Altogether a mean collection.

PLYMPTON. The Borough of Plympton is moſt enviably ſituated. The climature mild, almoſt, as that of the South of Europe. The ſcenery around it delightful; and the ſoil of a ſuperior quality; yet, in its nature, dry and clean. Proviſions of every kind abundant and cheap. The Town, or rather large genteel Village, is itſelf neat; its inhabitants reſpectable; and it is ſituated near a great public road, without being incommoded by it.

AUGUST

15.

TRAINING HEDGES.

AUGUST 12. (See MIN. 12.) Some older hedges, on the ſides of harveſt roads, whoſe boughs were grown too large, and reached too high, to be cut from the ground, I have had "pared" in the following manner.

Put two oxen to a waggon, and two men into it, with hooks of different lengths; placing the waggon cloſe to the hedgebank. In this ſituation, the men were level with their work; cutting out the larger boughs, with common hedge bills, and ſtriking off the ſpray, with lighter tools; the waggon proceeding with the work.

In this way, the two men cleared, in the courſe of yeſterday afternoon, not leſs than a hundred rods, ſufficiently to prevent the corn from being thraſhed out, or torn off the harveſt waggons, by the outhanging

 boughs.

15. TRAINING HEDGES.

boughs. A dispatch which could not have been obtained in any other manner.

Even in the training of younger hedges (of this Country), a waggon might be employed with advantage.

16.

RECLAIMING LAND.

August 15. Clearing arable lands from stones. The soils of this District are much incommoded with stones of different kinds; but chiefly with the slate rock, of which the Country may be said to be formed; and a species of chrystal —provincially "whitaker"—which is frequently met with in large blocks, either entire, or partially incorporated with the slate rock.

A field, now under fallow,—which has long been noted for sewl-breaking, I am clearing in this way. The plowman carries, in the body of his sewl, a parcel of small rods; and, where he finds a stone, sets up one

one of his marking ſticks. Two men follow, with ſhovels, mattocks, and crows, raiſing the *ſtones*, and baring the *rocks*, to be raiſed, at leiſure, by men accuſtomed to quarry work. Thus, at a comparatively trifling expence, the land is freed, plow-furrow deep, for ever, from obſtructions: not only of the plow, but of harrows; which would now be ſeen riding upon flat ſtones, from one end of the field to the other, were not a perſon employed to follow, and releaſe them from ſo aukward and unprofitable a ſituation: leaving, however, the ſtones upon the land; leſt this part of his employment ſhould be wanting, in future. 16. RECLAIMING LAND.

17.

AUGUST 27. CLEARING FOUL LANDS. (See MIN. 7.) This and another piece, ſtill fouler, and in a worſe ſtate of tillage, I have treated, and intend to treat, in the following manner. RECLAIMING LAND.

About a month ago, one of theſe fields, then in a ſtate of looſe broken ground, was laid

17. laid up into narrow ribs (the gardener's
RECLAIMING LAND. trenches) by a half plowing; with a wrested plow, and with the stern set TEN INCHES wide; forcing up the ridgets, as high and sharp as possible; in order to destroy the root weeds, by drought, and by breaking their field of pasturage; and to give the seeds of weeds an addition of air and surface to promote their vegetation.

About a week ago, the first-plowed part was harrowed across the ribs, with long-tined harrows;—levelling the surface completely, and following them with a roller and finer harrows, hung behind it: thus grinding down every clod, and effectually destroying every seedling weed which had vegetated.

TILLAGE. The surface is now thickly set with another crop of seedling weeds,—which I am turning under by ONE DEEP PLOWING, across the former ribs, and in narrow plits, but with a BROAD SHARE, and with a STERN TWELVE INCHES WIDE; thus moving every particle of the soil, about TEN INCHES DEEP (some inches deeper, perhaps, than it has ever been plowed before), beſore), leaving the ſurface rough and cloddy. 17.

MANURING.

Over this rough ſurface, I am ſpreading a moderate dreſſing of yard dung; to be dragged and rolled and harrowed, until the dung be effectually incorporated, with the freſh raw ſoil, brought up; thereby to meliorate it, and to *force* the ſeeds of weeds, with which it has, no doubt, been amply ſupplied, century after century.

FALLOWING.

The weed ſeeds having ſpent themſelves, and the crude ſoil having received the influence of the atmoſphere, the dreſſing will be turned in, with a mean-depth or ſomewhat ſhallow plowing; and the ſurface be ſuffered to remain in the rough ſtate, in which the plow leaves it, during winter.

In the ſpring, as ſoon as the clods have thrown out their ſeedling weeds, and the weather will permit, the ſurface will be ground down to powder, to provoke the remainder to vegetation; and, in due ſeaſon, be ſown with barley and ley herbage.

Thus, for the loſs of ONE YEAR'S RENT, theſe fields will probably be benefited for twenty years to come.

17. EIGHTEEN MONTHS FALLOW. 1794. The ſucceſs has anſwered the fulleſt expectation. The field which was managed more immediately under my own eye, is, I am of opinion, five pounds an acre better for the operation; reckoning on twenty years, from the time of performing it.

It is obſervable, that, in every caſe where circumſtances will allow it, an EIGHTEEN MONTHS FALLOW ſhould be broken up, in autumn, or early winter, by a rib plowing; ſuffering it to lie, in an expoſed ſtate, during winter. This, beſides employing the winter's froſts in the great work of purification, forwards the buſineſs of the enſuing ſummer, and renders the whole operation a matter of leiſure and conveniency; and, in the end, COMPLEAT: putting the ſoil in its moſt profitable ſtate of exertion, for a length of years. Under proper management and with the aſſiſtance of FALLOW CROPS, Lands, THUS EFFECTUALLY RECLAIMED, may not require a repetition of the operation, for half a century afterwards.

18.

HOING TURNEPS.

AUGUST 28. A field of twenty-four acres was sowing with Turneps, when I arrived here;—with too little tillage, too little seed, and some of it with dung much too long; the harrows drawing the seed into stripes and bunches. The consequence is, the crop is irregular, and the few plants which appear are nearly suffocated in wild Mustard, and other weeds.

Some light hoes were ordered to be made, from old sithe blades; and six of them were put into the hands of women, who had never hoed, and one into the hands of a man, who had.

The directions, in going the first time over the ground, were, to thin the clusters or bunches, and to check the weeds; without attempting to set the Turnep plants out, singly, or at full distances; and even, in doing this, to proceed slowly at the outset.

Hitherto,

18. HOING TURNEPS. Hitherto, they have performed this work better than was expected. Indeed, by adhering to the rules, here laid down, Turnep hoers will spontaneously grow out of them. By setting off slowly, and not attempting too great nicety, at first, the employment becomes pleasurable, and the eye and the hands are imperceptibly taught the art; especially if the greater errors which arise be, from time to time, pointed out, by one who is conversant in the operation.

They have now begun to go over the first-sown part, a second time; setting out the plants singly, and at due distances; namely ten to twelve inches apart (the hoes being eight inches long); except where two plants stand near each other, in a vacant space; in which case, both plants are permitted to stand *.

Hoing Turneps, with eight inch hoes, made from sithe blades, is moderate work for women (such hoes are light and pass freely

* For more particular remarks and directions, respecting this operation, see MID. ECON. Vol. II. P. 198.

freely through the soil); and, by proceeding on the principles here adopted, any woman, with an eye and hands, may be soon taught the art: will, in one full season, become a sufficient Turnep hoer. 18. HOING TURNEPS.

How eligible, in Countries where women are not employed in reaping, to teach them the use of the Turnep hoe. What avails the slowness of their work, the first season, compared with the introduction of so valuable a practice: especially to a large occupier; and, still more, to a man of large estate.

19.

SEPTEMBER 1. It is customary, here, to shoe working oxen; although they are rarely employed upon the road. The stoniness of the soils, and rockiness of the lanes and driftways, may account for the practice. SHOEING OXEN.

In the form of the shoes, or the method of setting them on, I see little new. A few parti-

19. SHOEING OXEN.

particulars of practice, nevertheless, require to be noticed. Having been cast, or thrown, and his legs bound together, in the usual manner, the animal is forced nearly upon his back, and his feet hoisted up to a convenient height, by means of a forked pole, some five feet long; the fork taking the bandage which binds the feet, the other end being fixed firmly in the sward, upon which they are usually thrown. This simple contrivance gives great firmness, steadiness, and conveniency to the operation.

That the individuals may be the more conveniently laid hold of, and trammelled, the team are driven to the place of shoeing, in their yokes, and hung together with chains, the hindmost chain being fastened to a large root, or stool, in the hedge; by the side of which they are usually placed; in order to prevent their running off, on seeing one of their companions thrown down and roughly treated, in their sight, —immediately under their eyes!

Today, the remaining three of a team, shoeing in this extraordinary way, being alarmed

alarmed and rendered savage, by seeing the savage treatment of their comrades, broke from their hold; ran off; the pair throwing down the single ox encumbered by his yoke;—dragged him;—broke off one of his horns, with its core close to his head; cut the sinew of his fore leg, almost through, with one of the hooks; and have thus *entirely spoilt him*. 19.

SHOEING OXEN.

Some means of facilitating the shoeing of oxen are much to be desired. I am of opinion that were rearing calves, which are intended for work, accustomed to have their feet taken up, and their hoofs beaten with a hammer; and were a repetition of this practice to take place, in the winter season, when the steers are in the yards, or in stalls, they might afterwards be shod as horses.

WORKING CATTLE.

Working cattle should also be accustomed, from their earliest age, to be driven and led about, singly; should be wholly reclaimed from a state of wildness; as working horses are.

The ox, under kind and generous treatment, is easily familiarized, and rendered docile.

20.

GENERAL WORK.

LONDON, 1794. Having, in the summer of 1790, spent some months at Maidstone, in Kent; to register the HOP CULTURE, and the other branches of Rural Economy; as they are practised in that fertile District; and having, in the Spring and early part of the Summer of 1791, paid some attention to the Farnham practice of cultivating hops, as well as to that and other Rural Subjects, in West Sussex; I judged it expedient to return to Farnham, early in September, in the same year, to be present at the picking and curing, in that District; in order to enable me, the better, to draw up a practical account of the management of the Hop; in a general account of the Rural Practice of the SOUTHERN COUNTIES; which I hope soon to offer to the Public.

IMPROVEMENTS SUGGESTED.

Before I left Buckland, I digested the ideas which I had collected, respecting the present

present ſtate and improvement of its charming demeſne. Many of thoſe ideas related, of courſe, to private concerns; many of them appear, in the foregoing Digeſt, of the practice of the Diſtrict at large; and others, in the preceding Minutes. Some few of them, however, have not yet been introduced into this Work; and theſe are inſerted, here. For what applies to the Barton of Buckland is more or leſs applicable to the lands of the ſurrounding Country, and may furniſh hints for thoſe of other Diſtricts. 20. IMPROVEMENTS SUGGESTED.

OBJECTS OF HUSBANDRY.

This, in ſoil and ſurface, is properly a SHEEP FARM. Sheep, Turneps, Barley, temporary Leys, and Wheat, ought certainly to be conſidered as PRIMARY OBJECTS. The DAIRY ſeems to ſtand ſecond; as being, in this ſituation, profitable in itſelf; and as a ſource of working cattle. But no part of it appears to be well adapted to the GRAZING OF CATTLE,

20. OBJECTS OF HUSBANDRY.

TLE, which preſents itſelf as a ſubordinate object; to be confined merely to the aged cows and oxen, which the farm itſelf throws off. A main object, on many accounts, is to keep the manager at home. Hence, adopt a courſe of tillage, ſuitable to the ſoil and ſituation; with liveſtock ſuitable, in ſpecies and proportion, to the crops: adhering as cloſely to this outline of management, as ſeaſons and circumſtances will permit. Under theſe regulations, the Hine would have little to take off his attention from the interior operations of the farm; except the diſpoſal of its immediate produce. He would have no riding about the Country to buy ſtock; nor any trifling away of his time, in ſelling them.

Farming and jobbing can ſeldom be united, with profit: even by a Principal; much leſs by an Agent.

RIVER BREAKS.

Some RIVER BREAKS are wanted to defend the meadow lands. Stones, not timber, appear to be the proper materials for theſe Breaks.

1794. Hitherto, piles and planks had been used, to confine the rapid Tavey within its channel; much valuable timber having been used, from time to time, in "weiring;" while the bed of the river is strewed with stones, fit for this purpose. 20. RIVER BREAKS.

I had one constructed, as a specimen, in the most difficult situation;—immediately in front of the Salmon Weir, and within the reach of its whirlpool, in times of floods; at one fourth of the expence which a timber break would have cost. It is built with *dry stones*, collected from the river bed.

The permanency of this loose stonework depends, entirely, on the *principle of construction*. The face of the Break is every way bulging towards the force of the current; which acts upon it, as superincumbent weight on an arch. The base line, some fifteen or twenty yards long, is the segment of a circle, with its outer or convex side to the water. The wall, from four or five, to two or three feet high, is carried up *battering*, very considerably, from the stream; not with a straight line,

 but

20. RIVER BREAKS.

but ſomewhat convex, and rounding off at the top,—until it forms nearly a horizontal paving. The ſtones are laid, with their larger ends inward; and not horizontally, but dipping, in ſuch a manner, as to lie ſquare with the face of the wall; which is thus placed in the poſture of *falling*, towards the bank of earth, that was rammed in firmly behind, as the wall was carried up. The whole to be filled in, level with the adjoining meadow; thick turf being firmly laid, in continuation of the pavement; that the water, when it overflows the meadow, may paſs ſmoothly over the break, and thereby prevent the adjoining ſward from being torn up, by a diſturbed current.

A violent flood diſplaced ſome of the uppermoſt ſtones, for want of the ground being filled up, and properly finiſhed, behind them; and the eddy of the Weir pool ſcooped away part of the gravel from the foundation, ſo as to endanger it; until large ſtones were thrown againſt it, for its defence.

Where there is a proper choice of ſtones; and

and if the top and foundation be from time to time attended to; a river Break, built on these principles, may endure for a length of years. 20. RIVER BREAKS.

BREED OF CATTLE. The present dairy cows, some few excepted, accord ill with the Barton of Buckland: which is entitled, in every point of view, to the finest breeds of liveſtock the Iſland at preſent poſſeſſes. The degenerate breed, now upon it, are unprofitable, even as dairy ſtock, and are altogether unfit, as molds for working oxen; the breeding of which ought to be a principal object in keeping them. Some of the oxen, the deſcendants of the old ſtock of the farm, are almoſt unexceptionable: their ſize being their principal deficiency. The preſent degeneracy of the cattle appears to have ariſen out of a wrong principle of management, of the late hines; namely, that of ſelling everything inclined to fatneſs, ſo as to fetch money; and buying in anything for cheapneſs, without regard to ſpecific quality *.

* This error in practice has been mentioned before; but it is of ſo treacherous and miſchievous a nature, it cannot be too often reprobated.

20. SALMON FISHERY. The Salmon Fiſhery, at preſent, is a nurſery of Poachers; owing not ſo much to the remoteneſs of its ſituation, with reſpect to the houſe, as to the ſkreens, of wood, which now riſe on either ſide of the river; and hide them, in a great meaſure, from detection. Under its preſent management, it is an object worth their attending to, and of courſe draws them off from honeſt, but leſs profitable, employments. The moſt eligible courſe to be taken appears to be that of throwing difficulties in their way; ſo as to make it not worth their attention. To attempt to prevent them by force, eſpecially while the mines remain open, would evidently be imprudent.

Perhaps, the men, who are employed in drawing the net, ſhould be paid not by the tide, or the number of times they draw it, but by the number, or weight, of the fiſh caught: thus uniting their own intereſt with that of their employer. Even night fiſhing might, by this means, be conſiderably checked; not ſo much by keeping watch, as by every pool being fiſhed *carefully*, before the night came on. Now, if the net be wetted, their hire is due.

Or *perhaps* deſtroy the net-fiſhing alto- 20.
gether; by placing obſtructions in the SALMON FISHERY.
pools; and depend ſolely on the Weir: which, if properly regulated and duly attended, would perhaps receive all the fiſh which enters the river; or, in much probability, a far greater number, than are now legally taken, by the weir and nets jointly. Giving a weir man a fixed proportion of the produce,—for his attendance during the fiſhing ſeaſon,—for ſeeing that the pools were kept guarded to prevent net fiſhing,—for keeping down the ſkreens,—and for attending daily and hourly, during dead water, to prevent ſpearing,—would, in this caſe, be requiſite.

At preſent, the Fiſhery is either neglected, or it interferes, unprofitably, with the ordinary buſineſs of the Farm.

On whatever principle a Fiſhery of this kind is conducted, the perſons employed in it ought to be rewarded, in proportion to the quantity taken; eſpecially when they are not immediately under the eye of their employer.

OCTOBER 30. Rode to MILTON ABBOTS; by TAVISTOCK and LAMERTON.

Some charming graſslands about Taviſtock; ſtill better before Lamerton; and yet more excellent, at Milton Abbots.

Conſiderable herds of fine oxen, and good fatting cows, are now in theſe grounds: ſome of which are ſtill full of graſs;—highly colored, and apparently of a ſuperior quality.

How extraordinary, that Plots, ſuch as theſe are, ſhould be ſcattered in ſo bleak and barren a Country. Between Lamerton and Milton, an unproductive Heath intervenes; the rich lands of the latter being nearly ſurrounded with ſuch Heaths, and overlooked by Mountains: the ſituation inhoſpitable in the extreme. The fertile lands of Lamerton and Taviſtock are inſulated in a ſimilar manner.

But

21. GEOLOGY.

But the extent of theſe lands, collectively, is ſmall: and in a ſurvey of the Rural Practice of the Weſt of England, they are rather a ſubject of admiration, than of importance.

22.

COATING BUILDINGS.

NOVEMBER 1. The ROUGHCAST work of this Diſtrict is executed in a ſuperior manner; being not only durable, but pleaſing to the eye.

Some lately done at Ivybridge is equal, in beauty, to dreſſed ſtone work. Mr. Stapleton's houſe, in this neighbourhood, done in a ſimilar way, has now ſtood upwards of half a century; and, excepting at the immediate foundation, and beneath ſome of the windows, where water has been ſuffered to lodge, the whole remains as firm as when firſt done; appearing to have acquired a ſtonelike texture. In both theſe caſes Chryſtaline gravel has been uſed;

 and

22. COATING BUILDINGS.

and both of them are falſe-jointed, to reſemble dreſſed ſtone work.

An intelligent workman, whom I accidentally converſed with on this ſubject, ſuggeſted an admirable *theory* of the operation of roughcaſting; making an accurate diſtinction between this and Stucco work.

STUCCO being laid on, *in a ſtate of paſte*, more or leſs air is unavoidably ſhut up,—let it be ever ſo well worked; and the very expanſion and contraction of this air, by heat and froſt, is ſufficient to break the texture of the Stucco. Beſide, let the working be done ever ſo carefully, cracks, though not evident to the eye, will be formed in drying; and if, by means of theſe microſcopic fiſſures (or of thoſe formed by the expanſion and partial eſcape of the confined air), water take poſſeſſion of the air cells, the periſhing and peeling become natural conſequences.

ROUGHCAST, on the contrary, being applied, *in a fluid ſtate*, and by little and little, fills up every pore, and cranny in the face of the wall; as well as in the face of every

every ſucceeding coat; which being ſuf- 22.
fered to dry, before another coat is added, COATING BUILDINGS.
the cracks, if any take place, are filled up; and *deep* ones, of courſe, are effectually prevented: whereas, the cracks of Stucco neceſſarily reach through the coat.

STUCCO evidently partakes of the nature of cement uſed, in a ſtate of paſte or mortar; LIQUID COATING, of cement poured into the wall, in a ſtate of grout.

STUCCO is analogous to the materials of a dam, or the bank of a canal, formed with earth, in a ſtate of paſte: ROUGH COATING, to the puddle of Canal Makers: to loam intimately mixed with water, and permitted to ſubſide in a liquid ſtate: thus preventing air cells; and forming a cloſe, homogeneous maſs.

23.

CHARLOCK, AS FOOD OF CATTLE.

DECEMBER 10. TURNEPS. (See MIN. 18.) Several acres of theſe Turneps were, in my abſence, omitted to be hoed. I found

23. CHARLOCK, AS FOOD OF CATTLE. found them, overgrown with Charlock,—a yard high, and as yellow as a Rape field: the feeds of the lower pods being fully formed. Part had been drawn by hand, according to the cuftom of the Country, and thrown in heaps: an expenfive and wafteful practice.

A few cart loads were ordered to be mown,—high enough to prevent, as much as poffible, the injury of the Turneps,—and low enough, to get beneath the pods of the Charlock; and were ftrewed over an adjoining pafture ground.

Sheep eat the tips of the leaves of the Turneps, partially cut off by the fithe; and alfo the leaves of the Charlock; but left the pods and the ftalks of the latter, in a great meafure untouched.

Cattle, however, preferred the Charlock; eating the whole up, clean; before they picked up the Turnep leaves.

Four or five acres kept about twenty head of young and ftore cattle, near three weeks. Had the food been given to them regularly, and more frugally than it was, it would have kept them, fufficiently as ftore store cattle, a month. This, added to the saving of the expence, compared with that of drawing, cannot be reckoned at less than twenty shillings an acre.

23. CHARLOCK, AS FOOD OF CATTLE.

They eat it so voraciously, that one or two of them were repeatedly blown, or sufflated, by it: and a heifer failed so much, while at this food, that it was thought right to have her butchered. On opening her, however, her disorder appeared evidently to have been of some duration; a part of her intestines being in a state of decay. The pungency of the Charlock might, or might not, have stimulated her disorder.

Be this as it may, it is sufficiently proved, that healthy cattle may be kept on Charlock in pod, with safety and profit*.

DECEM-

* Part of it, the rough Charlock or WILD MUSTARD (*Sinapis Arvensis*); part, the smooth Charlock, or WILD Rape (*Brassica Napus*).

24.

DECEMBER 10. The only useful idea I have been able to collect, from the late manager of this farm, is his method of cutting garden Cabbages.

Instead of clearing the stalk or stem from the lower leaves, and cross-slitting the crown or top of the stalk, in the usual manner,—he cuts out the body of the Cabbage, only; letting all the open, large, spreading leaves, remain upon the stem.

The consequence is a second, and perhaps a third, crop of *Cabbages*; not one, but many, upon a stem; forming, by the third crop, a Cabbage tree. There are now, in the garden of this place, several stems, with four, five, or more wellsized table Cabbages on each: and, applied to field Cabbages, which are cut early, the principle may be a good one. The old leaves continue to draw up the sap, until vigorous

vigorous ſhoots are formed; when they are obſerved to droop, decay, and fall at the foot of the plant; being, perhaps, in every ſtage of their decay, uſeful to the young progeny; in ſhading the ground, in keeping down the weeds, and in furniſhing a ſupply of mephitic gas to their riſing offspring: advantages which are loſt, in the ordinary method of treatment. Many of the plants are killed by the ſudden check of the ſap, and thoſe which ſurvive, throw out numerous, and of courſe, weak ſhoots; few of them ſwelling to any ſize, or taking the Cabbage form. 24. CABBAGES.

25.

DECEMBER 18. A SOCIETY of AGRICULTURE, I underſtand, is now forming in the South Hams. In my late excurſion, through that Diſtrict, I heard of a "Plowing Match," at Kingſbridge, and another, at Ivybridge; where Meetings of Country Gen- AGRICULTURAL SOCIETIES.

25. AGRICULTURAL SOCIETIES. Gentlemen, and substantial Yeomen, distributed REWARDS TO GOOD WORKMEN: a rational Institution, which, while it continues to adhere to this principle, cannot fail of proving beneficial to the Country.

If mere PRECEPTIVE SOCIETIES, without the power of EXAMPLE, IN THEMSELVES, can be materially serviceable to the advancement of Agriculture, their object, I am of opinion, ought to be that of ENCOURAGING GOOD HUSBANDRY, among PROFESSIONAL MEN: of searching for SUPERIOR HUSBANDMEN; and distinguishing them, in such manner, as to create a spirit of emulation; and of assisting such distinguished Managers to procure the requisite means of improvement. Thus placing them in a conspicuous light, and making them the honorable instruments of that example, which a mere preceptive Society has not, in itself, the power of setting.

But, on a LARGE ESTATE, this may be the best done, by its Proprietor. He knows, or ought to know, the individuals who are most worthy of being made the

distin-

distinguished leaders of its improvement: and, in this case, he can encourage them, according to their merit; without being liable to the cabals of Theorists and Adventurers, to which mixed Societies are ever subject. A few pounds expended, annually, among his own tenants, in stimulating them to accurate management, would, in most cases, pay him tenfold interest *. 25. AGRICULTURAL SOCIETIES.

ASSOCIATIONS OF LANDED GENTLEMEN.

These reflections suggest Institutions of a higher order. Let men of landed property associate: not so much for the particular purpose of ENCOURAGING GOOD HUSBANDRY among their tenants, as for the more general intention of ascertaining the suitable regulations, under which to conduct the MANAGEMENT of ESTATES. For

* In a Sketch of the RURAL ECONOMY of the CENTRAL HIGHLANDS of Scotland, which I had the honor of presenting, in 1794, to the BOARD OF AGRICULTURE, as a Report concerning that part of the Island, I pursued this idea; proposing to divide a large estate into Districts, or Officiaries; and to place a superior Manager in each, as a distinguished Leader, in Rural Improvements.

25. ASSOCIATIONS OF LANDED GENTLEMEN.

For ſeeing, evidently, not only in the Diſtrict under ſurvey, but in other Diſtricts of the Iſland, that a greater defalcation of public and private property is incurred, through the inaccurate management of landed property, than through the errors of cultivation, it belongs excluſively to the poſſeſſors of eſtates to rectify the impropriety *.

The

* I am deſirous of being fully underſtood. There are, in theſe Kingdoms, many Eſtates, as well as many Farms, in a ſtate of good management; they being either under the immediate direction of Proprietors, who have turned their attention to rural concerns; or of Agents, who have a practical knowledge of Rural Affairs, and who have no intereſts ſubverſive of, or diſtinct from, the good order and proſperity of the Eſtates under their care. But there will be little riſk in ſaying, that a majority of the larger Eſtates, throughout the Iſland, are under very diſſerent principles of management.

I am equally deſirous to be explicit, with reſpect to SOCIETIES OF AGRICULTURE. I have ſaid in another place (ſee the RURAL ECONOMY of the MIDLAND COUNTIES, Vol. I. P. 121.), that mixed Societies are capable of producing good, by aſſimilating the ſentiments of Proprietors and Occupiers. And I believe that Provincial Societies have ever been beneficial, *in the outſet*, to the Diſtricts in which they have been formed, by agitating the Subject, and tending to awaken the SPIRIT OF IMPROVEMENT.

The ſubjects, that would naturally offer themſelves to ſuch Aſſociations, are the following. 25. ASSOCIATIONS OF LANDED GENTLEMEN.

The preſent management of landed property, in the Diſtrict of Aſſociation.

The laying out of eſtates, into farm lands, or ſuch as are adapted to cultivation, and into woodlands, or ſuch as are fitteſt for the production of timber or coppice wood.

The ſuitable ſizes and characters of farms.

The ſpecies of tenancy.

The forms of leaſes.

The qualifications of tenants.

The proper ſeaſons and terms of removals, receiving rents, &c. &c.

The encouragement of good managers, and the diſcountenancing of bad ones.

The permanent improvement of farm lands, by draining, watering, &c. And their more temporary melioration, by manures, ſodburning, tillage, &c.

The plan, and conſtruction, of farm yards, and buildings.

 The

25. ASSOCIATIONS OF LANDED GENTLEMEN. The management of hedges.

The management of timber, woodlands, and plantations.

And the more general improvement of the given Diſtrict of Aſſociation ;—by

Public Embankments.

Public Drains.

Public Navigations.

Public Incloſures.

The melioration of Tithes, and

The Poor's Rate: as well as the regulation of

County concerns; and the ſupport of

The landed Intereſt; which has lain neglected and trampled on, by Commerce and Manufactures, until the Country is no longer able to provide ſuſtinence for its inhabitants *.

SEPTEMBER

* For a ſtriking evidence of the truth of this aſſertion, ſee the RURAL ECONOMY of the MIDLAND COUNTIES, Vol. II. P. 294.

26.

1792. SEPT. 24. The MONASTERY BARN of this place is perhaps the first to be found, at this day, in the Island: not in respect to size, though it is large, but in regard to the state of preservation,—both of its walls, and its roof. BARN OF BUCKLAND.

This Barn, having been built under the Pack-horse plan of Husbandry, was most inconvenient for carriages; having only one pair of doorways, in the middle of it; with a passage through, and a thrashing floor on either side of the roadway. The width of the barn (namely, twentyseven feet in the clear), not permitting waggons to turn within the area, the Corn has ever been thrown, from the waggons, upon the floors, and thence flung, from hand to hand, to either end of the barn! which is a hundred and fifty feet in length.

The obvious method of improvement was to break out doorways, towards the

26. ends; ſo as to divide the whole length of

BARN OF BUCKLAND. the barn, into ſix bays or mowſteads, with a floor between each two, in the *Engliſh* manner: an arduous taſk, which is now executing; and which will render it one of the firſt barns in the Kingdom.

NATURE OF CEMENT. The labor of cutting theſe doorways is nearly equal to that of cutting through ſolid rock, of equal thickneſs; namely, three feet. The cement is of an extraordinary quality: as hard almoſt as granite; eſpecially on the North ſide of the building. That of the South or rather South-Weſt wall is much more friable: a circumſtance which has been obſerved in other old buildings of this place; and which is entitled to Philoſophic enquiry.

27.

THE USES OF RILLS. SEPTEMBER 24. A Spring in the upper part of this Farm ſupplies the houſe with water. It alſo ſupplies a drinking pool, near

near the yards; and its natural courſe 27.
carrying it through a ſmall Strawyard, a THE USES OF RILLS.
trough is placed acroſs the rill, for the uſe of the yard cattle.

It has alſo, time immemorial, been led over ſome graſs lands, which lie below the yards,—on the float-and-drain principle.

But although this rill is ſeldom if ever dried up—leading it along the ſides of the Valley, through upland incloſures, which are deſtitute of water for ſtock, and their value of courſe thereby much depreciated,—does not appear to have been thought of.

In the courſe of laſt Summer, being deſirous to know if this rill could be carried through an intended ſuite of yards, on the ſide of the Valley, I took the level, and found not only that object to be attainable, but alſo that it may be led with eaſe into two waterleſs fields, which lie above theſe yards; and, through them, into four or five more (equally in want of water for ſtock), ſituated beyond them.

In aſcertaining theſe facts, I made uſe of a maſon's long level, inverted: a plummet

27. THE USES OF RILLS. hole being previously cut in the head of the standard; the crown of which being set upon the ground, the arms of the level were steadied by rods, in the horizontal position; and a carpenter's rule held across another rod, set up, at as great a distance as a clear sight would admit of, and at a height upon the staff, equal to the height of the level.

CONSTRUCTION OF A NEW LEVEL. Finding this a most simple and perfect instrument, but difficult to adjust, by reason of its instability, I have since had a FRAME LEVEL made, on the same principle; namely, with a straight edge, or top rail, answering to the base board of the long level; with a broad piece falling down from the middle of it, answering to the standard; and with two end pieces or legs, to supersede the use of the rods; together with a bottom rail, eight or nine inches from the ground, and with diagonal braces, to keep the whole firm, and prevent the middle or plumb line from getting out of the square, with the straight edge of the top rail; which is seven or eight feet long, and

and the height about four feet *. And, as 27.
an improvement of the rule and rod, I contrived a CROSS STAFF; namely, a slip of thin deal, about five feet and a half long, with a cross piece, about two feet long and three inches wide, fixed in the edge of it, at the exact height of the level; the top of the staff rising twelve or eighteen inches above the upper edge of the cross piece, that the hand of the person who holds it up may not interfere with the view †.

CONSTRUCTION OF A NEW LEVEL.

CONDUCTING MADE RILLS.

With this instrument, I have lately traced the FLOWING LEVEL of the intended rill, for watering the yards, and the grounds beforementioned.

To ascertain the proper fall of a rill of this intention, I previously took the running level of the antient floating Leat of the meadows ‡; and finding its fall irre-

* Half a rod long, and a quarter of a rod high, are eligible dimensions, when great accuracy is required. But a shorter length, as one third of a rod, is more handy.

† This cross piece should be of white wood, as deal, or be painted white, that it may be the more distinctly seen, at a distance.

‡ See Vol. I. P. 206.

27. gular, I took it in two places, where the variations were greatest. In the first, the fall was twentyseven inches, in one hundred and ten feet; which is nearly one inch, or one foot, of fall, to fifty inches, or fifty feet, in length. In this part the current is in a degree rapid; the fall much too great for the general intention. The fall, in one hundred and ten feet of the other part, is barely six inches; which is only one measure of perpendicular height to two hundred and twenty of horizontal length. But in this part, the motion is too sluggish: the surface of the water is nearly smooth; barely dimpling; no ripple, or agitation appears. The fall is evidently too little for a water course, in which there is not a constant stream.

CONDUCTING MADE RILLS.

PROPER FALL OF RILLS.

I have therefore fixed upon ONE MEASURE IN A HUNDRED, as the proper fall of a water course, into which water is occasionally thrown; for the purposes of watering lands, filling drinking pools, cisterns, &c. &c.

To adjust the level to this descent, I measured one hundred feet in length, and having

having nicely ascertained the DEAD LEVEL, I depressed the range of the top bar, one foot below the upper edge of the cross piece of the staff, and, while in that position, I marked the situation of the plumb line, on the face of the level; the plummet hole being made wide for this purpose: thus *fixing* the FLOWING LEVEL. 27. PROPER FALL OF RILLS.

With this descent, I have traced a line, from an intended reservoir, and from point to point, through the fields of one side of the farm, and find that it reaches, even with this descent, within every field: and that three fourths, or a larger proportion, of the surface are *capable* of being floated, from this intended pool.

To see the actual motion of water falling one in a hundred, I have had fifty yards of the upper end of the line opened; and find the current fully sufficient; a lively rippling stream; more active perhaps than is necessary. But the leakage being the less, the quicker the water moves, we may safely conclude, that one foot of fall in a hundred feet of length is nearly perfect.

By

27. PROPER FALL OF RILLS. By the fame means, I have alfo found that, from a fimilar refervoir to be formed near the fource of the rill, water might be conveyed to every field, and almoft every acre of the oppofite fide of the farm.

USES OF RESERVOIRS. The ufes of thefe refervoirs will be thofe of having in readinefs, during the fummer months, when the rill is weak, a body of water to throw into drinking pools, cifterns, &c.: a weak current turned into a dry trench is abforbed by its perforations and fiffures, for fometime, at leaft, after it is turned in: whereas a body of water, rufhing quickly along it, not only in part efcapes abforption, but tends to fill up the leaks: and, in winter, thefe refervoirs will be ufeful in fcouring the trenches, and in hoarding up bodies of water, for the purpofe of irrigation.

In fetting out thefe rills, I have laid the head or upper end of each, from two to three feet below the intended furfaces of their refpective refervoirs, when full. Hence, by means of a portcullis floodgate, a body of water, two or three feet deep, and

and the whole extent of the surfaces of the basons, may be poured into the rills, faster or slower, as occasion may require. 27. USES OF RESERVOIRS.

28.

SEPTEMBER 30. The Florists of this District have an effectual and ready way of DESTROYING EARTH WORMS, in their knots and borders; by the means of an infusion of wallnut-tree leaves. The process is this:---fill a vessel nearly full, with leaves, gathered in the first or second week of September;---cover them with water, and let them stand two or three days; until the water has acquired a blackish green color. With this infusion, the beds and alleys are watered, by means of the common watering pot. The worms presently rise to the surface, and die in apparent agony.

DESTROYING EARTH-WORMS.

It strikes me that this interesting fact may be turned to a profitable purpose, in the forming of DRINKING POOLS. It is probable,

DRINKING POOLS.

28. DRINKING POOLS. probable, that leaves of the walnut, ſpread under the clay, would have the ſame effect as the lime, which is now in uſe *.

Reflecting on this ſubject, it appears to me further probable, that the uſe of clay, in making pools, may be diſpenſed with. Thus:---form the baſon; puddle with the beſt of the excavated mold; ſtrew on leaves; and pave with liquid mortar; made up with their infuſion,---if required.

The baſon form of the pit is an objection to puddling; and could not, perhaps, be effected otherways, than progreſſively with the pavement; by puddling above each ring, and bedding the ſtones in the medicated matter; pouring in liquid cement, where it might appear to be wanted. Or, perhaps, the medicated batter would in itſelf be ſufficient.

This is a ſubject of great importance, in upland ſituations. Forming drinking pools with clay and lime (great as was the diſcovery) is difficult and expenſive; and any means of ſimplifying the proceſs would be valuable.

SEP-

* See York. Econ. Vol I. P. 146.

29.

SEPTEMBER 30. FARM BUILDINGS. Where a blank is given, — where the ground may be chofen,—where there are no buildings already erected,—or, where there are given buildings, if they ftand in the defired fituation,—few difficulties can arife, in laying out a Farmery.

LAYING OUT FARMERIES.

But where the fite is given, — where there are principal buildings already fixed on the fpot,—and thefe on aukward ground, and in aukward fituations with refpect to each other, as they are on this farm, it requires great ftudy and invention to render the yards and additional buildings convenient, or commodious.

FARMERY OF BUCKLAND.

In this cafe, the capital barn, already mentioned, is fituated between the dwelling houfe, and a range of fpacious office buildings,—on the fide of a fteep hill; the out

'29. out buildings above,---the houſe below---

FARMERY OF BUCKLAND. the barn;---with other offices, at a conſiderable diſtance.

The deſirable object, here, was to collect the whole into a compact form, in the immediate vicinity of the barn. And this has been effected, by forming a ſemi-octagon yard, in the front of the principal range of buildings; and incloſing it with a line of cattle ſheds; the area of the yard being formed into a receptacle for the dung of the ſheds and ſtables.

This form of a farm yard, though I have been led to it by circumſtances, cannot perhaps be improved; even where a blank ſite is given; except by that of a compleat octagon.

CATTLE YARDS. An OCTAGONAL YARD is warm, and is much more commodious than a ſquare one; by reaſon of the ſharp inconvenient angles being cut off; and octagonal ſheds are equally commodious; each ſide having its range of ſtalls, with fodder houſes in the angles, between them: a gangway, in this caſe, running from end to end, before the heads of the cattle, and through the ſtore houſes;

houses; which have doors opening to the road, on the back or outer side of the sheds, to receive the food;---whether it be hay, straw, roots, or other material. 29. CATTLE YARDS.

30.

HANGING DOORS.

OCTOBER 5. The doors of the store houses of these sheds are hung to open outward; to prevent a waste of room, and to render them more secure against intruders. To increase the security, they are hung with a fall to the catch; and to prevent their being injured by the weather, when open, they have also a fall, backward, under the eaves of the building. To effect this, the balance point is placed in the midway, between the two extreme positions of the door; which, being set at right angle to the line of the building, has a fall to either hand *.

The

* See MID. ECON. Vol. II. P. 79. for practical rules on this subject.

30. HANGING DOORS. The hooks and catches are laid into blocks of moorſtone, and worked up into the jambs of the doorways; the material of building being a coarſe ſchiſtus, or ſlate ſtone.

The hooks of the new doorways of the barn I am likewiſe laying into moorſtone; receſſes being hewn out of the jambs to receive the blocks; which are large, and fixed firmly in their places;---firſt, by means of wedge-ſhaped ſtones, driven in above them; and, afterwards, by wedging them in more firmly, with thin pieces of iron; forcing out the cement, at every crevice.

AN EFFECT OF RUST? It is obſervable, that the hooks of the original doors of the barn, which are in like manner laid in ſtone, have moſt of them burſt their bounds, and broken off more or leſs of the outer parts of the ſtones they are reſpectively laid in. A ſenſible and experienced ſtone maſon is of opinion, that theſe fractures are occaſioned by the ruſting of the iron; having, he ſays, carefully traced the effect, in ſeveral inſtances.

But

AN EFFECT OF RUST.

But may not this effect be cauſed by the 30.
ſuſceptibility of metals, with reſpect to heat and cold? Or may not the miſchiefs, in the inſtance under notice, have been done by the jarring of the heavy doors, blown violently to, by the wind? I have, however, obſerved ſimilar fractures, in caſes where the laſt ſuggeſted cauſe could not ſo eaſily operate.

Facts, which require a ſucceſſion of ages to produce them, are too intereſting to be paſſed without attention. The effect here noticed is obſervable in many ancient buildings, and the operation of the ruſt of iron is not, perhaps, accurately underſtood.

31.

HANGING DOORS.

OCTOBER 13. Doors hung on hooks laid into the wall, as above deſcribed, require to be hung in *rabbets*. For, if they are hung in *between* the jambs, rain and ſnow will beat in: if they *lap over*, on the

 out-

31. HANGING DOORS. outside, they are exposed to the weather, are in harm's way, and are unsightly. A rabbet, of due dimensions, obviates these inconveniences. And I have found that, for ledge doors, made of inch boards, and hung to fall back under the eaves, in the manner above mentioned, three inches deep, each way, are the proper dimensions.

32.

LIMING LAND.

OCTOBER 28. Last year, I had the lime, for wheat, set about the field, in waggon-load heaps; with the intention of mixing with it the velled Beat, or the ashes that might arise from it, as the season should render most convenient. But I left the Country, before I had an opportunity of seeing the operation, properly performed.

This year, similar heaps being set about, I have had them covered, thickly, with unburnt Beat, collected with the team rake, or "drudge," of the Country; and the whole

whole duly " melled" or mixt, in the Devonſhire manner *; with a ſmall deviation in this caſe. 32. LIMING LAND.

The operation being purpoſely begun before the middles of the heaps were fallen, they were firſt pulled abroad, with a hack; thus giving a rough mixture to the unſlacked knobs of lime and the wet Beat, under which they were deeply buried. This brought on a quick diſſolution of the lime; whoſe heat, of courſe, operated in the deſtruction of weed ſeeds and animalculæ; and, while the heat was at its height, the whole were intimately mixed together; thus ſaving, by one eaſy proceſs, the endleſs labor of two tedious operations.

33.

OCTOBER 28. (See MIN. 27.) In conducting this rill through an open grove of tall trees, I have found ſome difficulties: not only the *ground* but the *trees* were given. CONDUCTING RILLS.

* See the Article LIME, Vol. I. Page 158.

33. CONDUCTING RILLS. PRACTICAL DIRECTIONS.

given. By purſuing the following methods, theſe difficulties have been overcome.

Having, by means of the frame level and croſs, aſcertained the general deſcent, or flowing level, through the whole extent of the grove; and having, in this operation, gained a general idea of the requiſite direction of the rill, by means of ſtakes placed at the ſeveral ſtations of the croſs ſtaff, wherever clear views could be caught through the openings between the trees,—the intermediate ſpaces, between the ſtakes, were traced by the eye, ſo as to endeavour to follow the natural level of the ground, without forming abrupt bends in the channel;—parrying between the two.

The ſuppoſed line being thus ſet out, the ſurface of the ground was cleared two or three feet wide on either ſide of it, from leaves and other incumbrances, and the top ſoil removed for manure; thus making a hollow pathway through the grove, ſome four or five feet wide.

The next operation was to level this pathway; which was likewiſe done by the eye, from ſtake to ſtake; paring off the pro-

protuberances, and casting or wheeling them into the hollows. 33. CONDUCTING RILLS.

To come at the true line, and to render the flowing level perfectly uniform, a narrow pathlet, the width of the spade, was formed on the upper side of the broad pathway. This pathlet was formed, with the frame level in hand; sinking trenches in the still protuberating parts, and raising banklets in the hollows: thus *fixing* the exact flowing level, at each level's length; and, at the same time, forming the face, or lower side of it, in such manner as to ease the bends, and give a smooth flowing line to the rill.

In order to bring the business of forming the bed of the rill to a certainty, and thereby to render any further superintendance unnecessary, yet to prevent error in the execution, I formed a gauge for the laborers to work by.

This gauge consists of a board, forming the segment of a circle; the chord or greatest length being three feet, the greatest depth twelve inches. This gives the dimensions of the bed of the rill. To keep

33. CONDUCTING RILLS. the bottom of it, exactly true to the flowing level, so that the current or stream may be perfectly uniform,— this gauge is fixed under a mason's short level; the end of one of the arms projecting, three or four inches, beyond one end of the gauge.

The trench being sunk, to nearly its proper depth, by the eye, kept on the adjusted margin, the projecting end of the level is placed on the same marginal guide, and the plummet line being brought to the perpendicular (and the base of the level of course rendered horizontal), the bottom of the trench is finished, *with certainty*.

This evening, I have had the water turned into the upper part of the trench thus formed, by two common laborers, who never before, perhaps, took a level in their hands. The current is not only desirable, as to descent; but is perfectly uniform,—*without alteration*.

Hence the practicability and certainty of this method of forming the channels of rills,—as well as the eligibility of one measure in a hundred, for the descent or fall,— are fully ascertained.

The

The dimenfions above ftated,—namely, three feet wide and one foot deep,—(a fize fully fufficient for any purpofes, at prefent intended by this rill) I have adopted as the fitteft for the part which paffes under trees, and which will be liable to be choaked by leaves and falling twigs. But a part which croffes an open grafs ground, and where cattle will frequently pafs and repafs, I have had formed by a fhallower gauge: namely, a fegment four feet wide and eight inches deep; the bank on the lower fide of it being made broad, and flatly convex; to prevent the cattle from treading in the fides: and, to give it more immediate firmnefs, it is turfed with the fods, taken from the part which is now the bed of the rill. 33. CONDUCTING RILLS.

34.

DECEMBER 8. The laying out and forming of ROADS have engroffed a principal part of my attention, during the laft two or three weeks; and, fo far as relates LAYING OUT ROADS.

34. LAYING OUT ROADS.

to convex roads, on a deſcent, I have brought this uſeful art to method and a degree of certainty.

In the forming of roads, as in the conducting of rills, the frame level and croſs are accurate and ready guides.

The given points of the intended road having been marked, the moſt deſirable line, whether as to utility or ornament, is to be ſet out, with tall ſtakes placed at equal diſtances, as ten paces from each other. Theſe preparatory ſteps having been taken ſome days previous to the commencement of the work,—in order to give time for deliberate adjuſtments,—the level and the croſs are placed at the oppoſite extremities of the line, or as near them as a clear ſight can be caught from the one to the other; and the level being deliberately adjuſted to the croſs, the ſituation of the plumb line is marked, on the face of the level; and thus the rake or degree of DESCENT is determined and *fixed*; and, of courſe, a uniformity of deſcent, if required, may thereby be accurately preſerved, in every part of the line. If this wind much, the

34. LAYING OUT ROADS.

the degree of inclination or deſcent will be diminiſhed, as the length of line is encreaſed; and, if an exact uniformity be required, an allowance ſhould be made for ſuch deviation. But, if the declivity be long, relaxations in the line of aſcent, at ſuitable diſtances, have their uſe for heavy carriages, and are not diſpleaſing to the eye.

The degree of deſcent being determined, the next ſtep is to try if the line marked out correſpond with it. This is done by keeping the level in its place, and ſetting up the croſs at the foot of each ſtake, or at the feet of as many as occaſion requires.

If the marked line deviate, much, from the line of general level; ſo as to render the road inconvenient, or encreaſe, unneceſſarily, the expence of making it, a freſh line is ſet out; endeavouring to parry, between the true line of direction, and the true line of deſcent.

The line of direction being finally determined on, and adjuſted, a ſtrong ſtump, or ſlender pile, two feet or more in length, is entered, with an iron crow, at the foot of each ſtake; and driven down to the general

34. general rake of the intended ſurface of the road, when finiſhed.

LAYING OUT ROADS.

This is readily done, by placing the feet of the level, on this intended line of ſurface, and putting the foot of the croſs upon the head of each ſtump; continuing to keep the level to the rake line, and to drive the ſtump, until the arms of the croſs are ſeen to range exactly, with the ſtraight edge of the level; or, which is frequently more expeditious, eſpecially where the ſubſoil is ſtoney, by placing the foot of the croſs againſt the ſide of the pile, and raiſing or lowering it, until the raking level be caught; then marking, and ſawing off, the head of the ſtump: proceeding in this manner, until each ſtake is ſupplanted by a pile.

Where the ground is very rough and uneven, it is convenient to break down the protuberances, by the eye, previouſly to the adjuſtment of the piles.

The piles being adjuſted, a regular trench or pathway is formed, the whole length of the line of road ſet out, at a depth below the heads of the ſtumps, equal to the intended thickneſs of the covering materials:

materials: namely, in private roads and ordinary cases, one foot: leaving the piles standing in the middle of the trench or pathway; showing one foot of their length above the intended bed of the road, with another foot, or a sufficient length in the ground, to keep them firmly in their places, until the road be finished; the heads of the piles being the requisite guide to the covering. 34. LAYING OUT ROADS.

This trench or pathway being the true middle line of the bed of the road, an unerring guide is given to the workman, and the business of the artist is at an end. The rest is mere labor, which may be performed, by ordinary workmen, under general directions.

FORMING ROADS.

The BED OF THE ROAD I make flat, or nearly so; the outer edges, only, dipping somewhat beneath the general level; the convexiture of the road, itself, being given with the rough foundation materials.

35.

COPPICE WOOD. 1793, JANUARY 29. There are, now, on this demesne, fortyfive acres of overgrown COPPICE WOOD; namely, wood of about thirty years growth.

AGE OF CUTTING. The lands of this Diſtrict being in general unfriendly to the Oak, after it attains a certain growth, much of the ſpray and upper branches of this wood are beginning to decay. Inſtead of encreaſing in value, it is probably getting worſe, every year;—eſpecially with reſpect to its bark, which is at preſent a valuable part of it. Twenty years, I find, is the uſual growth of coppice wood, here, and every circumſtance weighed, it is perhaps, on the whole, the moſt eligible.

RENTAL VALUE. The uſual price of coppice wood, at twenty years growth, has been of late years ten to twelve pounds, the "cuſtomary acre"

acre" of the country *; for wood growing on land of a quality, equal to that of arable lands, which are worth ten or twelve ſhillings the *ſtatute* acre. Of courſe, woodlands afford, to their proprietors, little more than half the annual rent of farm lands, of equal quality. 35. RENTAL VALUE.

For ſuppoſe coppice wood of twenty years growth ſells for ten pounds the provincial acre,—this is but barely equivalent to ſeven ſhillings an acre, received annually for farm lands; as, in the courſe of twenty years, the intereſt of the ſeveral annual ſums received, and the accumulating intereſt thereupon ariſing, amounts to nearly half the principal: and, if a farther reduction be made for the difference between the provincial and the ſtatute acre, we ſhall bring down this nominal rent of ten ſhillings, an acre, a year, to little more than five.

Twenty pounds, an acre, have been offered for twenty acres of the beſt of this coppice wood; under the conditions of being

* The "CUSTOMARY ACRE" of this Diſtrict is calculated on eighteen feet to the perch: five provincial acres being about equal to ſix ſtatute acres.

35. RENTAL VALUE. being allowed two years for the felling of it; — and to pay at Christmas for the quantity taken down in the preceding year; agreeably to the usual custom of the District.

This farther delay of the receipt of the principal, and the attendant loss of interest, is a farther reduction of the annual rent of the land; yet is seldom, perhaps, taken into the account, in calculating the net produce of woodlands.

On calculation, I find that twenty pounds an acre, for wood of thirty years growth, does not neat more than seven shillings and nine pence an acre, received annually, and put out, at simple interest, at five percent. At four percent, and reckoning nothing for interest on the accumulating interest (which in a course of years would amount to a considerable sum), this price does not neat more than eight shillings and five pence an acre, a year, received annually as rent; even supposing the whole money to be paid down at the time of sale.

RECLAIMING COPPICE GROUND. About thirty acres of this tract of wood-land lies on a culturable slope; and would be-

be worth, in a ſtate of full cultivation, fif- 35. RECLAIMING COPPICE GROUND.
teen to twenty ſhillings an acre: whereas, in a ſtate of woodland, it has probably never paid more than one third of the money; and is not, in reality, worth more than half of it.

The propriety of reclaiming it, from its preſent unprofitable ſtate, admits not of diſpute; and, the means of bringing it into cultivation is the only point which remains to be determined.

To dig up the roots entirely, ſo as to admit the plow, in the firſt inſtance, would not only be expenſive; but, by bringing up the ſubſtrata, the cultivated ſoil would be debaſed, and rendered unproductive for a courſe of years.

But, by clearing away the whole, level with the ground, or a little within the ſurface of it; and dreſſing this freed ſurface with lime, in order to diſſolve, the more readily, the leaves and decayed wood with which it is thickly covered; and by giving a degree of evenneſs to the ſurface with the harrow and the roller; ſowing ſuitable graſs ſeeds between the operations; a ſheep-walk

35. RECLAIMING COPPICE GROUND. walk would be immediately obtained; and, in a few years, when the roots were decayed, and a turf formed over them, the land might be broken up with ease and profit *.

36.

COPPICE WOOD. FEBRUARY 13. (See the last MINUTE.) A few days ago, I sold the whole of this coppice wood, at the high price of twenty two pounds ten shillings an acre; and under the following favorable conditions †.

CONDITIONS OF SALE. The whole to be taken down in two years; namely, in the years 1793 and

1794.

* For former Remarks on this Method of Reclaiming Woodlands, see YORK. ECON. Vol. I. page 316.

† These Conditions are Inserted, here, for the general purpose of giving the Reader an opportunity of comparing them with those of other Districts; and to assist, eventually, in drawing Forms of CONDITIONS OF SALES; which, as FORMS OF LEASES, are at present, in a degree vague and unfixed.

1794.—One hundred pounds of the purchaſe money to be paid down each year, previouſly to the commencement of the cutting; one moiety of the remainder of the amount of what ſhall be taken down in each year, at Midſummer; the other moiety at the enſuing Chriſtmas. The purchaſer to be allowed a ſquare perch for each tree ſtanding among the coppice wood, and a quarter of a perch, for each ſtandle of the laſt cutting. To finiſh the cuttings, by Midſummer, and to clear the ground, by the Chriſtmas following, in each year, &c. &c. 36.

CONDITIONS OF SALE.

Previouſly to this advantageous bargain, I had an offer of twenty pounds an acre, for the whole, to be taken down in five years.

SALE OF COPPICE WOOD.

The difference between theſe two prices appears, on a ſuperficial view of them, to be little more than a hundred pounds. But if the intereſt of money, and the growth of the ſucceeding wood be taken into the calculation, the ſuperior advantages of the latter will be found to amount to more than two hundred pounds: as appears in the following ſtatement.

36.
SALE OF COPPICE WOOD.

First, forty five acres, at 20l. an acre, and taking down nine acres a year.

	Princ. £.	Int.		£.	s.	d.
1st Year,	180	00	Growth of Wood at 8s.	3	12	0
2d	180	9	———	7	4	0
3d	180	18	———	10	16	0
4th	180	27	———	14	8	0
5th	180	36	———	18	0	0
	900 Prin.	90		54	0	0

90 Interest
54 Growth of Wood.

£.1044 the total Advantage, at the end of five years.

Secondly, forty five acres at 22l. 10s. and twenty two and a half acres, a year.

	Princ. £.	s.	d.	Int. £.	s.	d.		£.	s.	d.
1st Year,	506	5	0	00	0	0	Growth of Wood,	9	0	0
2d	506	5	0	25	6	3	———	18	0	0
3d	00	0	0	50	12	6	———	18	0	0
4th	00	0	0	50	12	6	———	18	0	0
5th	00	0	0	50	12	6	———	18	0	0
	1012	10	0	177	3	9		81	0	0

177 3 9 Interest
81 0 0 Growth of Wood.

1270 13 9 total Advantage at the end of five years.
1044 0 0 as above

£.226 13 9 superior Advantage *.

FEBRUARY

* Those Statements are published, for the instruction of those, to whom calculations of this kind may not be familiar. The use of them is obvious.

37.

FEBRUARY 14. The ſide walls of an ancient monaſtic building having fled from the upright,—by the buttreſſes in front having given way at the foundation, and by the back wall being impelled forward, by a load of earth and a road, behind it,—(the ground, on the outſide, being ſeveral feet higher than on the inſide) I have ſecured, in the manner hereafter deſcribed.

What rendered this caſe the more difficult was the circumſtance of both walls requiring ſupport; yet both of them inclining the ſame way; ſo that there was no *tie* to be got, nor any *purchaſe* to be had.

If the front wall had been ſtayed, by freſh buttreſſes; ſtill the back wall (againſt which the preſſure immediately acted) would have remained, in a degree unſupported. There are, in this, as in other Gothic buildings, no binding beams to the roof; nor any other tie between the two

37. SECURING BUILDINGS.

walls, than the floor beams of a chamber. Beſide, buttreſſes, in front, would have been inconvenient, and unſightly; and, like other ſupports on the *outſides* of buildings, would have been liable to the drip of the eaves, and to the effects of the weather.

The expedient, which I hit upon, was that of raiſing ſtrong BUTTRESSES, on the INSIDE OF THE BUILDING, againſt the back wall; which is thus firmly ſtayed, and effectually prevented from farther inclination; and, at the ſame time, firm purchaſes are obtained, for the purpoſe of tying in the front wall; which has been done in ſuch a manner as will probably be the means of prolonging the duration of the building,—a few more ages of time.

The ties, in this caſe, are large oak floor-beams; which are ſecurely fixed, in front, to the old buttreſſes; and, to the back wall, by means of large blocks of granite or moorſtone; in ſhape, the lower fruſtums of ſquare pyramids. Theſe blocks are laid in, fluſh with the outſide of the wall, and with their baſes outward; beds or receſſes having been accurately cut out of the rocklike

rocklike ſubſtance of the wall, to receive them. 37.

SECURING BUILDINGS.

Through theſe blocks, paſs ſtrong iron bars, or pins; which are firmly ſtrapped to the ends of the beams (bearing on the tops of the buttreſſes); and which are ſecured, and the ties drawn tight, by means of ſtrong wedges or keys, drawing againſt broad firm diſks of iron, bearing againſt the perforated blocks; which thus operate as dovetails to the ties.

BUILDING BUTTRESSES.

In building theſe buttreſſes, the foundations, as well as each courſe of ſtones, were made to dip towards the wall, in the ſame proportion as the buttreſſes incline, or batter: the courſes being kept at right angle to the line of batter, or face of the buttreſs:—a principle which ought not to be deviated from. For, by adhering to it, the reſiſtance is rendered the greateſt; and, by placing the buttreſs in a falling poſture, towards the wall, it ſettles the more firmly againſt it; while, by toothing the one into the other, as has been done in this caſe, the whole ſettles, intimately and firmly, into one incorporate maſs.

38.

SHEEP FARMING.

TEMPORARY GRASS-LANDS.

FEBRUARY 16. On a farm on which SHEEP are a principal object, TEMPORARY LEYS productive of sheep feed become, likewise, an object of the first magnitude. The practice of mowing, the first year, leys intended for five or six years duration, is a crime for which nothing, but necessity, is admissible as an excuse. By this improvident step, the sward or turf is rendered thin of plants, for several succeeding years. Not only the more delicate species of herbage, which seldom fail to rise after a short course of aration, are liable to be checked or smothered, by the luxuriant growth, and impervious shade, of cultivated herbage; but the cultivated herbs, themselves, are in some certain degree weakened, and their number decreased; especially if the soil be much exhausted, or be out of tilth.

On

On this farm, a ſtriking inſtance of the miſchief ariſing from the practice of mowing ſuch leys, the firſt year, is at this time moſt evident. The young ley grounds, which were mown laſt ſummer, may be ſaid to be now unoccupied; except by daiſies, groundſel, and a few other weeds. One of them, though the land is of a ſuperior quality, is not worth, for the coming year, five ſhillings an acre. Whereas, had it been paſtured down, cloſe, laſt ſpring and ſummer, it would, in all probability, have been worth five times that rent---for this and ſeveral ſucceeding years,---as a ſheep paſture. 38. TEMPORARY GRASS-LANDS.

To every farm, on which cultivated leys, of five or ſix years duration, make a part of the plan of management, the moſt deſirable appendage is a ſufficiency of MEADOW LANDS, or PERENNIAL MOWING GROUNDS, to furniſh the farm with a ſupply of hay, without being under the neceſſity of mowing temporary leys, the firſt year; and happily circumſtanced is the farm, whoſe ſituation, with reſpect to the quality and quantity of water it commands, enables it PLAN OF FARMING.

38. to produce, by IRRIGATION, a ſufficiency of hay, to carry its requiſite liveſtock, through the winter months.

WATERED MEADOWS.

The demeſne lands of this eſtate are fortunately in this ſituation. Some twenty or thirty acres of them have been more or leſs watered, time immemorial; and with water of a ſuperior quality.

NATURE OF WATER.

The effects of the ſlate-rock waters of this Diſtrict are ſuperior to thoſe of any others I have had an opportunity of obſerving; the chalk waters of Wiltſhire and Hampſhire excepted. There are ſlopes of hills on this and the ſurrounding farms, which are now as green and *groſs*, to the eye at a diſtance, as the rankeſt wheat in May *.

STUDYING SITES OF IMPROVEMENT.

Seeing theſe advantages, I have been aſſiduous to aſcertain the facts reſpecting the poſſibility of watering the different parts of this eſtate; and I found, ſome time ago (ſee MIN. 27.), that almoſt every acre of it is *capable* of being flooded, artificially, by running water. The QUANTITY OF WATER,

* It is everywhere obſervable, and is moſt intereſting, that the ſteeper the ſlope, the more obvious is the effect.

WATER, however, that can be conveyed to it, though ſufficient to furniſh paſturing ſtock, with a valuable ſupply of beverage, is too ſmall for the purpoſes of irrigation. 38.

STUDYING SITES OF IMPROVEMENT.

But the miſchiefs ariſing from the practice of mowing ley grounds, the firſt year, having lately preſſed more cloſely on my mind, I have been ſtudying, with redoubled attention, the capacity of the different grounds of this farm, with reſpect to water. And I have diſcovered, that a ſufficiency of them, to anſwer, fully, the purpoſes required, are capable of receiving an abundant ſupply of water; and that ſuch a ſupply may be brought to them, at a ſmall expence.

WATERING SLOPES,

But the waters which are already within the farm, claiming the firſt attention, I have, hitherto, been endeavouring to turn them to the beſt advantage; by conducting them properly over the lands which moſt command them.

This has been effected by taking the water out of its natural channel, at different heights, and conveying it to the ſeveral ſtages of the ſlopes, over which theſe lands are

38. are spread, by means of main floats, leats, or artificial rills, for the purpose of feeding the floating trenches, which distribute and spread the water over the faces of the slopes.

WATERING SLOPES.

PROCESS OF IRRIGATION.

In setting out and forming these conducting channels, I have found the frame level and cross safe and ready assistants; and the descent of one measure in a hundred most eligible;—as giving a lively motion to the water, and a firm bottom to the channel, without wearing away its sides.

In conducting channels of this intention, across grounds much varied in surface, and where a degree of ornament is required to be joined with use, as was the case in this instance, some attention is requisite. If the ground be implicitly followed with the level, not only a circuitous length of channel and a waste of land, but short angular unsightly bends, are produced. If, on the contrary, straight lines are attempted across a varied surface, the labor of raising the hollows, and sinking the knolls, is great, and the beauty of the line is wholly lost. Hence, where the ground does not naturally

rally afford the given line, the MIDDLE COURSE is requisite to be chosen. 38. PROCESS OF IRRIGATION.

In this instance of practice, I have found it best to set out the line, first by the level, crooked or straight, as the ground directs; then, to give it the required direction, by the eye; and, afterward, to correct the eye with the plummet; lest the line should lie much too high or too low, in any particular part:—for a steepsided trench is liable to be trodden in by cattle, and a sharp ridgey bank is equally liable to be torn down by their tread: while, over a shallow trench, and a broad swelling bank, they step without injury.

LAYINGOUT WATERED LANDS.

But, in watering the hangs of hills where a blank site is given, and where no fences already exist, there are few cases, perhaps, in which the main floats should be liable to the passage of stock. The uppermost is, of course, laid as high as the flowing level from the source will allow, and necessarily divides the watered from the unwatered lands; and is, of course, a *given* line of fence. If the valley be narrow, or the foot of the slope, which commands the water,

38. LAYING OUT WATERED LANDS.

water, be short, one main floating trench is sufficient. For by running parallel trenchlets along the face of the slope, at once to collect the dispersed waters, from above, and to distribute them more evenly below; and by letting down a supply of water to the lower trenchlets, when the upper side of the slope is sufficiently watered; one main float is sufficient to supply a field's width of land. And, if a continuation of the slope require it, another main float, and another fence, may, and in general ought to run parallel to the first.

There are two reasons why fences of this sort should be placed on the *upper side* of the floating rill. The water is more easily let off, into the working trenches, than it would through a fence; and especially through a hedge; whose roots, and the holes of the vermin they harbor, would be the cause of a continual waste of water.

Viewing fences, thus winding along the wavy surface of a slope, in the light of ornament, a light in which they ought to appear within this demesne, an additional motive, for running them along the side of a wavy a wavy rill, ariſes. If the broad ſwelling bank, which ought to accompany ſuch a rill on the lower ſide, were formed into a walk,—determined in width, and always kept dry, by a working trench, on its lower margin,—the bank would be rendered firm, by the preſſure of the foot, and, in this inſtance, a delightful ſtroll will be obtained, at an eaſy coſt. 38.

LAYING OUT WATERED LANDS.

39.

PLOWING WITH TWO OXEN.

FEBRUARY 20. I have at length the pleaſure of ſeeing a TWO-OX PLOW compleatly in its work. Two oxen, in yoke, with a ſingle chain paſſing from it, to the draft iron of the plow, and driven, with whip reins, by the plowman, have been employed, during the laſt fortnight, in giving the firſt fleet plowing of turnep grounds: a work which they perform with eaſe and diſpatch.

This is the ſimpleſt and cheapeſt plow-

team

39. team I have yet ſet to work. The yoke and ſingle chain, if made light and well fitted to the oxen, are, for a two-ox plow, in light work, much preferable to collars, traces, and ſplinter bars; which are complex, expenſive, and for ever entangling with the reins; and the ſplinter bars are a heavy incumbrance, at the head of a light ſwing plow.

PLOWING WITH TWO OXEN.

SEPTEMBER, 1794. This ſummer, I have had two of theſe admirable plow-teams, in full work: employing them, chiefly, in ſtirring fallows; which they do with great effect: plowing eight or nine inches deep, with plows which clear their work. To make the labor the leſs, and the operation the more effective, the ſlices are cut narrow; not more than ſix or ſeven inches wide; by which means this cheap and eaſy plowing becomes nearly equal to ſpade work;—more effective than any number of the partial plowings, uſually given to broken ground, in this Diſtrict.

MARCH

40.

MARCH 12. In the Autumn of 1791, I designed and set out, and have now brought into a train of finishing, a suite of FARM YARDS and BUILDINGS, on a large scale. See MINUTE 29. FARMERY OF BUCKLAND.

I have not leisure to register, in detail, the minutiæ of this improvement; but a few particulars strike.

A DUNG YARD of a semi-octagon form, inclosed, on one side, with cattle sheds, and, on the other, by a line of stables and farm offices; with opposite gates and a carriage road, by the side of the latter; is, in every point of view, in which I have yet seen it, very eligible. CATTLE YARDS.

BATTERING FOUNDATION WALLS. The surface of this yard, by reason of the form of the ground (see page 317.), necessarily rises, in one part of it, nine or ten feet, above the road, which passes on the outside of the sheds; consequently, the weight of earth, BUILDING.

from lodging upon them; and thereby to 40.
elude, as much as poſſible, the decay of the CATTLE SHEDS.
timber.

The proper WIDTH OF A STALL, for two middle-ſized working oxen, is ſeven feet. Cows, though of ſmaller ſize than oxen, require as much or more room, for the conveniency of milking them, and ſuckling their calves. A danger of making ſtalls too wide is that of the cattle turning round in them; and by that means placing themſelves, in an aukward and dangerous ſituation, with reſpect to their fellows. This danger, however, is to be guarded againſt by a poſt riſing in the middle of the ſtall, immediately before the ſhoulders of the cattle; in a line with the front poſts of the PARTIAL PARTITIONS*: and a poſt in this place may be found uſeful to faſten calves to, during the time of ſuckling.

The proper LENGTH OF STALLS, for Devonſhire oxen, of the larger ſize, is nine feet; namely, three feet the width of the trough, and ſix feet the platform, or reſting

* See Mid. Econ. Vol. I. P. 33.

carried up; but very much battering, or 40.
falling back towards the ſheds; the angle DUNG PITS.
of inclination, from the perpendicular, being not leſs than thirty degrees. The foundation of this wall was dug, and the courſes of ſtones laid, not horizontally, but at right angle, or ſquare, with the line of reclination; the earth being firmly rammed in behind, as the wall was carried up. The uppermoſt or coping ſtones are large and ſtrong; ſerving as bonds to the wall, and as a buttreſs to the convex pavement, above mentioned; which preſſes againſt theſe coping ſtones, on one ſide, and againſt thoſe which form the outer edge of the platforms of the ſtalls, on the other, as an arch bears on its butments.

On a ſtage below this principal dung-yard, and on the upper ſide of the barn, a STRAWYARD, for looſe cattle, and ſtore ſwine, is ſhaped out of the ſlope of the hill on which this farmery is ſituated. And behind the range of offices, which form one ſide of the dung yard, is another ſtraw yard. And between theſe two ſtraw yards is a MILKING YARD.

40. WATERING YARDS.

These three yards are WATERED, by means of the made rill, which has been spoken of, in MINUTE 27; and which passes through these yards, in channels, partially or wholly open, for the use of stock; and thence through a covered drain, to its natural channel. In passing through the principal strawyard, it runs along the top of a dwarf wall, or offset (at the foot of a fence wall), twelve or fifteen inches high, from the level of the yard; and about fourteen inches wide; with a channel, six inches deep on the back part, shelving upward to an angle in front; and divided by upright stones, placed edgeway across the rill; which has, here, a considerable descent: consequently, each obstruction forms an eddy, small pool, or drinking place; eight or ten head of cattle being able to drink, at the same time, and with the most perfect conveniency.

Finding, by experience, that too copious a supply of water is, on many accounts, troublesome, in a rill of this intention, I ascertained the exact size of the stream required, by means of gauges of different dimensions,

menſions, ſet acroſs the channel. And having found, that a bore of two inches diameter gave the deſired ſupply, I have fixed a ſtone, perforated with a bore of this diameter, in a penſtock of oak, and placed this acroſs the channel, above the yards, with a waſte water channel, immediately above it; ſo that an inordinate ſupply of water, ſent down, by rains or otherwiſe, is effectually prevented. 40.

WATERING YARDS.

FARM YARD ECONOMY.

In this yard, the ſtall cattle are to be watered, and to be allowed to amuſe themſelves, in the middle of the day; while the ſtore ſwine are collecting in the dung yard, whatever the ſtalls or the ſtables may afford them; being carefully kept out of that yard, while the cattle are in their ſtalls: a principle of management, which can never be departed from, with propriety.

YARD LIQUOR.

The ſuperfluous rain water, or YARD LIQUOR, of theſe ſeveral yards, paſs off, in the following manner. That of the dung yard (as well as thoſe of the inferior yards) paſſes, firſt, into the principal ſtraw yard; in a pit, or hollow part, of which it makes its firſt depoſit. From hence the collected

40. YARD LIQUOR.

waters will be led through paved courts, and a ſtable yard,—collecting in their paſſage, and by proper aſſiſtance, in times of rain, the ſulliage which ſuch places are ever accumulating,—to a common receptacle; where, having depoſited their groſſer feculencies, they will fall immediately into the main float that has been mentioned, mix with its ſtream, and aſſiſt in fertilizing the meadow lands which lie below theſe yards,

INDEX.

INDEX

TO THE

TWO VOLUMES.

A.

ABSTRACT RIGHTS, West Devon, i. 48.
Acre, Customary, its Contents, ii. 333.
After Grass, West Devon, i. 211.
Agricultural Practices of Districts; Reflections on their Origins, i. 131.
——— Societies, Remarks on, ii. 301.
Agriculture, a Branch of Rural Economy, i. 55.
———, West Devon, i. 98.
———, South Hams, i. 292.
———, on the Improvement of, South Devon, i. 317.
———, Vale of Exeter, ii. 116.
———, West Dorset, ii. 141.
Analysis of Slate Rock, i. 16.
——— of Sea Sands, i. 154.
——— of Waters, wanted, i. 209.
Appearance of the Country, West Devon, i. 40.
——— of the South Hams, i. 289.
——— of South Cornwall, ii 9.
——— of the Mountains of Cornwall, ii. 15.
——— of Exmore, ii. 79.
——— of the Vale of Exeter, ii. 110.
——— of West Dorset, ii. 138.
Apples, Disposal of, by Number, i. 301.
———, Remarks on, as a Food of Swine, N. i. 223.
Apprentices, West Devon, i. 110.
———, their improper Treatment, i. 111.

A a 4 Arrange-

Arrangements and Tables of Agriculture, ii. 249.
Arrish Mows, Method of Making, i. 171.
Artificial Grasses, i. 202.
——— Rills, West Devon, i. 61.
Associations of Landed Gentlemen, proposed, ii. 303.
Auction of Devonshire, i. 71.

B.

BARK, its Market in West Devon, i. 56.
Barley, Thrashing, in West Devon, i. 183.
———, and its Management, West Devon, i. 191.
Bampton, and its Environs, ii. 87.
———, Barrow, ii. 88.
Barn of Buckland, ii. 307.
Barnstaple and its Environs, ii. 69.
——— to South Moulton, ii. 70.
Barometer, its Uses, i. 129.
Barrow of Bampton, ii. 88.
Battering Foundation Walls, Remarks on, ii. 351.
Beaminster Down, Views from, ii. 139.
Beans, Vale of Exeter, ii. 118.
Beasts of Labor, West Devon, i. 113.
——— ———, South Hams, i. 293.
Beasts of Labor, South Cornwall, ii. 7.
——— ———, Vale of Exeter, ii. 116.
——— ———, West Dorset, ii. 142.
——— ———, South Somerset, ii. 219.
——— ———, the Oxen of Devon excellent as, i. 242.
Beat Burning, i. 144.
Beating Axe, i. 141.
Beech, its Natural Characters, i. 66.
Bees, Remarks on, ii. 222.
Biddeford and its Environs, ii. 57.
——— to Barnstaple, ii. 65.
Blackdown Hills, ii. 174.
Bleeding Cattle for the Slaughter, i. 247.
Blue Slates — see List of Rates, i.
Boar or Eagre, Remarks on, N. ii. 180.
Bodmin, ii. 10.
——— to Buckland, an Excursion, ii. 10.
Boiling the Food of Swine, i. 258.
Box Clubs, i. 29.
Breast Plow, i. 142.
Breed of Cattle, West Devon, i. 240.
——— ———, South Somerset, ii. 221.
——— Sheep, West Devon, and Remarks thereon, i. 159.

Breeding

Breeding Cattle, West Devon, i. 243.
——— ———, Remarks on West Devon, ii. 247.
——— Swine, West Devon, i. 255.
——— Sheep, West Devon, i. 264.
——— Livestock, on the Improvement of, South Devon, i. 316.
Brent Tor, a remarkable Eminence, N. ii. 22.
Bridge of Biddeford, and Extraordinary Erection, ii. 57.
Brook, Artificial of Plymouth noticed, ii. 244.
——— of Plymouth, described, ii. 269.
Brooks Artificial, their Antiquity in Devonshire, ii. 271.
——— ———, Remarks on, ii. 272.
Buckland, Flock of Sheep, i. 262.
——— to Bodmin, an Excursion, ii. 3.
——— Place described, ii. 235.
——— Farm described, ii. 237.
———, Improvements of, suggested, ii. 286.
——— Barn, ii. 307.
——— Farmery, ii. 317.
——— Farmery, further Remarks on, ii. 351.
Building Materials, West Devon, i. 27. and 62.
——— ———, Vale of Exeter, ii. 112.
——— against Banks of Earth, ii. 351.
——— the Sides of Pits, Remarks on, ii. 355.
Buildings, Remarks on Securing, ii. 339.
Burning Beat, i. 145.
——— off the Heath of Wastes, ii. 31.
Burnt Clay, Remarks on, as a Manure, ii. 101.
Busses, or Grass Calves, West Devon, i. 249.
Butter, West Devon, i. 249.
Buttresses, on the Situation of, ii. 340.
———, on Building, ii. 341.

C.

CABBAGES, Remarks on Cutting, ii. 300.
Calculations on the Sale Value of Coppice Wood, ii. 337.
Callington, ii. 10.
Calstock, Village of, ii. 240.
Calves, West Devon, i. 248.
Canal Proposed, between Plymouth and Biddeford, ii. 38.
——— ———, Vale of Exeter, ii. 106.

Canker,

Canker, Remarks on, i. 220.
Carriage done on Horseback, i. 113.
Carrying Corn, on Horseback, i. 176.
Cart Horses, West Devon, i. 117.
Cattle, West Devon, i. 239.
—— of Devonshire described, i. 240.
——, Conjectures on the Native Breed of, in this Island, i. 241.
—— of Cornwall, i. 243.
——, South Hams, i. 302.
——, on the Improvement, of South Devon, i. 316.
——, South Cornwall, ii. 7.
——, of the Mountains of Cornwall, ii. 14.
——, Dartmore, ii. 26.
——, of South Moulton, ii. 75.
——, Vale of Exeter, ii. 119.
——, West Dorset, ii. 149.
——, South Sedgemore, ii. 182.
——, South Somerset, ii. 220.
——, Skirts of Dartmore, ii. 243.
——, Valley of the Tamer, ii. 247.
——, Remarks on the Short-horned Breed, ii. 248.
——, of Buckland, Remarks on Breeding, ii. 291.
Cattle affect Charlock or Wild Mustard, ii. 297.
——, Bleeding, for the Slaughter, i. 247.
——, Breeding, West Devon, i. 243.
——, Fatting, West Devon, i. 246.
——, Rearing, West Devon, i. 245.
—— Sheds, their proper Width, ii. 352.
—— Stalls, their proper Dimensions, ii. 351.
——, Working, West Devon. i. 116.
Cement, Remark on its Nature, ii. 308.
Chalk, West Dorset, ii. 131.
Charlock, as Food of Cattle, ii. 297.
Cheese, West Devon, i. 254.
Cherry, a Coppice Wood, in West Devon, i. 85.
Chesnut, a Coppice Wood, in West Devon, i. 84.
Chemistry, applicable to the Analysis of Waters, i. 209.
———— of Agriculture, applicable to Tanning, i. 96.
Chinese Policy, with respect to Mines, i. 40.
Cider Rooms, i. 224.
—— Press of Devon, i. 228.
——, General Observations on, i. 233.
—— Management, Improvement of, South Devon, i. 315.

Clay,

Clay, Burnt, Remarks on, as a Manure, ii. 161.
Clearing Arable Land from Stones, ii. 276.
Climature, West Devon, i. 11. and 129.
———, South Cornwall, ii. 4.
———, Mountains of Cornwall, ii. 11.
——— of Dartmore, its Means of Improvement, ii. 31.
———, its Means of Improvement, on the lower Lands of Dartmore, ii. 35.
———, Okehampton to Torrington, ii. 53.
———, Environs of Biddeford, ii. 64.
———, Biddeford to Barnstaple, ii. 68.
———, Dulverton to Tiverton, ii. 91.
———, Vale of Exeter, ii. 100.
———, West Dorset, ii. 128.
———, Vale of Taunton, ii. 167.
———, South Somerset, ii. 216.
———, Valley of the Tamer, ii. 241.
Clouting Cream, Method of, i. 247.
——— ———, Remarks on, i. 251.
——— ———, Remarks on its probable Continuance, ii. 120.
Coating Buildings, General Remarks on, ii. 295.
Cob Walls, Method of Forming, i. 62.
———, Vale of Exeter, ii. 111.
Colic of Devon, described, i. 235.
Colonization, Remarks on, ii. 224.
Common Rights, East Devon, ii. 135.
Commonable Lands, Improvement of, ii. 153.
Commons, their Cultivation in West Devon, i. 32.
———, Cultivation of, North Devon, ii. 46.
———, General Remarks on their Cultivation, ii. 132.
Conditions of Sale of Coppice Wood, ii. 336.
Conducting Made Rills, ii. 311.
——— ———, Further Remarks, ii. 323.
Conversion of Coppice Wood, i. 95.
Coppice Fences, on Pruning, ii. 266.
——— Grounds, Remarks on Reclaiming, ii. 334.
——— Wood, Species of, West Devon, i. 84.
——— ———, Management of, i. 90.
——— ———, Age of Cutting, ii. 332.

Coppice

Coppice Wood of Buckland, ii. 332.
———, Conditions of Sale of, ii. 336.
———, Rental Value of, ii. 332.
Cordwood, Dimensions and Price, i. 95.
———, Selling by Weight, N. i. 95.
Corn Mills of Devon. i. 30.
Corn Stacks, Form of, i. 178.
———, Thatching, i. 178.
——— Swaths, Method of Turning, i. 173.
———, Method of Binding, i. 174.
Cornish Wain, i. 120. and ii. 7.
Cornwall, Excursion in, ii. 3.
———, General Observations on, ii. 10.
———, Stroll into, ii. 293.
Covering Materials, West Devon, i. 64.
Course of Practice, West Devon, i. 135.
Course of Crops, West Devon, i. 136.
Crewkerne to Chard, N. ii. 125.
Crooks. i. 121.
Crops, West Devon. i. 134.
———, South Hams, i. 295.
———, South Cornwall, ii. 7.
Crops, Vale of Exeter, ii. 117.
———, West Dorset. ii. 144.
———, Vale of Taunton, ii. 170.
Cultivated Herbage, and its Management, i. 202.
Cultivating Leys, Remarks on, i. 311.
Cultivation, its Probable Progress in Devonshire, i. 32.
——— of Commons, North Devon. ii. 46.
Customary Acre, its Contents, ii. N. 333.

D.

DAIRY Management, West Devon, i 248. and ii. 148.
———, Vale of Exeter, ii. 120.
———, District, ii. 123.
———, Men, West Devon, ii. 150.
Dairies, Letting, Remarks on, ii. 150.
Danmonian Husbandry, Retrospective View of, ii. 225.
———, Peculiarities of, ii. 226.
Dartmore, and its Uncultivated Environs, ii. 17.
———, its present Value, ii. 27.

Dartmore,

Dartmore, Improvements of, proposed, ii. 29.
———, Ride on the Skirts of, ii. 242.
Deer, Wild, formerly common, in West Devon, i. 165.
Destroying Earth Worms, ii. 315.
Devizes, ii. 214.
Devonshire Cattle, compared with other Breeds, i. 240.
——— Colic, Remarks on, i. 235.
District, West Devonshire, i. 7.
———, South Hams, i. 277.
———, North Devonshire, ii. 41.
———, Vale of Exeter, ii. 97.
———, West Dorset, ii. 123.
———, Vale of Taunton, ii. 163.
———, Plymouth to Buckland, ii. 235.
———, Valley of the Tamer, ii. 239.
———, Skirts of Dartmore, ii. 242.
———, Environs of Tamerton, ii. 245.
———, Banks of the Tavey, ii. 264.
———, Buckland to Plymton, ii. 273.
———, Milton Abbots, ii. 294.
Districts Agricultural, i. 2.
——— Natural, i. 2.
——— of West of England, i. 5.
Dog of the West Devon Shepherds, i. 266.
Doors, Remarks on Hanging, ii. 319.
———, Further Remarks on Hanging, ii. 321.
Dorsetshire Breed of Sheep, i. 261.
Draining proposed, as an Improvement of Dartmore, ii. 33.
Dray of Devonshire, i. 120.
Drinking Pools, Remarks on Forming, with Walnut-tree Leaves, ii. 315.
Driving Oxen, i. 116.
Drudge, or Team Rake, i. 125.
Duchy of Cornwall's Rights on Dartmore, ii. 25.
Dulverton and its Environs, ii. 82.
——— to Tiverton, ii. 85.
Dung, West Devon, i. 153.
——— Pit of Buckland, ii. 354.

E.

Earth of Heath, Remarks on, as a Manure, ii. 162.
——— Walls, Vale of Exeter, ii. 113.

Earth

Earth Worms, Method of destroying, ii. 315.
Eighteen Months Fallow, Eligibility of, ii. 280.
Elevation, West Devon, i. 10.
———, South Hams, i. 278.
———, South Cornwall, ii. 3.
———, Mountains of Cornwall, ii. 10.
———, Dartmore, ii. 21.
———, Vale of Exeter, ii. 98.
——— West Dorset, ii. 126.
———, Vale of Taunton, ii. 166.
———, South Somerset, ii. 216.
Elm of Hedgerows, Remarks on, ii. 105.
——— Timber improved by judicious Lopping, ii. 115.
Embankment near Bideford, ii. 62.
Employments, West Devon, i. 28.
Established Practices, their Importance, i. 135.
Estates, West Devon, i. 57.
———, Laying out, West Devon, i. 59.
———, their Management, West Devon, i. 58.
———, their Management, with respect to the Sizes of Farms, i. 103.
———, Management of, Vale of Exeter, ii. 111.
Excursion in Cornwall, ii. 3.
Excursion, through North Devonshire, ii. 41.
Exmore, its Appearance, ii. 79.
Extent, West Devon, i. 9.
———, South Hams, i. 277.
———, Dartmore, ii. 20.
———, Vale of Exeter, ii. 98.
———, West Dorsetshire, ii. 126.
———, Vale of Taunton, ii. 165.

F.

FACE of the Country, West Devon, i. 40.
———, South Hams, i. 289.
Fair of Tamerton, ii. 246.
——— Plymton, ii. 274.
Fairs for Stock, West Devon, i. 185.
——— of West Devon, Remark on, ii. 248.
Fall of Rills ascertained, ii. 312.
Fallowing, a successful Instance of, i. 140.
——— proposed as an Improvement of South Devonshire, i. 312.
———, Process of, ii. 278.
——— Eighteen Months, its Eligibility, ii. 280.
Farms, Disposal of, i. 69.
———, Occupying, i. 70.
———, Selling, for three Lives, i. 71.

Farms,

Farms, their Characters, West Devon, i. 98.
——, Sizes of, West Devon, i. 101.
——, General Observations on the Sizes of, i. 102.
——, Plans of, West Devon, i. 104.
——, Management of, West Devon, i. 130.
——, Management, South Hams, i. 294.
——, South Hams, i. 292.
——, Vale of Exeter, ii. 116.
——, West Dorset, ii. 141.
——, South Somerset, ii. 219.
Farm Apprentices, their political Value, i. 112.
—— Buildings, Vale of Exeter, ii. 112.
—— Lands, Laying out, West Devon, i. 60.
—— ——, their History, West Devon, i. 100.
—— ——, their Distribution, Vale of Exeter, ii. 111.
—— Yard Management, West Devon, i. 179.
—— —— —— ——, on the Improvement of, South Devon, i. 312.
—— Yards, on the Improvement of, South Devon, i. 308.
—— ——. General Economy of, ii. 357.
Farm-Yards of Buckland, Final Remarks on, ii. 351.
—— ——, on Watering, ii. 356.
Farmers, West Devon, i. 104.
——, South Hams, i. 292.
——, West Dorset, ii. 142.
Farmeries, West Devon, i. 60.
—— ——, Remarks on Laying out, ii. 317.
Farmery of Buckland, ii. 317.
—— —— ——, further Remarks on, ii. 351.
Fatting Cattle, West Devon, i. 246.
—— Sheep, West Devon, i. 270.
—— Swine, and Remarks thereon, i. 257.
Felling Coppices, i. 93.
—— Timber, an Instance of shameful Practice, i. 88.
Fences, West Devon, i. 65.
—— Danmonian, their probable Origin, &c. i. 66.
——, South Hams, i. 288.
——, South Cornwall, ii. 7.
——, East Cornwall, ii. 14.
——, Okehampton to Torrington, ii. 53.
——, Vale of Taunton, ii. 169.
——, Danmonian, its Termination, Vale of Taunton, ii. 169.
——, on Pruning, ii. 266.
——, further Remarks on Training, ii. 275.

Fence

Fence Mounds, as an Improvement of bleak Situations, ii. 31.
Fish, West Devon, i. 35.
—— Poachers, ii. 261.
Fishery of the Tavey, ii. 260.
—— ——, Improvement of proposed, ii. 292.
Flowing Level of Rills ascertained, ii. 313.
Fodder Straw, West Devon, i. 184.
Food, West Devon, i. 27.
Form of Lease, South Devon, i. 77.
—— ——, on the Improvement of, South Devon, i. 309.
Forming Roads, Remarks on, ii. 331.
Fossils, West Devon, i. 18.
——, West Dorset, ii. 150.
Foundation Walls, on Battering, ii. 351.
Fowls, West Devon, i. 272.
——, Remarks on their Fecundity, i. 273.
Foxtail, Meadow, wanting, N. i. 205.
Frame Level Constructed, ii. 310.
—— ——, its Use in Conducting Rills, ii. 310.
—— ——, its Use in Laying out Roads, ii. 328.
Free Stone, West Devon, i. 18.
Frome, ii. 209.
—— to Devizes, ii. 210.
Fruit Liquor, West Devon, i. 213.
—— ——, General Observation on, i. 233.
Fuel, West Devon, i. 28.
Furniture of Pack Horses, i. 121.
Furze, Dwarf Trailing, N. i. 37.
Furzes of South Cornwall, ii. 9.

G.

GAME, West Devon, i. 165.
Gate Posts, Devonshire, N. ii. 114.
Gateways, Devonshire, N. ii. 115.
Geese, South Sedgemore, ii. 182.
General Principle, in the Management of Estates, i. 152.
—— Remarks on the Progress of Cultivation, in Devonshire, i. 32.
—— —— on the Salmon, i. 36.
—— —— on the Danmonian Fence, i. 65.
—— —— on Letting Farms by Auction, i. 73.
—— —— on Taking down Coppice Wood, i. 93.
—— —— on the Sizes of Farms, i. 102.

General

General Remarks on the Pointed Shovel, &c. i. 127.
——— on Provincial Practices, i. 131.
——— on Sodburning, i. 146.
——— on the Application of Lime, as a Manure, i. 160.
——— on the Breeds of Cattle, in this Island, i. 241.
——— on North Devon, ii. 77.
——— further on North Devon, ii. 93.
——— on the Lands of the Vale of Exeter, ii. 105.
——— on the Cultivation of Commons, West Dorset, ii. 132.
——— on Hedgerow Timber, ii. 154.
——— on the Southern Parts of Somersetshire, ii. 215.
——— on the Danmonian Husbandry, ii. 225.
——— on Coating Buildings, ii. 295.
——— on Conducting Rills, ii. 323.
——— on Laying out Roads, ii. 327.
——— on the Rental Value of Coppice Wood, ii. 332.
General Remarks on Watering Slopes, ii. 345.
——— on Life-Leasehold, i. 44.
——— on Seminating Wheat, i. 190.
——— on the Turnep Culture, i. 197.
——— on Orchards and Fruit Liquor, i. 233.
——— on Cornwall, ii. 16.
Geological Remarks on the Limestone of West Somersetshire, ii. 175.
———, South Somerset, ii. 217.
———, West Devon, ii. 242.
——— on the Country round Milton Abbots, ii. 294.
Glastonbury, Vale of, ii. 200.
Goad, &c. for driving Oxen, N. i. 118.
Goats, Mountains of Cornwall, ii. 14.
Gradation of Farms, Remarks on, i. 102.
Grass Calves, West Devon, i. 249.
Grasses Cultivated, i. 202.
Grasslands, and their Management, West Devon, i. 204.
———, South Hams, i. 299.
———, Vale of Exeter, ii. 118.

Grasslands, West Dorset, ii. 146.
Grazing, West Devon, ii. 247.
——— Grounds of Milton Abbots, ii. 294.
Gurry Butt, i. 121.

H.

HABITATIONS, West Devon, i. 27.
———, Vale of Exeter, ii. 109.
———, West Dorset, ii. 138.
Hams, their probable Origin, i. 33.
Handbeating, i. 142.
Hanging Doors, Remarks on, ii. 319.
———, Further Remarks on, ii. 321.
Harrows of West Devon, i. 125.
Harvested Crops, their Management, i. 179.
Harvest Holla, West Devon, N. i. 170.
Harvesting, West Devon, i. 166.
———, South Cornwall, ii. 9.
———, Management of West Devon, General Remarks on, i. 173.
Hatherly, ii. 48.
Hawthorn, uncommon, in West Devon, i. 85.
Hay Harvest, West Devon, i. 209.
Hedges, West Devon, i. 65.
———, on Pruning, ii 266.
———, Training, ii. 275.
——— Management on the Improvement of South Devon, i. 308.
——— Mounds, Guarding, ii. 275.
Hedgerows, South Hams, i. 288.
———, Vale of Exeter, ii. 113.
Hedgerow Timber, Vale of Exeter, ii. 115.
——— Timber, Management of, proposed, ii. 154.
Hedgewood, Management of, West Devon, i. 95.
Herbage of Dartmore, Improvement of proposed, ii. 31.
Hewing Wheat, West Devon, i. 168.
Hogs, West Devon, i. 257.
Homestall Management, i. 179.
Homesteads, West Devon, i. 60.
Hoing Turneps introduced, ii. 281.
Hoops, for Cider Casks, N. i. 91.
Horses, Working, West Devon, i. 115 and 117.

Horses, West Devon, i. 238.
——, Tax on, Proposed, ii. 220.
—— of the Cornish Mountains, ii. 241.
Horse Barrow, ii. 88.
Hours of Team Labor, i. 119.
House Lamb Breed of Sheep, i. 261.
——, their Quality, i. 263.
——, a Remark on, i. 265.
Housing Stacks by Hand, i. 180.
Hundred Courts, West Devon, i. 21.
Hundreds, Names of, Remarks on, ii. 244.
Husbandry Danmonian, its Termination, Vale of Taunton, ii. 170.

I.

IMPLEMENTS, West Devon, i. 119.
——, South Hams, i. 294.
——, South Cornwall, ii. 7.
——, Vale of Exeter, ii. 117.
——, West Dorset, ii. 143.
Improvement, Spirit of, West Devon, i. 106.
Improvements, their slow Progress, i. 61.
—— proposed, South Devon, i. 308.
—— of Dartmore proposed, ii. 29.
—— of Devonshire proposed, by a triple Canal, ii. 107.
——, West Dorset, ii. 152.
—— of Sedgemores, Remarks on, ii 183.
——, Preliminaries of, ii. 249.
—— of Plows, ii. 253.
——, a general Principle, on introducing, ii. 255.
—— of Buckland suggested, ii. 286.
——, how best promoted, ii. 302.
——, on Studying the Site of, ii. 344.
Inclosures, West Devon, i. 31.
——, their probable Origin in Devonshire, i. 31.
——, State of, South Hams, i. 287.
——, South Cornwall, ii. 6.
——, Mountains of Cornwall, ii. 13.
——, Okehampton to Torrington, ii. 53.

INDEX.

Inclosures, State of, Vale of Exeter, ii. 108.
——————, West Dorset, ii. 131.
——————, Vale of Taunton, ii. 169.
——————, South Somerset, ii. 217.
Inhabitants, West Devon, i. 24.
Inland Navigation, South Hams, i. 284.
—————— requisite as an Improvement of Dartmore, ii. 37.
—————— proposed, between Plymouth and Biddeford, ii. 38.
——————, Vale of Exeter, ii. 106.
——————, Vale of Taunton, ii. 168.
Introduction of Improvements, the Cautions necessary to, ii. 255.
Irrigation, its History in West Devon, i. 206.
———, West Dorset, ii. 147.
———, its Advantages, ii. 144.
Irrigating Slopes, Practical Remarks on, ii. 345.

L.

LABORERS, West Devon, i. 107.
Lambs, their time of dropping, West Devon, i. 264.
Lambs, the time of Weaning, West Devon, i. 264.
Landed Estates, West Devon, i. 57.
——————, their Management, West Devon, i. 58.
Landed Gentlemen, Associations of, proposed, ii. 303.
Langport, ii. 196.
Larch, its probable Value, in West Devon, i. 87.
Launceston, ii. 5.
Laying Land down to grass, practical directions on, ii. 159.
—————— to grass, Remarks on, ii. 342.
——— out Estates, West Devon, i. 59.
——— Farmeries, ii. 317.
——— Farm Lands, West Devon, i. 60.
——— Farm Lands, Vale of Exeter, ii. 111.
——— Roads, ii. 327.
——— Townships, N. ii. 138.
——— Watered Lands, ii. 347.
Leases, Forms of, West Devon, i. 77.
Leat of Plymouth, noticed, ii. 244.
——————, described, ii. 269.
Leats of Potwater, West Devon, i. 61.
Leskard, ii. 10.

Letting

Letting Farms, in West Devon, i. 73.
———, by Auction, general Remarks on, i. 73.
Level, a new one constructed, ii. 310.
Ley Grounds, Remarks on, i. 311.
———, on the Improvement of, South Devon, i. 314.
———, on Mowing, the first Year, ii. 342.
Life Leasehold, Tenure described, i. 43.
———, its Disadvantages, i. 44.
———, its Means of Annihilation, i. 47.
Life Leases, Mode of Selling, i. 71.
———, Conditions of, i. 72.
———; their Estimate Value, i. 72.
Lime, West Devon, i. 136.
——, General Remarks on the Application of, i. 160.
——, Method of Spreading, i. 159.
——, necessary as an Improvement of the lower Lands of Dartmore, ii. 37.
——, Preparation of for a Manure, i. 158.
——, separating the Ashes of, i. 157.
Liming Land, an Instance of Practice, ii. 322.
Lime Kilns, West Devon, i. 156.
Lime Kilns, Biddeford, ii. 58.
———, Bampton, ii. 87.
———, Calstock, ii. 240.
Limestone, West Dorset, ii. 130.
———, West Somerset, ii. 176.
———, South Somerset, ii. 217.
Linhays, described, i. 61.
List of Rates, i. 319.

M.

MANAGEMENT of Coppices, i. 90.
——— of Estates, a Branch of Rural Economy, i. 54.
——— of Estates, West Devon, i. 58.
——— of Estates, with respect to the Size of Farms, i. 103.
——— of Estates, Vale of Exeter, ii. 111.
——— of Estates, General Principle of, i. 152.
——— of Estates, a Principle suggested, ii. 157.
——— of Estates, Improvements of proposed, ii. 303.
——— of Farms, West Devon, i. 130.

Management of Farms, South Hams, i. 294.
——— of Farms, Vale of Taunton, ii. 170.
——— of Hedgewood, West Devon, i. 95.
——— of Grasslands, i. 205.
——— of growing Crops, West Devon, i. 164.
——— of the Soil, West Devon, i. 137.
——— of Soils, South Hams, i. 295.
——— of Soils, an Improvement of, West Dorset, ii. 159.
——— of Timber, in West Devon, i. 88.
——— of Woodlands, a Branch of Rural Economy, i. 55.
——— of Woodlands, West Devon, i. 87.
Manor Courts, their Advantages, i. 22.
———, West Devon, i. 49.
Manorial Rights, a singular one in Devonshire. i. 32.
———, West Devon, i. 49.
Manors, West Devon, i. 21.
Manufactures, West Devon, i. 28.
———, Village, their Advantages, i. 50.
——— should go hand in hand with Agriculture, i. 51.
Manufactures declining, their Effects on the Poor's Rate, i. 290.
———, South Cornwall, ii. 6.
———, Vale of Exeter, ii. 109.
———, West Dorset, ii. 145.
———, South Somerset, ii. 218.
Manures, and their Management, West Devon, i. 153.
———, South Hams, i. 297.
———, South Cornwall, ii. 8.
———, North Cornwall, ii. 14.
———, proposed as an Improvement of Dartmore, ii. 34.
———, Vale of Exeter, ii. 117.
———, West Dorset, ii. 145.
———, Improvements by, suggested, West Dorset, ii. 160.
Manuring Fallows, ii. 279.
Markets, West Devon, i. 165.
——— of Biddeford, ii. 61.
——— of Taunton, ii. 190.
Marsh Lands, Remarks on their Formation, ii. 179.
Marl, West Dorset, ii. 146.
Meadow Foxtail wanting, West Devon, N. i. 205.

Meadow

Meadow Lands, West Devon, i. 204.
——— Plants, West Devon, N. i. 204.
Melling Lime, Method of, i. 159.
Mill Leats of Devonshire, ii. 271.
Milton Abbots, Ride to, ii. 294.
Minerals, West Devon, i. 19.
Mines inimical to Agriculture, i. 19.
——, their Effect on Society, i. 39.
——, their Profit to the Lord of the Soil, i. 49.
——, South Cornwall, ii. 5.
—— in East Cornwall, ii. 12.
Mining, its present Seat, N. i. 39.
Misseltoe, unknown, in West Devon? i. 222.
Moorside Farmers, Objects of, ii. 27.
Moory Earth, Remarks on, as a Manure, ii. 162.
Moulton, South, and its Environs, ii. 75.
————, to Dulverton, ii. 78.
Mounds of Hedges, on Guarding, ii. 268.
Mountains of Cornwall and Devonshire, ii. 1.

N.

NATIONAL Domain of West Devon, i. 20.
Natives of Devonshire, their Habitudes, i. 25.
Natural Boundaries, West Devon, i. 9.
Navigation, Inland, see INLAND NAVIGATION.
Newport, Borough of, ii. 16.
North Devon, District of, ii. 41.
————, General Remarks on, ii. 93.
Nutwell, ii. 103.

O.

OAKBARK, its Market, in West Devon, i. 96.
——, its Characteristics, in West Devon, i. 86.
—— Timber shamefully lopped, Vale of Exeter, ii. 115.
Oats, West Devon, i. 193.
Objects of Husbandry, West Devon, i. 133.
——— of Husbandry, Vale of Exeter, ii. 117.
——— of Moreside Farmers, ii. 27.
——— of Husbandry most eligible, at Buckland, ii. 286.

Occupiers of Devonshire, i. 70.
——, West Devon, i. 104.
Octagonal Yards, Remarks on, ii. 318.
——, further Remarks on, ii. 351.
Okehampton and its Environs, ii. 43.
—— to Torrington, ii. 45.
Orchards, and their Management, West Devon, i. 213.
——, General Observations on, i. 233.
——, South Hams, i. 300.
——, South Cornwall, ii. 8.
——, East Cornwall, ii. 15.
——, their Character, near Dulverton, ii. 82.
——, Vale of Exeter, ii. 119.
——, West Dorset, ii. 147.
——, Danmonian, their Termination, N. ii. 148.
——, Danmonian, their Termination, Vale of Taunton, ii. 171.
——, Vale of Taunton, ii. 171.
——, on Breast Plowing, ii. 164.
Orchard Grounds, Remarks on their Application, i. 222.
Orchard Grounds, on the Improvement of, South Devon, i. 315.
Oxen, as Beasts of Labor, in West Devon, i. 116.
——, Method of driving, i. 116.
——, Breaking in, N. i. 118.
——, a favorite Team, West Devon, i. 118.
——, Remarks on Shoeing, ii. 283.
——, Remarks on Training for the Yoke, ii. 285.
——, on Plowing with a Pair, ii. 349.

P.

PACKHORSES, West Devon, i. 115.
——, on the comparative Dispatch of, N. i. 115.
——, South Hams, i. 293.
Padstow Hill, ii. 50.
Paring Spade, i. 142.
Paring and Burning, general Remarks on, i. 146.
Pasturage of Dartmoore, ii. 25.
Peat, charred for the Use of Blacksmiths, N. ii. 25.
Peeling Coppice Wood standing, i. 93.
Pigs, West Devon, i. 257.

Pilchard

Pilchard Fishery, i. 35.
Pillars of Sheds described, ii. 352.
Pitching Corn Sheaves, i. 177.
Plan of Management, West Devon, i. 130.
——, Vale of Exeter, ii. 117.
——, West Dorset, ii. 143.
——, an Improvement of West Dorset, ii. 158.
——, Vale of Taunton, ii. 170.
— of Farming, with respect to Grass Land, ii. 343.
— of Farms, West Devon, i. 104.
Plans of Management, Reflections on their Origin, i. 131.
Planting Orchards, i. 218.
——, proposed in West Devon, i. 86.
——, South Devon, i. 310.
——, as an Improvement on Dartmore, ii. 30.
——, West Dorset, ii. 154.
Plow of West Devon, i. 123.
——, further Remarks on, ii. 252.
——, of the South Hams, i. 294.
——, of South Devon, on Improvement of, i. 311.
Plow, of Devonshire. Remarks on its Origin, ii. 253.
Plowing, in West Devon, i. 138.
——, with Whip Reins, ii. 265.
——, with two Oxen, ii. 349.
Plow Team, West Devon, i. 116.
——, Hours of Work, i. 119.
——, South Hams, i. 293.
——, Skirts of Dartmore, ii. 243.
Plymouth, i. 23.
—— to Bucklead, ii. 235.
—— Leat, noticed, ii. 244.
——, described, ii. 269.
Plymton, fine Situation of, ii. 274.
Poachers of Fish, ii. 261.
Political Divisions, West Devon, i. 21.
—— Economy, its prime Object, i. 40.
—— of the Chinese, i. 40.
——; the rational Alliance of Agriculture and Manufactures, i. 51.
——; Remarks on the Woollen Manufacture, ii. 110.

Poors

Poors Rate, West Devon, i. 50.
——— assisted by Village Manufactures, i. 50.
———, South Hams, i. 290.
———, encreased by a declining Manufacture, i. 290.
Potatoes, and their Culture, i. 198.
Potts of Pack Horses, i. 122.
Potwater Leats, West Devon, i. 62.
Poultry, West Devon, i. 272.
Pound House, or Place of manufacturing Cider, i. 224.
Practices, their slow Progress, i. 198.
Preliminaries of Improvement, ii. 249.
Private Property, West Devon, i. 43.
Produce of Wheat, by the Acre, West Devon, i. 191.
——— of Barley, by the Acre, i. 193.
Productions, West Devon, i. 34.
———, politically viewed in West Devon, i. 38.
———, South Hams, i. 258.
———, South Cornwall, ii. 6.
———, Dartmore, ii. 24.
Productions, Vale of Exeter, ii. 108.
———, West Dorset, ii. 137.
———, Vale of Taunton, ii. 168.
———, South Somerset, ii. 218.
Prognostics ill attended to, West Devon, i. 129.
Propagation of Woodlands, West Devon, i. 85.
Proprietors, West Devon, i. 57.
——— occupying Lands, Reflections on, i. 70.
Provident Societies, i. 29.
Provincial Practices, general Remarks on, i. 131.
Possessory Rights, West Devon, i. 43.
Public Works, West Devon, i. 29.
——— Vale of Exeter, ii. 106.

Q.

QUANTOCHILLS, ii. 172.

R.

RABBETS of Doorways, their Use, ii. 321.
Rabbits, West Devon, i. 271.

Rabbit

Rabbit Warrens proposed as an Improvement of Dartmore, ii. 35.
Rain, its Effect on Natural Scenery, ii. 70 and 71.
—— of West Devon, Remarks on, ii. 262.
Rape Seed proposed, as a Crop for Dartmore, ii. 33.
Rates, List of i. 319.
Rearing Cattle, West Devon, i. 245.
—— Swine, West Devon, i. 245.
Reclaiming Land from Stones, ii. 276.
—— —— from Weeds, ii. 277.
—— the Soil, Remarks on, i. 312.
—— Coppice Grounds, ii. 334.
Reed, its Eligibility, as a Covering, i. 64.
——, Method of making up, i. 182.
Remarks on the slow Progress of Improvements, i. 61.
—— on the Wages of Farm Laborers, i. 106.
—— on Horseback Carriage, i. 113.
—— on the Devonshire Plow, i. 123.
—— on Tools of Husbandry, i. 129.
—— on the Origin of provincial Practices, i. 131.
—— on established Practices, i. 135.
Remarks on the registering of the Harvest Management, N. i. 174.
—— on the slow Progress of Practices, i. 198.
—— on Bleeding Cattle for the Slaughter, i. 247.
—— on the Term Dufs, N. i. 249.
—— on Scalding Cream, i. 251.
—— on the Devonshire Method of fatting Swine, i. 257.
—— on the native Breed of Sheep, in Devonshire, i. 259.
—— on the House Lamb Breed of Sheep, i. 265.
—— on the Shepherding of Sheep, i. 267.
—— on the Washing of Sheep, i. 269.
—— on the Fecundity of Fowls, i. 273.
—— on Townships, i. 283.
—— on the Effect of declining Manufactures on the Poors Rate, i. 290.
—— on the Renewal of Sward, i. 311.
—— on wholly reclaiming the Soil, i. 312.
—— on the Improvement of Ley Grounds, i. 314.

Remarks

Remarks on the ſubſtantial Improvements of Agriculture, i. 317.
——— on Examining the Surface of a Country, ii. 98.
——— on the Hedgerow Elm, ii. 105.
——— on the Incloſure of Vale of Exeter, ii. 108.
——— on the Alliance of Huſbandry and the Woollen Manufacture, ii. 110.
——— on the Diſtribution of Farm Lands, Vale of Exeter, ii. 111.
——— on the probable Continuance of Clouting Cream, ii. 120.
——— on the Congeniality of Soils and Stock, ii. 121.
——— on letting Dairies, ii. 150.
——— on laying Land to Graſs, ii. 159.
——— on Burnt Clay, as a Manure, ii. 161.
——— on the Moory Earth of Heaths, as a Manure, ii. 161.
——— on the Limeſtone of Weſt Somerſet, ii. 176.
——— on the Formation of Marſh Lands, ii. 179.
——— on the Improvement of Sedgemores, ii. 183.
Remarks on Travelling in Rain, ii. 193.
——— on the Wooll Manufacture, ii. 219.
——— on the Colonization of this Iſland, ii. 224.
——— on the Rodborough Stone, ii. 242.
——— on the Names of Hundreds, ii. 244.
——— on Surveying a Diſtrict, ii. 246.
——— on the Plow of the Herald, N. ii. 253.
——— on the Introduction of Improvements, ii. 255.
——— on the Rains of Weſt Devon, ii. 262.
——— on Made Brooks, ii. 272.
——— on Cutting Cabbages, ii. 300.
——— on Societies of Agriculture, ii. 301.
——— on the Nature of Cement, ii. 308.
——— on Laying out Farmeries, ii. 317.
——— on the Effect of Ruſt, ii. 321.
——— on the Rabbets of Doorways, ii. 320.
——— on Reclaiming Coppice Grounds, ii. 334.
——— on Calculating the Value of Coppice Wood, ii. 337.
——— on ſecuring Buildings, ii. 332.

Remarks

Remarks on the General Economy of Farm Yards, ii. 357.
Removals, West Devon, i. 82.
Rent, West Devon, i. 82.
Rental Value of Coppice Wood, ii. 332.
Reservoirs, their Use to Made Rills, ii. 314.
Retrospective View of South Devon, i. 305.
———— of the West of England, ii. 221.
Right of Depasturage on Dartmore, ii. 25.
Rills, Artificial, West Devon, i. 61.
——, the various Uses of, ii. 308.
——, on Conducting, ii. 311.
——, proper Fall of, ii. 312.
——, Practical Remarks on Conducting, ii. 323.
River Breaks of Buckland, ii. 288.
———— Method of forming with Stone, ii. 289.
River Fish of the Tavey, ii. 259.
Roads, West Devon, i. 30.
——, South Hams, i. 285.
——, South Cornwall, ii. 5.
——, Mountains of Cornwall, ii. 13.
——, Vale of Exeter, ii. 107.
——, West Dorsetshire, ii. 131.
——, General Remarks on Laying out, ii. 327.
——, Remarks on Forming ii. 331.
Roborough Stone, Remarks on, ii. 242.
———— Hundred, Conjectures respecting its Etymon, ii. 244.
Roller of West Devon, i. 125.
Rough Cast, West Devon, i. 64.
———— General Remarks on, ii. 295.
Rural Economy defined, i. 53.
—— Practices, Reflections on their Origins, i. 131.
Rust, Remarks on its Effect, ii. 320.

S.

SALE of Coppice, Calculations on, ii. 337.
————, Conditions of it, ii. 336.
Salmon, its Habits, i. 36.
———, its Value as a National Produce, i. 36.
——— Fisheries, West Devon, i. 35.
——— Fishery of the Tavey, Improvement proposed, ii. 252.
——— Weir of the Tamer, ii. 240.
———— of the Tavey described, ii. 256.
Scalding Cream, Method of, i. 249.

Scalding

Scalding Cream, Remarks on, i. 251.
Sea Sand of Devonshire, i. 154.
——, Analysis of, i. 154.
—— Winds, their Effects, ii. 66.
Securing Buildings, Remarks on, ii. 339.
Sedgemore, South, ii. 178.
Sedgemores, Conjecture on their Formation, ii. 179.
——, Remarks on their Improvement, ii. 183.
Seed Process, West Devon, i. 164.
—— of Wheat, West Devon, i. 187.
Seed Weeds, Means of Extirpating, i. 140.
Selling Farms for Three Lives, i. 71.
Semination, West Devon, i. 164.
—— of Wheat, West Devon, i. 187.
Servants, West Devon, i. 108.
Setting Sun, its Use as a Prognostic, i. 130.
Shearing Sheep without washing, i. 269.
Sheds for Cattle, their proper Dimensions, ii. 352.
Sheep, West Devon, i. 259.
——, House Lamb Breed of, i. 261.
—— of Buckland Place, i. 262.
——, Remarks on selecting Varieties of, i. 262.
Sheep, South Hams, i. 102.
——, on the Improvement of South Devon, i. 316.
——, South Cornwall, ii. 7.
——, Mountains of Cornwall, ii. 14.
——, Dartmore, ii. 25.
——, Okehampton, ii. 44.
——, Vale of Exeter, ii. 121.
——, Remark on their Congeniality with Soils, ii. 121.
——, West Dorset, ii. 151.
——, South Sedgemore, ii. 182.
——, South Somerset, ii. 221.
——, Skirts of Dartmore, ii. 243.
——, Tamerton Fair, ii. 248.
Sheet Cows, Remarks on, ii. 2 3.
Shepherding Sheep, West Devon, i. 266.
Shepherds' Dog of West Devon, i. 266.
Shipton and its Environs, ii. 205.
—— to Frome, ii. 206.
Shocks, Setting up, West Devon, i. 170.
Shoeing Oxen, Remarks on, ii. 283.
Short Crooks, i. 122.
Shovel, pointed, General Remarks on, i. 127.
Sites of Improvement, on studying, ii. 344.
Situation, West Devon, i. 9.

Situation,

Situation, South Hams, i. 277.
———, Dartmore, ii. 22.
———, Vale of Exeter, ii. 97.
———, West Dorset, &c. ii. 125.
———, Vale of Taunton, ii. 165.
Sizes of Farms, West Devon, i. 101.
———, General Observations on, i. 103.
Skim Cheese, West Devon, i. 254.
Skirting, Method of, i. 144.
Slate Rock, i. 15.
———, analized, i. 16.
—— Covering of Devon, see LIST OF RATES.
Slating Walls, i. 63.
Sledge of Devonshire, i. 120.
Slopes, Practical Remarks on Watering, ii. 345.
Sodburning, West Devon, i. 141.
———, General Remarks on, i. 116.
———, applicable to Waste Lands, i. 151.
———, as an Improvement of Heathy Lands, ii. 32.
Soils, West Devon, i. 13.
——, Management of, West Devon, i. 137.
——, Unreclaimed, West Devon, i. 139.
——, South Hams, i. 280.
Soils, South Cornwall, ii. 4.
——, Mountains of Cornwall, ii. [illegible]
——, Dartmore, ii. 23.
——, Vale of Exeter, ii. 101.
——, West Dorset, ii. 129.
——, Vale of Taunton, ii. 16[illegible].
——, South Sedgemore, ii. 181.
——, Skirts of Dartmore, ii. 243.
——, clearing, from Stones, ii. 276.
——, reclaiming, from Weeds, ii. 277.
—— Process, an Improvement of, West Devon, ii. 159.
———, South Hams, i. 296.
Somersetshire, Journey through, ii. 185.
———, General View of its Southern Parts, ii. 215.
Somerton and Environs, ii. 198.
——— to Shipton, ii. 198.
Societies, Provident, i. 29.
——— of Agriculture, Remarks on, ii. 301.
———, a Hint offered to, i. 317.
Society, State of, Vale of Exeter, ii 109.
South Hams, the District of, i. 275.

South Devon, Retrospective View of, i. 305.
South Devon, Improvements proposed for, i. 308.
South Moulton and its Environs, ii. 75.
———— ———— to Dulverton, ii. 78.
———— Sedgemore, ii. 178.
Spade, or Paring Spade, i. 142.
Sparrows, West Devon, i. 165.
Spayed Heifers, not in Use, West Devon, i. 117.
*Spaying not practised, i. 252.
Speculative Commerce, its Mischiefs, i. 102.
Spirit of Improvement, West Devon, i. 106.
Stock, West Devon, i. 134.
Stacks, Housing by Hand, i. 150.
Stalls of Cattle, their proper Dimensions, ii. 353.
Stannary Laws, want Revising, i. 19.
State of Husbandry, South Cornwall, ii. 9.
———— ————, Environs of Biddeford, ii. 64.
———— ————, North Devon, ii. 94.
———— Society, West Devon, i. 23.
———— ————, Vale of Exeter, ii. 109.
Stock, Dartmore, ii. 25.
———— Fairs, West Devon, i. 185.
Straw for Fodder, i. 124.
—— Yards of Buckland, ii. 355.
Stream Work, a Description of, ii. 12.
Stucco, General Remarks on, ii. 296.
Studying the Site of Improvement, ii. 344.
Subjects of Agricultural Survey, i. 4.
Subplow, South Hams, i. 296.
Subsoil, West Devon, i. 15.
————, South Hams, i. 282.
————, South Cornwall, ii. 5.
————, Dartmore, ii. 24.
————, Vale of Exeter, ii. 104.
————, West Dorset, ii. 130.
————, Vale of Taunton, ii. 169.
Succession, West Devon, i. 136.
————, South Hams, i. 295.
———— of Arable Crops, on the Improvement of, South Devon, i. 310.
————, West Dorset, ii. 144.
Surface, West Devon, i. 10.
————, South Hams, i. 278.
————, South Cornwall, ii. 4.
————, Mountains of Cornwall, ii. 11.
————, Dartmore, ii. 22.
————, Vale of Exeter, ii. 98.

Surfaces, Methods of Examining, ii. 98.
——, West Dorset, ii. 127.
——, Vale of Taunton, ii. 166.
——, South Somerset, ii. 216.
Survey of Devonshire, described, i. 71.
Surveying a Country, General Remarks on, i. 1.
——, Remarks on the Mode of Travelling, ii. 193.
—— a District; the Outlines soon caught, ii. 246.
Swimbridge, Valley of, ii. 72.
Swaths of Corn, Method of Turning, i. 173.
——, Method of Binding, i. 174.
Swine, Remarks on Apples as the Food of, N. i. 223.
——, West Devon, i. 253.
——, a new Breed of introduced, i 256.
——, on boiling the Food of, i. 258.
——, on the Improvement of, South Devon, i. 316.
——, Vale of Exeter, ii. 121.
——, South Somerset, ii. 222.

T.

TABLES of Crops, &c. their Use, ii. 249.
Tamerton and its Environs, ii. 245.
—— Fair, ii. 246.
Tanning, an Object of Chemistry, i. 96.
Tavistock, i. 23.
Taunton, Market of, ii. 190.
——, Town of, ii. 189.
—— to Somerton, ii. 191.
Tax on Horses Proposed, ii. 220.
Team Labor, Hours of, i. 119.
Team Rake, or Drudge, i. 125.
Temple, a deserted Village, ii. 15.
Temporary Leys, and their Culture, i. 202.
——, Remarks on, i. 311.
——, Remarks on mowing the first Year, ii. 342.
Tenancy, South Hams, i. 290.
Tenure, West Devon, i. 43.
Thatching Corn Stacks, i. 178.
Thrashing Wheat, in West Devon, i. 181.
—— Barley, in West Devon, i. 183.

Tillage, South Cornwall, ii. 8.
———, West Devon, ii. 252.
——— of Fallows, ii. 278.
Timber, its Management, in West Devon, i. 88.
——— Trees, Species of, West Devon, i. 84.
——— ———, their proper Management suggested, ii. 154.
Tithes, West Devon, i. 49.
Tiverton to Taunton, ii. 185.
Tools of West Devon, i. 127.
Tormenting, Operation of, i. 296.
Torrington and its Environs, ii. 54.
——— to Biddeford, ii. 55.
Towns, West Devon, i. 23.
———, South Hams, i. 284.
———, South Cornwall, ii. 10.
———, East Cornwall, ii. 15.
———, West Dorset, ii. 137.
Townships, West Devon, i. 22.
———, South Hams, i. 283.
———, Remarks on, i. 283.
———, Vale of Exeter, ii. 106.
Tradition respecting the Cultivation of Commons, ii. 132.
Tradition, Note on its Authenticity, ii. 133.
Training Hedges, ii. 275.
Travelling, Remarks on, ii. 193.
Trowbridge, ii. 212.
Turnep Crop, on the Improvement of, South Devon, i. 313.
——— Culture, General Observations on, i. 197.
Turneps and their Culture, West Devon, i. 194.
———, South Hams, i. 299.
———, Vale of Exeter, ii. 118.
———, Hoing of, introduced, ii. 281.
———, Mowing the Weeds of, ii. 297.
Two-Ox Plowteam, ii. 349.

V.

VALE of Exeter, District of, ii. 95.
———, Character of, defined, ii. 99.
——— of Taunton, District of, ii. 163.
——— Glastonbury, ii. 200.
——— Trowbridge, ii. 212.
Vegetating Process, West Devon, i. 164.
Velling, Method of, i. 143.
Venville Right, its Nature, ii. 26.

Vermin,

Vermin, West Devon, i. 165.
Village Manufactures, their Benefit to a Country, i. 50.
Villages, West Devon, i. 24.
———, West Dorset, ii. 137.

W.

WAGES, West Devon, i. 108.
——— of Farm Laborers, General Remarks on, i. 108.
Waggons, West Devon, i. 119.
Wain of Cornwall, i. 120. and ii. 7.
Walnut Tree Leaves, their Effect on Earth Worms, ii. 315.
——— ———, their probable Use in forming Drinking Pools, ii. 315.
Washing of Sheep, Remarks on, i. 269.
Waste Lands improveable, by Sodburning, i. 151.
Water Mills Bars to Improvement, ii. 273.
Waters, West Devon, i. 12.
——— of West Devon, their Effect on Land, i. 208. and ii. 344.
———, their Analysis desirable, i. 209.
———, South Hams, i. 279.
———, Dartmore, ii. 23.
———, Vale of Exeter, ii. 101.
———, West Dorset, ii. 128.
Waters, Qualities of, West Dorset, ii. 147.
———, their different Qualities, with Respect to Land, ii. 344.
——— of Farm Yards, Disposal of, ii. 357.
Watered Meadows, and their Management, West Devon, i. 206.
——— ———, their Advantages, ii. 344.
——— ———, Laying out, ii. 347.
Watering Proposed, as an Improvement of Dartmore, ii. 33.
——— Slopes, Practical Remarks on, ii. 345.
——— the Yards of Buckland, ii. 356.
Weather, West Devon, i. 129.
Weeding, West Devon, i. 164.
West Devon, District of, i. 7.
——— ———, Natural Characters of, i. 8.
West of England divided into Districts, i. 5.
——— ———, Retrospective View of, ii. 223.
Wheat, West Devon, i. 186.
———, South Hams, i. 297.
———, a new Variety of, i. 297.
———, Vale of Exeter, ii. 118.
———, General Observations on Seminating, i. 190.

Wheat, Hewing, i. 168.
——, Thrashing, in West Devon, i. 181.
Whip Reins, on introducing, ii. 265.
Whitaker, i. 16.
Wild Mustard affected by Cattle, ii. 297.
—— Oats, Instance of Extirpation, i. 140.
Winnowing, Method of, West Devon, i. 184.
Wolves, Tradition respecting, ii. 132.
Woodlands, West Devon, i. 83.
——, their Management, in West Devon, i. 87.
——, East Cornwall, ii. 15.
——, Okehampton to Torrington, ii. 53.
——, Vale of Exeter, ii. 114.
Woollen Manufacture, Remarks on, ii. 219.
Working Cattle, West Devon, i. 116.
——, the Devonshire Breed excellent as, i. 242.
——, a Mode of Treatment suggested, ii. 285.
—— Horses, West Devon, i. 115. and i. 117.
Workpeople, West Devon, i. 107.

Y.

YARCOMBE, Valley of, N. ii. 127.
Yard Liquor, Disposal of, ii. 357.
Yard, Octagonal, Remarks on, ii. 318. and 351.
Yoke, of Devonshire, its admirable Construction, i. 125.

FINIS.

WORKS

Written by the same AUTHOR,

AND

To be had of the PUBLISHERS of these Volumes;

(In two Volumes, Octavo,)

THE RURAL ECONOMY

OF

NORFOLK;

comprising the MANAGEMENT of LANDED ESTATES, and the PRESENT PRACTICE of HUSBANDRY, in that County.

ALSO,

(In two Volumes, Octavo,)

THE RURAL ECONOMY

OF

YORKSHIRE;

Comprizing the MANAGEMENT of LANDED ESTATES, and the PRESENT PRACTICE of HUSBANDRY, in the agricultural Districts of that County.

ALSO,

(In Two Volumes Octavo,)

THE RURAL ECONOMY

OF

GLOUCESTERSHIRE;

including its DAIRY: together with the Dairy Management of NORTH WILTSHIRE; and the Management of ORCHARDS and FRUIT LIQUOR in HEREFORDSHIRE.

ALSO,

(In Two Volumes Octavo,)

THE RURAL ECONOMY

OF

THE MIDLAND COUNTIES;

including the Management of LIVESTOCK, in LEICESTERSHIRE, and its Environs; together with Minutes on AGRICULTURE and PLANTING, in the District of the Midland Station.

*** *For some Account of the general Design of which the Four last Works form Parts, see the Address prefixed to the* RURAL ECONOMY *of* NORFOLK.

ALSO,

(In Two Volumes Octavo,)

PLANTING
AND
RURAL ORNAMENT.

Being a Second Edition, with large Additions, of PLANTING and ORNAMENTAL GARDENING, a Practical Treatise.

www.ingramcontent.com/pod-product-compliance
Lightning Source LLC
Chambersburg PA
CBHW032318280326
41932CB00009B/852